Portraying Elizabeth

Glenda Jackson studies a portrait of Elizabeth while on location at Parham House, Storrington, West Sussex, during the filming of *Mary, Queen of Scots* (Everett Collection Inc.)

Portraying Elizabeth

Elizabeth I on stage and screen,
and the actresses who have played her

Anton Burge

Copyright © 2020 Anton Burge

The moral right of the author has been asserted.

Apart from any fair dealing for the purposes of research or private study, or criticism or review, as permitted under the Copyright, Designs and Patents Act 1988, this publication may only be reproduced, stored or transmitted, in any form or by any means, with the prior permission in writing of the publishers, or in the case of reprographic reproduction in accordance with the terms of licences issued by the Copyright Licensing Agency. Enquiries concerning reproduction outside those terms should be sent to the publishers.

Matador
9 Priory Business Park,
Wistow Road, Kibworth Beauchamp,
Leicestershire. LE8 0RX
Tel: 0116 279 2299
Email: books@troubador.co.uk
Web: www.troubador.co.uk/matador
Twitter: @matadorbooks

ISBN 978 178901 861 5

Cover: Glenda Jackson in make-up for *Elizabeth R* (Keystone Press)
Back Cover: Sarah Bernhardt in *Queen Elizabeth* (World History Archive)

British Library Cataloguing in Publication Data.
A catalogue record for this book is available from the British Library.

Printed and bound in the UK by TJ International, Padstow, Cornwall
Typeset in 11pt Adobe Garamond Pro by Troubador Publishing Ltd, Leicester, UK

Matador is an imprint of Troubador Publishing Ltd

For
Deborah Smith
Sheila Ruskin
Rosemary Cordingley
Brenda Longman
Gail Steele
&
Stephen Wicks

Bette Davis in *The Virgin Queen*
(World History Archive)

"Elizabeth wasn't a woman of her time,
she was a woman of *all* time"
Anna Massey

Contents

	Acknowledgements	XI
	Foreword by Zenaida Yanowsky	XIII
	Introduction: "Who is she? ... We remember our history through our drama"	XV
	Elizabeth: Fact & Drama	XX
1.	An Actress Prepares: Anna Massey (Includes an interview with Anna Massey)	1
2.	The Sentimentalisation of Elizabeth: Sarah Bernhardt	19
3.	The Schiller Influence: Florence Eldridge & Harriet Walter (Includes an interview with Harriet Walter)	25
4.	The Queen's Head: In the Image of Elizabeth: Flora Robson & Bette Davis	44
5.	Are you a Mary or an Elizabeth?: Helen Mirren	61
6.	Elizabeth: Heroine or Villainess?: Jean Simmons, Cate Blanchett & Greta Scacchi (Includes an interview with Greta Scacchi)	69
7.	The Body of the Queen: The Playing of Elizabeth & Other Tudor Women: Vanessa Redgrave & Joely Richardson	95
8.	The Portrait as Cameo: Elizabeth as a Supporting Role: Judi Dench, Lalla Ward, Quentin Crisp, Jenny Runacre, Eileen Atkins & Felicity Dean (Includes interviews with Eileen Atkins & Felicity Dean)	103
9.	Elizabeth: The Whole Story: Glenda Jackson & Anne-Marie Duff (Includes an interview with Glenda Jackson)	128
10.	The Queen in Comic Relief: Miranda Richardson (Includes an interview with Miranda Richardson)	152
11.	The Return of the Queen: Actresses who have Played Elizabeth Twice: Flora Robson, Bette Davis, Glenda Jackson	

& Cate Blanchett 156
Conclusion: 'The Daughter of Debate' 173
Appendix I: Queen Elizabeth's Locket Ring 176
Appendix II: The Interviewees: Biographies of Eileen Atkins,
Felicity Dean, Glenda Jackson, Anna Massey,
Miranda Richardson, Greta Scacchi & Harriet Walter 179

Sources 186

Acknowledgements

MANY PEOPLE HAVE HELPED ME IN THE MAKING OF THIS BOOK AND I am most grateful for all the advice and inspiration I have received. To Dame Eileen Atkins, Glenda Jackson, Dame Harriet Walter, Greta Scacchi, Felicity Dean, Miranda Richardson and the late Anna Massey, who were kind enough to give up their time and let a novice interviewer interview them, I am forever indebted.

In particular I would like to thank Deborah Smith for her generous commitment and patience: no one could have been more helpful. My thanks also to Sheila Ruskin for her advice and insight, and, not least, to Stephen Wicks for his belief in the project. And I do appreciate the encouragement given by Rosemary Cordingley, Zenaida Yanowsky, Barbara Hann, Isabella Gardiner, Ann Pinnington, Brenda Longman, Gail Steele, Alan Strachan, Peter Warrick, Carol Royle, Alma Gaoaen, Fiona Drake, Milly Ellis, Vikki Turney and Oliver Sharpin.

Finally I would like to thank the Alamy Photographic Agency for all their help with images, ArenaPAL, Alice Pennefather, Brendan McGinty, The Royal Opera House, the Ensemble Theatre, and all those at Troubador Publishing including Joe Shillito, Sally Brigham, Hayley Russell, Sophie Morgan, Hannah Dakin, Jonathan White, Jeremy Thompson and Lauren Bailey.

Zenaida Yanowsky in Will Tuckett's production of *Elizabeth* at
The Royal Opera House, 2018
(Photo by Alice Pennefather ©Alice Pennefather)

Foreword

Zenaida Yanowsky

Here is a book that I wish I had read before I undertook my own portrayal of Elizabeth I.

Anton elegantly braids historical fact with layers of emotional research to explore a century and more of performance, considering the actors' intuitions and experiments which gave rise to innumerable depictions of this marvellous woman for all time.

Zenaida Yanowsky
London, 2019

Vanessa Redgrave in *Anonymous* (Everett Collection Inc.)

Introduction

*"Who is she? ... We remember our history through our drama"**

IN THE FIRST INTERVIEW I CONDUCTED WITH HARRIET WALTER IN March 2008, I asked her where one starts in preparing to play a woman so multilayered, so complex and so often performed as Elizabeth I. She replied, "I was influenced first of all by the fact that so many people had performed her, and that so many portraits exist of her and that somewhere there was

---

*   Harriet Walter

an individual called Elizabeth... and I thought, who is she?" Indeed – who is she? In terms of our dramatic reconstructions of Elizabeth's life we have come a long way from the affectations of Sarah Bernhardt in 1912, in which the French star forced her own grandiose personality upon that of the Queen, in the hope that the medium of film would bring 'The Divine Sarah' immortality. In other ways, we have come full circle, and perhaps nothing has changed from that bygone era when acting was more about personality, and historical research was something for the costume department.

It seems that Elizabeth (1533–1603) has been strangely and often badly served by dramatists, and frequently been presented as an adjunct to the drama that was her cousin Mary, Queen of Scots' life. Or she is seen as someone to be reshaped, reinterpreted and often rehashed, as if her own consummate reinvention of herself in the latter half of her reign gives writers carte blanche to elaborate on what is already one of the most fascinating life stories in history.

The role of Elizabeth has become a pinnacle by which to judge many an actress's credentials, just as we might consider her Cleopatra or Lady Macbeth. In a market that is still unresponsive to the needs of actresses, especially as they age, Elizabeth can be the Hamlet of a part into which an actress can sink her artistic teeth. So, as we might judge her Ranevskaya, her Hedda Gabler or her Mother Courage, the interpretation of Elizabeth is now seen as the jewel in the crown of many a career, winning stage awards, Emmys and Oscars.

Elizabeth has been deciphered, unravelled and decoded in a wide variety of ways, variously as villainess, martyr, heroine and sometimes even comic turn. All these versions are staggeringly different, dictated not only by the performer and writer, but also by the context of the time in which the material is produced. One fact, though, has become increasingly clear: Elizabeth is reinterpreted with every age that discovers her, therefore she is always altering and always updating, on occasion going out of fashion, sometimes becoming *the* fashion, but ultimately never losing our interest. As changes in our own history are often reinterpreted by focusing on hers, the role of Elizabeth can become as relevant now as it was in her lifetime.

Two main dramatic representations of Elizabeth have coloured and influenced writers more than any other: Friedrich Schiller's *Mary Stuart*, first performed in Germany in 1880, in which the two rival Queens, Elizabeth and Mary Stuart, meet; and Maxwell Anderson's *Elizabeth the Queen*, written in 1930, in which Elizabeth's love affair with the youthful Earl of Essex is the focus of the drama. Both these works stress Elizabeth's advancing age, her decaying appearance and her barrenness; yet, although sharing common themes, these very different portrayals have steadily changed people's perception of Elizabeth in a way no amount of documentary evidence has ever been able to. Even now when the majority of people have a loose idea of the historical facts of Elizabeth's life, they will staunchly hold an opinion influenced by Cate Blanchett's, Miranda Richardson's or Judi Dench's interpretations, and these and many more have their core in either, or sometimes both, of these works. So, it was revealing of Harriet Walter to state that "We remember our history though our drama". Often what we think is true has very little foundation in fact. Does this matter? Is that not the nature of drama?

In the time span covered in this book, 1912 to the present day, it is apparent that casting an actress as Elizabeth depends more upon her bankability and the public's perception of her personality, than her physical credibility in the role. As Anna Massey would comment, it is often "the actress of the age" playing the part. Considering the wealth of portraiture and descriptions of the Queen, it is sometimes staggering to see actresses whose looks are poles apart from the recognised likeness of Elizabeth, yet these casting choices have given us some of our most memorable Queens: Bette Davis, Glenda Jackson, Cate Blanchett, Greta Scacchi and Flora Robson, to name a few. And certainly, in terms of character, we rarely have an actress of such individuality in the role, with some having more in common with Mary Stuart and admitting this fact themselves.

Many of the actresses who have played Elizabeth are associated with toughness: Helen Mirren for her work in *Prime Suspect*; Judi Dench for 'M' in the Bond films; and Glenda Jackson, who had won an Oscar for playing the free-thinking Gudrun in *Women in Love*. And in 1939, when she first took on the role, Bette Davis was cinema's No 1 dramatic actress, with a reputation for being challenging both on film and off. Robson, Blanchett, Scacchi, Walter, Atkins and Massey would all continue to align their careers with forceful heroines as well as meeker incarnations. So, as far as casting directors are concerned, the actress playing Elizabeth needs to be of a certain character, and her physical likeness is of lesser importance. This at least is refreshing and allows attention to be paid to the lengths the actress will go to in order to convince with a physical likeness. All these choices and more have led to some absorbing results and some problems. It is worth pondering that as Elizabeth has become more accessible and supposedly understood, she has also become more romantic, humane, vulnerable and 'normal'. And as history is rewritten across our screens and on our stages, Elizabeth's own command of her life comes under question: had some of the decisions, political or personal, created by dramatists, actually been made, history – her own and England's – would have been markedly different. So, finding the 'real' Elizabeth, behind all these masks and in all the different interpretations, is even more complicated.

Although the essence of this book is to study the performances of the chosen actresses, each one of these Elizabeths starts with the written word and, just as Shakespeare created Cleopatra, various writers have created their own Elizabeth, so I have tried, while discussing the stage or film representations of the Queen, to also tell the *real* story of what was happening at that point in the drama. Dramatists have to make certain choices when tackling any historical character, not only about what to leave out, but often what to add.

Depictions of Elizabeth's life have increased since the 1970s. Writers and performers have attempted to reveal the woman behind the crown. We have Elizabeth the lover; Elizabeth taking on the mantle of the Virgin Mary and reclaiming her virginity; Elizabeth on the brink of dementia; Elizabeth as a caustic sparring partner; and Elizabeth as a frustrated feminist. It would seem that Elizabeth the war leader and dominating force of 16th-century Europe has gradually been replaced by a new model, often hunted and haunted, sentimental, sexualised and human. Strangely, during the 1980s, when Margaret Thatcher modelled herself as a second Elizabeth I, defeating the Argentine Armada in the attempted invasion of the Falkland Islands, the only major portrayal of the Queen on stage or screen was Miranda Richardson's comic 'Queenie' in the *Blackadder* series.

By discussing Elizabeth with several leading actresses, we learn not only about the research and problems an actress has to deal with, but also her understanding of the Queen. It may be a well-trodden path, but the journey to Elizabeth is unexpected: just because it is often a plum part doesn't mean a star performance emerges. All the actresses I was fortunate enough to speak to were fervent in their admiration of Elizabeth, but some admitted that one of the chief problems they had in common was the difficulty of playing the text (fiction) after they had researched their subject and knew the historical background (fact). They could see what was gained by not playing the truth of the situation, but this created an Elizabeth conundrum where their own views felt straitjacketed by those of the playwright. On the other hand, would drama be improved if it was dictated to by historical fact? Perhaps the example of Robert Bolt's *Vivat! Vivat Regina!* best answers this: a successful play in its day, steeped in accuracy, but rarely performed since it premiered; whereas Schiller's *Mary Stuart* has found greater favour and is regularly revived. The imagined scene when the two Queens meet continues to enthral and mislead its audiences.

If one thing were to link all of these women portraying Elizabeth, it would be their intellectual insight into her character and their desire to be as true as possible, each relishing the challenge of Elizabeth and the question: "How do you start to play a woman so far removed from yourself?"

Flora Robson in *Fire Over England* with Vivien Leigh (Everett Collection Inc.)

Elizabeth: Fact and Drama

OVERALL, THE AREAS OF THE QUEEN'S LIFE DEPICTED ON STAGE AND screen focus on the more human elements of her story: the relationship with Mary Stuart, Elizabeth's early struggles and her later reign are frequently reinterpreted in an attempt to throw new light upon her life. Depictions of the story of England and her success as a ruler are less frequently drawn, except when England and Elizabeth's power are threatened, as with the Spanish Armada. The middle years of her reign, when England began to build itself into a superpower in the eyes of the world, are often ignored by writers.

1533... Elizabeth born at Greenwich Palace, to Henry VIII and his second queen Anne Boleyn. Henry VIII playfully wraps a hand around the laughing Anne's neck in *Young Bess*, as if to indicate that the "little" neck (as she described it herself the night before her execution) will not bear the weight of its head for much longer. This image of Anne's vulnerable neck was repeated in the Royal Shakespeare Company's (RSC) 1998 production of *Henry VIII*, in which the play closes with a final circle of light on Anne's neck before blackout.

1536... Anne Boleyn executed after being found guilty of trumped-up charges of adultery. Henry marries Anne's lady-in-waiting Jane Seymour, and Elizabeth is declared illegitimate, along with her half-sister Mary from Henry's first marriage. The death of Elizabeth's mother is probably the single most significant event in her life, creating her distrust of marriage and men, and an association of sex with death. Birth of Edward, Elizabeth's half-brother. In *Anne of the Thousand Days* the baby Elizabeth is featured with Anne Boleyn, emphasising Anne's role as an unusually doting mother. As the credits roll we see the infant Elizabeth alone, walking in the gardens of a royal palace, as Anne's voiceover prophesies: "Elizabeth shall be a greater queen than any king of yours."

1544... Elizabeth and Mary restored to the succession. The previous year, Henry had married his sixth and final wife, Katherine Parr, who did much to create an air of harmony in the King's relationship with his family in his final years. This is summed up in a tableau of family life in the film *The Six Wives of Henry VIII*, each child at some form of study, aided by Katherine, as the King looks on contentedly.

1546... Henry VIII dies. Edward becomes King Edward VI.

1547... Elizabeth goes to live with Katherine Parr, of whom she is fond. Katherine remarries, to Thomas Seymour, one of Jane Seymour's brothers, and brother of Edward Seymour, Protector of the King, until Edward comes of age and can rule in his own right.

1548... Rumours reach Katherine of a supposed affair, or at least a flirtation, between Thomas and Elizabeth, and Elizabeth is sent away from the household. Katherine dies in childbirth. A symbolic 'rape' of Elizabeth, by Thomas, is featured in 'The Lion's Cub', the first episode of *Elizabeth R*, implied by the slashing of Elizabeth's gown as she is chased by Thomas in the garden of Katherine's residence at Chelsea.

1549... Thomas Seymour (known as 'a worm in the bud') arrested on charges of treason, which include trying to kidnap the King and overthrow his own brother, Edward Seymour, the Lord Protector, and seize power. He is later executed: although Edward Seymour refuses to sign the death warrant of his brother, Edward VI is less reserved. Rumours persist concerning Elizabeth's part in the plot and she, along with everyone connected with Thomas, is questioned. Nothing comes of the interrogation and Elizabeth moves to Hatfield House, where she remains, sporadically, until 1588.

1553... With the death of Edward VI, the Protestant Lady Jane Grey is proclaimed Queen*. The Catholic Princess Mary rallies support, aided by Elizabeth, and is herself proclaimed Queen; Jane has reigned for only nine days. In the film *Elizabeth*, Mary is portrayed as an embittered, paranoid despot, ugly, dwarf-like, in contrast to the beautiful Elizabeth. Their relationship is strained to breaking point. This distrust, chiefly concerning Elizabeth's legitimacy, has more to do, for Mary, with the memory Elizabeth evokes of Anne Boleyn and the hardships she inflicted upon her. Elizabeth, always wisely looking ahead, backed Mary's claim to the throne: if she had favoured Jane Grey, she would have called into question her own claim as heir to the throne – did she also wonder whether the ageing Mary would probably be too old to bear children?

1554... Lady Jane Grey executed, and Elizabeth sent to the Tower to be questioned, on the premise that she has been involved in a plot, led by Thomas Wyatt, to overthrow Mary and put Elizabeth on the throne. The dangerous and overwrought relationship between the half-sisters is documented in *The Virgin Queen* (2006), *Elizabeth R* and *Elizabeth*, each drama favouring Elizabeth and presenting Mary in a negative light, surrounded by popish, dark influences, and each showing the famous moment of Elizabeth refusing to enter the Tower, and sitting on the steps in the rain stating: "Better sit here, than in a worse place, for God knoweth where you will bring me." By May she has been moved and is under house arrest in Woodstock.

1556... The Dudley plot is thwarted by Mary. The plan was again to overthrow

---

* An attempt by Edward VI to keep the Protestant religion, knowing that his half-sister Mary would undo all the work he and Henry VIII had done in breaking from Rome and the Catholic faith.

the Queen and crown Elizabeth – memories of being heir to the throne and the focus of other men's lust for power would play a great part in Elizabeth's later refusal to name her successor, and throw a light on her relationship with Mary Stuart. Philip II of Spain, Mary's unpopular husband, intervenes when Mary wishes to have Elizabeth tried for treason. The sometimes playful, sometimes dangerous early association between Philip and Elizabeth forms part of 'The Lion's Cub', exploring Philip's attraction to his sister-in-law, his suspicions that Mary might not have long to live, and that Elizabeth would be an attractive and powerful second wife.

1558... Mary dies, childless and unpopular, strengthening the belief that women are not fit to rule. Elizabeth is proclaimed Queen of England; she receives the news at Hatfield, while sitting under an oak tree. "This is the Lord's doing; it is marvellous in our eyes." She appoints William Cecil as her chief minister. In *Elizabeth R*, Elizabeth is seen walking in the grounds of Hatfield, composing herself, hoping that there will be news of Mary's death, as we hear the gentle rumble of horses' hooves. William Cecil approaches and hands Elizabeth Mary's coronation ring, and joyfully, with a peal of laughter, she tosses her hat into the sky.

1559... Coronation of Elizabeth. "She's her father's daughter," comments one spectator, in Paula Milne's script *The Virgin Queen*, as Elizabeth takes her place on the throne (an image influenced by the famous Coronation portrait); the speaker is answered: "Look closely, sir – her eyes are her mother's." Parliament opens dialogue with various countries to arrange a suitable match for the new Queen. Elizabeth states that she will never marry.

1560... The Queen's early reign is rocked by scandal, as Robert Dudley*, her favourite, and Master of Horse (an appointment that caused much envy and dislike) is rumoured to be responsible for the death of his wife, Amy Robsart, who was found with a broken neck at the bottom of a staircase at their residence. This is where Elizabeth's story begins in *Mary, Queen of Scots*: it is suggested that she is probably having an affair with Dudley, only to be informed of the loss of his wife. She sends him away from court and

---

*   He would be created Earl of Leicester in 1664 and occupy apartments over the Queen's own at court.

has him tried. "Hide nothing," she tells Cecil. Once again, the association of sex and death is prevalent.

1562... Elizabeth falls ill with smallpox, a condition that claimed an abundance of lives during her reign. (The following year the plague would claim a quarter of the population of London.) She declares Dudley (proved innocent of any implication in his wife's death) as her successor. In 'The Marriage Game', the second episode of *Elizabeth R*, the Queen is shown being swaddled in red flannel and placed before the fire, to sweat out her sickness. Her ministers, appalled at the thought of Dudley on the throne, are thrown into chaos trying to find a replacement and act against their mistress's wishes. If she survives, the need to get Elizabeth married and pregnant cannot be ignored any longer.

1563... Mary Stuart, Queen of Scots returns to her homeland. She seeks safe passage through England but is refused by Elizabeth and her council. This incident proves one of the primary bones of contention between the rival Queens in *Mary, Queen of Scots*. Adding insult to injury, Elizabeth's navy hijacks one of Mary's ships and takes the Scottish Queen's stable of horses. It is not highlighted that Mary's chief desire is to be proclaimed Elizabeth's successor despite the fact she hasn't put her own kingdom in order.

1564... Elizabeth's favourite, Robert Dudley, created Earl of Leicester. He will go on to begin an affair with Lettice Knollys*, the Queen's married cousin, and in time they will marry.

1565... Mary Stuart marries Henry, Lord Darnley, Elizabeth's cousin. In both *Mary Stuart* biopics, the match is seen accurately as a love match that turns sour when his true character is revealed. Elizabeth is presented as a shrewd negotiator who has set her cousin up with a delinquent husband.

1567/8... Darnley murdered. It is presumed that Mary plays a part in the act. Further muddying the water, Mary makes a disastrous marriage with the Earl of Bothwell, almost certainly Darnley's murderer. Both biopics of Mary show this match as a love match, this time inaccurately: in actual fact Bothwell

---

* Her son is the future Earl of Essex, favourite of Elizabeth in her later years.

rapes Mary to secure marriage, control and power over her, a far cry from the intimate love scenes Vanessa Redgrave embarks upon with Nigel Davenport. Rebellion in Scotland, and Mary is forced to abdicate. Her son with Darnley, the infant James, will rule in her place. In *Mary, Queen of Scots* Elizabeth falls to the floor on hearing the news of the birth and declares, "The Queen of Scots is lighter of a fair son, and I am but barren stock." Back in England, Elizabeth continues to be courted by ambassadors from most of the crowned heads of Europe, seeking her hand in marriage. Mary flees Scotland, taking refuge in England, refusing passage to France and safety, only to be placed under house arrest; she will remain in captivity for the rest of her life.

1569... Northern rebellion. The Queen will experience trouble with the north of her realm, where Catholicism is more prominent, throughout her reign. The Duke of Norfolk is executed for plotting to overthrow Elizabeth and place himself on the throne with Mary Stuart as consort.

1570... Dukes of Anjou and Alençon offer their hands in marriage to Elizabeth, to strengthen relations with France. Francis Drake begins the first of his expeditions, initially bringing booty back from the Spanish.

1572... Marriage negotiations with France (although Elizabeth is approaching forty, will soon be past childbearing and has always stated that she will live and die a virgin) are called off when the world hears of the St Bartholomew Day's Massacre in Paris.

1578... Robert Dudley, who has spent the Queen's reign trying to win her hand in marriage, finally marries Lettice Knollys in secret. When Elizabeth hears of the union the following year, her rage knows no bounds. "I have heard the Queen speak roughly before... I don't know where she learns such language," says a member of her council in *Elizabeth R*. In *The Virgin Queen* (TV), Lettice is presented, not just as Elizabeth's cousin but also her friend and confidante, in the first episode – in fact, with the use of clever direction, the viewer is led to believe that Lettice, at first, is Elizabeth.

1579... Negotiations with France resume, and again marriage to Alençon is proposed, though Elizabeth is now forty-six, and the chances of a safe pregnancy and birth are highly unlikely. Her council is losing hope of any sort of alliance with any state, but Elizabeth continues to play suitor off against suitor, as she has done since her coronation. It is over this period that images of the Queen become more widespread and paintings of her start to embody elements of iconography that will cement her lasting presentation as Gloriana, the Virgin Queen: paintings such as the Ermine Portrait and the Sieve Portrait, in which her chastity is represented by the sieve, an association with the story of Tuccia, who proved her virginity by carrying water in a sieve without spilling a drop. This is counteracted by depictions of Elizabeth as a mother to her people. In Hilliard's Pelican Portrait the Queen wears a pendant of a pelican at her breast, the pelican being reputed to feed her young with the flesh of her own breast. And a third strand is introduced: that of Elizabeth as a great power in the world. Globes, and images of England's crusades, are often depicted, particularly in the Armada Portrait of 1588. Very few images, after the Darnley Portrait of 1575, show Elizabeth as just a woman who is also a queen; this is roughly the point, when she was in her early forties, where goddess takes over from mortal. In *The Golden Age*, the imagery of Elizabeth continually depicts her as above mortality, and it is only when her life is threatened, either by attempted assassination or when her country is threatened with invasion, that glimpses of the woman, whom we observed being repressed at the close of *Elizabeth*, return.

1580... Drake knighted on the *Golden Hind*, and relations with Spain worsen. Negotiations continue for the betrothal of Elizabeth and Alençon.

1581... Elizabeth is now forty-eight. Alençon finally visits the English court, but his journey is in vain as Elizabeth tells him that she cannot marry him. The Queen's age is seen as a repeating point of reference as Elizabeth is courted by Alençon in *Elizabeth I*. Dudley interrupts an intimate moment between the two, with news that literature has been published that speaks of Elizabeth's "advancing years".

1585... The Babington Plot is foiled. The conspiracy to murder Elizabeth and place Mary Stuart on the throne paves the way for the Scottish Queen's eventual demise. In Schiller's *Mary Stuart*, Cecil states that "[Mary's] life is death to you, her death your life".

1586... The Dutch war continues. Elizabeth supports the Dutch against Spain.

1587... Elizabeth signs the death warrant of Mary Stuart: the main sources of evidence, the Casket Letters (of which only forged copies remain), depicting Mary and Bothwell as the murderers of Darnley, seal the Scottish Queen's fate. Even after signing the death warrant, Elizabeth still prevaricates. In *Vivat! Vivat Regina!* she asks Davison, the messenger, what he will do with the death warrant now that she has signed it. "Take it to Lord Shrewsbury," he replies. "You do it without my authority and I shall put you in the Tower for it... until such time as the world recognises that it was not my desire," Elizabeth answers.

1588... As predicted, Spain launches the Armada (the execution of Mary is all the Catholic Spanish need to declare war on the English). Elizabeth gives her famous Tilbury Speech. The weather is in the English's favour and the Spanish are crushed. In *The Golden Age* the Queen addresses her subjects, dressed in full armour, resembling Joan of Arc, her long tresses flying in the wind, a far cry from the real picture of the fifty-three-year-old Queen, bewigged and wearing a breastplate. **Death of Dudley.** "Sweet Robin dead?" questions the Queen in *Elizabeth R*, before putting away his 'Last Letter' and falling to the floor uttering croaking sobs, majesty and vulnerability creating a moving tableau.

1589... 'The Faerie Queene' by Edmund Spenser published. The image of Elizabeth as Gloriana seems complete, though there are segments that question her ability as a ruler, shining a light on the Queen's later reign.

1590s... A period when time begins to creep up on the Queen in the shape of the deaths of many of those who have supported her throughout her reign, chiefly Cecil and Hatton, and the emergence of new powers in her court: Essex[*] (Dudley's stepson) and Raleigh. Both these strong-willed men will lead campaigns with varying degrees of success over the coming decade.

1592... Raleigh marries Bess Throckmorton, and a furious Elizabeth has them imprisoned in the Tower. "Dirty little lovemaking," snaps an imperious Elizabeth from her four-poster bed, as Bess begs for Raleigh's life in *The Virgin Queen* (film). "It is reason enough for two to die, Raleigh and his wench!"

---

[*] Essex was chiefly concerned in the continuing difficulties in Ireland.

1595-6... Deaths of Drake and Hawkins, after their last failed expeditions.

1598... Death of Cecil. His son Robert becomes the Queen's new chief minister. The Queen's relationship with Essex is becoming increasingly strained as he demands more power in Ireland and grows in popularity, threatening Elizabeth's authority. In *The Private Lives of Elizabeth & Essex* an increasingly vulnerable Elizabeth bellows at Essex, "You dare turn your back on Elizabeth of England? You dare?" Then the Queen promptly slaps Essex, just as in reality Elizabeth boxed Essex's ears, in front of her council. Whereas on celluloid Essex is presented as a charming hero, a favourite with the court, the reality was somewhat different: Essex was dashing and popular with the people, but his high-handed ways, and demands upon the Queen's revenue, caused much dislike among her courtiers, and wore thin with Elizabeth herself.

1601... After more failed campaigns, and a failed rebellion in Ireland, Essex, seen by many as out of control, is sent to the Tower and is executed in November. The Queen makes her final speech, her 'Golden Speech' to Parliament. In the final episode of *Elizabeth R* ('Sweet England's Pride'), the lines "To be a king and wear a crown, is a thing more glorious to them that see it, than it is pleasant to them that bear it," are played with particular poignancy, as Elizabeth, dressed in the costume of the famous Ditchley Portrait, addresses her court. These lines are reiterated in *The Virgin Queen* (TV) some thirty-four years later.

1603... Death of Elizabeth. *The Virgin Queen* (TV) shows Elizabeth in her final years as a paranoid neurotic, fearful of assassination, prowling her court, wearing a breastplate, striking out randomly with a heavy sword. The final episode makes much of the Queen's ring, supposedly bearing a portrait of Anne Boleyn, in its closing shot; in fact, the ring also bears a likeness of Elizabeth herself (see Appendix I). In *Elizabeth I*, Elizabeth actually meets her successor, James VI of Scotland, an event that never happened in life.

1

An Actress Prepares

❦ *Anna Massey* ❦

"I don't think she was that complex, just in a complex situation"
Mary Stuart 1996

EILEEN ATKINS FEELS THAT ACTING TECHNIQUE HAS IMPROVED considerably since she played Elizabeth – stagecraft, accents and emotional insight have been honed to a greater degree; if this is so, are the Elizabeths of now better than those of yesteryear? And if better prepared today, are the actresses tackling Elizabeth better informed about her, and what might the starting points and sources be for them? With so much material readily available, preparation to play Elizabeth must prove not only daunting to a performer – tackling a role so locked in the world's imagination – but also baffling when choosing what source material to use. Elizabeth isn't the sort of part where an actress can simply choose to play what is set before her on the page*; a performer must also possess a firm background knowledge of her.

All of the actresses I spoke to, and many of those I researched, had an admiration for the Queen before playing her and were delighted at the challenge of such a formidable and rich subject. Some, like Anna Massey and Bette Davis, had a girlhood interest in her, their research beginning with an

---

* As discussed with Eileen Atkins, it can also prove dangerous to bring too much research into the rehearsal process; at some point research must be set aside.

interest in Elizabethan portraiture. Massey's technique of line learning and preparation for a role took her away from the script completely, focusing instead on the visual elements that make up the character's existence. Imagery was at the centre of Massey's process: "For example," Massey states in her autobiography *Telling Some Tales*, "if the line was, 'The Siamese cat sat on the Paisley rug', I would picture the scene in my mind, filling out the whole room where the action is taking place, not just the room but the entire house… The same thing happens with my method of acting. You have a strong background of images from which the words and thoughts spring. This not only helps you to learn the text, but it helps you to remember it in-depth. You also create for yourself the whole world and background of the character, from when they were very young… It is like taking photographs with an emotional camera." And so it was with Elizabeth: maps, paintings, letters, books were all devoured by Massey to create such a photograph. Visuals aside, the problem facing any actress who does her research is that often the knowledge acquired is at odds with what is in the script. This can cause dilemmas, as Harriet Walter continually found when rehearsing and performing in *Mary Stuart*, as the Queen's actions in the play were not substantiated in historical fact. Playing Elizabeth is not the same as playing Lady Macbeth or Cleopatra and, although these women existed, it would be unlikely that a performer would research beyond what is in Shakespeare's texts. Elizabeth is probably the most frequently portrayed of all historical women, though what is presented is often a distortion of the truth, and not just because of the choices of the writer. Publicity and design continually present us with new versions of Elizabeth. For example, when promoting *Elizabeth I*, HBO sold the show on a depiction of a semi-clad Elizabeth in the arms of a Photoshopped Robert Dudley, played by Jeremy Irons. Mirren's Queen becomes a fantasy figure, rather 17th century in her softness and curvaceousness – she could have been inspired by a Peter Lely portrait*. She looks back at us, full of sexual mystery, just as Moll Flanders might. Entertaining this may be, but this, and the tag line, 'The hardest thig to govern is the heart', wouldn't have been out of place promoting Sarah Bernhardt's movie back in 1912. Perhaps the poster was inspired by an 18th-century interpretation by Vroom Cornelius of the Queen as Diana, the goddess of hunting, a part Elizabeth might well have played in a masque at court, but the representation is far removed from the idea of the most powerful

---

* Court painter to Charles II and famed for his depictions of court ladies and many of the King's mistresses, including Nell Gwynne.

woman of the 16th century. It is a fantasy, as is this view of her. In *The Virgin Queen*, Bette Davis insisted, as she had in *The Private Lives of Elizabeth and Essex* in 1939, on being as authentic as Hollywood could be at that time, with costumes and wigs, and this is one of the problems with her performances, as they often don't match the wishes of her directors. Michael Curtiz and Henry Koster cared little for historical accuracy: their chief objective was to make exciting movies for pre- and post-war audiences. Portraying Elizabeth in an authentic and realistic light was down to Davis, her knowledge and instinct alone creating a performance that would have been even more effective if tempered by a strong director willing to stand up to a star used to getting her own way.

In 2006 Anne-Marie Duff followed in Glenda Jackson's footsteps by playing the life of the Queen from Princess to grave. This allowed both actresses to put Elizabeth in a more accurate light, because the frame in which Elizabeth is cast is more truthful, with more space to explore her history. Cate Blanchett's Elizabeth follows on from Bette Davis's in terms of presentation, with a lush Hollywood epic that set the scene in the opening frames by giving us the relevant information on cards and then taking liberties with the facts as an exciting, romantic and powerful story unfolds, though often less extraordinary than the real one. Elizabeth emerges triumphant because of the force of character of the actress, but how much is Queen and how much is player? Blanchett might have steeped herself in everything that was available to her to study Elizabeth, including other actresses's performances, but she is no more accurate than Glenda Jackson nearly thirty years earlier.

When researching the Queen many start with the exterior. But if the wealth of portraits of Elizabeth can be seen as the YouTube footage of the Tudor period, can one ever really get to the real woman behind the masks? Especially as even these were privy to her own controlled censorship. And the commentators of the time have to be examined with caution: some write to flatter, others to insult. One could be wooed by Edmund Spenser's epic poem 'The Faerie Queene' in which Elizabeth is represented as Gloriana, the personification of glory, whose castle is the aspiration for the poem's chief characters; or could a more accurate description be that of a German visitor to court, Paul Hentzner: "Next came the Queen, very majestic; her face oblong, fair, but wrinkled; her eyes small, jet-black and pleasant; her nose a little hooked; her lips narrow and her teeth black; her hair was an auburn colour, but false; upon her head she had a small crown. Her bosom was uncovered, as all the English ladies have it till they marry. Her hands were slender, her fingers rather long, and her stature neither tall nor low; her air was stately, and her manner of speaking mild and obliging." Both might hold conflicting views, but neither is inaccurate.

So, what did other actresses playing Elizabeth use for research? For Bette Davis and Flora Robson, both of whom stated that they heavily researched the role, it was J. E. Neale's landmark *Queen Elizabeth*, to this day still considered one of the greatest biographies of the Queen. Agnes Strickland's 'Queens of England' series, although not always reliable, is also an admirable character study of Elizabeth. But for earlier actresses, some of the literature about Elizabeth was still influenced by the views of Charles Dickens and Jane Austen, two writers whose antipathy towards the monarch still stings across the centuries.

These, however, are starting points for building a character, but before that can happen the fit between actress and role has to be considered. Mostly this creates a happy marriage, but sometimes, as with Helen Baxendale in *In Suspicious Circumstances: An Evil Business* (a reconstructed drama investigating the mysterious death of Amy Robsart) and Joely Richardson in *Anonymous*, it does not. Other failures are more often than not confined to cameo performances. These include Athene Seyler's affected Queen in the 1935 film *Drake of England*; dressed to resemble a satin fairy on a Christmas tree, Seyler's big moment comes at the knighting of Drake on the *Golden Hind*, a performance that owes nothing to research; Irene Worth in *Seven Seas to Calais*, another Drake-inspired biopic from 1962 showing the knighting of Drake; and, perhaps worst of all, Agnes Moorehead in the 1957 release *The Story of Mankind*, directed by Irving Allen, which is a lamentable reconstruction of Elizabeth. The production, made on a shoestring budget, was released by Warner Bros (the studio that made *The Private Lives of Elizabeth and Essex* in 1939) and used sets and costumes kept in stock from the earlier film for the segment on William Shakespeare and the court of Elizabeth I. Moorehead, in one of Davis's costumes, is usually an excellent actress, who carved out a niche for herself in supporting roles, but here she plays the Queen as a pantomime despot, who bellows with a transatlantic accent, "Where is that actor-poet?!" after a heated debate with the Spanish ambassador. The performance is played at a continuous level of screech and gives no insight into Elizabeth, only that of an actress poorly directed. Davis herself would get further use from the costume at a charity event in the late 1960s, though this time wearing a rubber scalp mask instead of shaving her head.

By the 1970s, a whole library on Elizabeth was forming: historical novelist Margaret Irwin had written her trilogy on the early life of Elizabeth, the first of which was the source for the 1953 movie *Young Bess*; Neville Williams and Alison Plowden* produced excellent works on Elizabeth and the Tudor period, which highlighted a change in the interest in the Queen, a shift from ruler to woman, much of this due to the influence of Elizabeth Jenkins' brilliant biography *Elizabeth the Great*; a work that was invaluable to many of the actresses playing the Queen, *Punch* called it "the most intimate portrait of Elizabeth".

The BBC's six-part series *Elizabeth R* marked a sea change in the representation of Elizabeth. Although the sets may seem naive to today's cynical eye, they, along with the costumes, are more accurate than the lavish idea of Tudor England of later Hollywood blockbusters. And within this authentic setting the role of Elizabeth is also played with a greater sense of truth. This is achieved not only by Glenda Jackson, a stickler for accuracy in all things to do with the Queen's appearance, but also by Elizabeth Waller's meticulous costumes, for the first time re-created costumes that were copies of those worn by the Queen in her portraits: we see dresses replicating the Phoenix, Armada, Sieve, Ditchley and Darnley Portraits, so instead of modern takes on Elizabeth's wardrobe, the Queen is presented to us as she had looked. Along with this, most importantly, the script of the series was inspired by many of the Queen's own writings as well as recorded quotations. It gives Elizabeth a strength sometimes missing in other characterisations and proves that Elizabeth was her own best speech writer, giving Jackson's performance a weight that others' lack. Eileen Atkins' Elizabeth in *Vivat! Vivat Regina!* is also an exception, and this too relies on actual reported speech.

By the 1990s and beyond, when Elizabeth is being characterised in numerous studies and writings, sexualising her is the flavour of the time. One could say the process has almost returned to the sentimentalisation of Sarah Bernhardt's Queen. Of course, as Eileen Atkins advises, you can only play what is on the page, but just by looking at the chronology of the Queen's life it is enlightening to observe the licence dramatists continually take with her history.

---

*   Alison Plowden would also pen the final episode of *Elizabeth R*.

❦ *Anna Massey* ❦

"Flawless in her acting sense of regal solitude"
Mary Stuart **1996**

When it was announced that the French film star Isabelle Huppert would be making her British stage debut on the Lyttelton stage at the National Theatre in 1996, there was huge expectation placed upon the actress and the production by the world press. *Mary Stuart*, adapted by Jeremy Sams, bringing Schiller's text bang up to date, was chosen as a star vehicle for her, and the brilliantly concise, less showy Anna Massey was picked as her co-star. The production had its faults, chiefly its leading lady, who delivered her lines at such a rattling pace that words were lost and the meaning of speeches forfeited for Gallic passion. Fortunately, as the production progressed Huppert slowed down and settled into her part, but some of her dramatic choices did not sit well with the rest of the production, and certainly not with her fellow actors.

Ably directed by Howard Davies, Anna Massey's "bitterly regal" Elizabeth, in contrast, is at the peak of her powers: cunning, seductive and ultimately terrified, she possessed what one reviewer called an "ice cold and lonely brilliance" that showed the weight of Elizabeth's isolation. Her Elizabeth had an air of girlish charm about her, curdled by age and responsibility, and a bitter humour that was perfectly placed within the dangerous context of the piece. John Peter in *The Sunday Times* called it "the finest creation in Davies's production: tragic sensibility meets political duplicity. Elizabeth knows the score. She knows Mary must die, but she wants to shuffle off the responsibility… [she] superbly suggests the regal cunning of the Queen, her pity for Mary, and her frustration that she, a prisoner, seems more free than her captor, who is a slave to expediency." Peter goes on to pinpoint the failing the play can't rid itself of: "This woman [Elizabeth]… has taken the political risk of meeting her notorious rival and allowed her unavoidable execution to look like the result of personal spite."

The set, designed by William Dudley, was made up of a bevy of painted, sliding flats – no doubt similar to how the production was originally staged – creating the air of tension and uncertainty that any 16th-century palace no doubt possessed, and his costumes merged the 16th century with the 18th, producing a prevailing sense of the ever-changing yet consistent nature of power.

An image of Fotheringhay Castle looms over the proceedings, but its most famous prisoner sadly fails to dominate the play. Huppert's Mary – barefooted, hair running free, never still, always whipping up an air of anxiety – is an exhausting creation, and pitted against the disdainfully still Massey (ably assisted by a wonderfully devious Tim Piggot-Smith in the guise of Robert Dudley) she has little hope of engaging the audience in Mary's plight and eventual self-created martyrdom. Such differing approaches in the production's leading ladies' work jar, and are ultimately its chief failing, along with the fact that the speed of Huppert's delivery makes her incomprehensible. So, as *Mary Stuart* develops, sympathy towards the Scottish Queen recedes, and the performance of the night belongs to Massey's razor-sharp Elizabeth, certainly not Schiller's intention when he wrote the play, but something that seems to be shifting the axis of popularity from Mary to Elizabeth as the piece is more frequently produced.

> "Elizabeth wasn't a woman of her time, she was a woman of all time"

Anna Massey's passion for Elizabeth was infectious. Her knowledge was faultless and vast. It was obvious, after an interview that lasted much longer than expected, that she still had much to say on the subject, and that there was still more work to be done in her own mind, as an actress. She had obviously felt frustrated by some of the confines of the play *Mary Stuart* and how it was produced, and felt that another stab at "the most dignified person who trod the globe", in a different vehicle, still wouldn't exhaust all she had to express on the part.

The manner in which Massey worked (turning the text into images, so that it might come to light in her mind) was detailed beyond the call of duty. Her theory, certainly unique amongst the actresses I interviewed, rooted Elizabeth in her mind's eye, and she didn't question the text by saying, 'Elizabeth didn't do this, so I therefore feel uncomfortable doing this'. Massey knew so much about Elizabeth that she easily separated fact from fiction as part of the process of drama, and she knew the world that the Queen inhabited, giving her work a weight that informed the audience that she understood this. By becoming Elizabeth so convincingly, she commanded the stage as a woman emotionally thwarted and trapped by the demands of her position, those she has placed upon herself, and her own fear of emotional commitment.

Portraying Elizabeth

Interview with Anna Massey

Anna Massey as Elizabeth

"THE CANVAS THAT ELIZABETH GIVES YOU IS VAST. IN ORDER TO work on any part I always work in minute detail which then builds up into the character, whoever that may be. The book that gave me the most information about Elizabeth – the woman, not the queen so much, but the woman – was Elizabeth Jenkins' *Elizabeth the Great* (1958). I found it incredibly helpful. As a reader you really feel that you get to know her, almost as if she were being interviewed. It tells you about her daily life, her character, for instance her terrible temper: she would rage at one moment and the next all would be fine. No royal ever slept in a room on their own – either there was a servant at the door, or one also sleeping in the chamber – so her privacy was very threatened. I imagined from this that somebody like Elizabeth would find that very difficult, an intrusion of privacy, even though it was the norm for royalty, especially as she had spent some time imprisoned. The book gives wonderful insight into her daily life – the fact that every morning, just as we would go jogging or do yoga, she did a galliard, which is incredibly strengthening to the muscles, not only to keep fit. So she was something of a health fanatic – not only in order to keep healthy, but to keep alive. I was also helped by the fact that I had done a massive amount of costume drama on television and was aware of how little comfort there was then. Elizabethan furniture, also their carriages, along with the clothes were all very uncomfortable – and all these elements brought up an enormous number of images for me to work from.

Then, in the process I work with, I imagined going through a day as Elizabeth. You have to make her as humanly believable as possible, because you are in an extraordinary situation. So you use any link of understanding you have – for instance Elizabeth had a nanny and I also had a nanny. Confidantes, women, were around her always from the outset, so I can, to a degree, understand that feeling of someone always being there. You also have to remember that you *are* the Queen of England: you don't have to play it – you are it. The rest of the cast are playing the 'in awe'. You have to remember what your motives are for each scene, for example with Aubespine, the French ambassador, all that one has to do, for the play within the play, is to come on and your intention is to get Aubespine to do your will. So you're not actually daunted by it – however terrified I was doing the play at the National, all I am doing is getting him to do what I want him to do. You're not playing being Queen Elizabeth. And of course you're used to getting people to do what you want them to do, so you're *playing* him. You don't have to look at him all the time, just occasionally, which can be quite frightening: you're not imploring him, you're telling him, and you know *damn* well that you will win! You have that confidence and ability and you have that training. And amongst all that, the link is that you had Nanny back in your little room and you had a galliard with Christopher Hatton in the morning, so you bring on stage a world that is very replete with activity and action and images. The camera in your mind is quicker than your speed of thought, so you need as many pictures as you can possibly have because you could run out of pictures, and you mustn't let that happen. So the woman that you are, Elizabeth, is a very simple mechanism and you, as an actor, know it.

Then when I'm off stage, I don't mix very much with the other actors during the performance. I usually go back to my dressing room and write myself notes of what I didn't achieve during that time on stage. But it can be difficult at the National Theatre because you have a run of performances and then you can be off for a couple of weeks, with the way it works in repertory. This can make one very nervous and I think that was part of the trouble with Isabelle's[*] Mary: she often went too fast, which was a problem when acting in another language.

I believe the *core* of Elizabeth, and I actually don't think she was that complex, she was just put into a terribly complex situation, by which I mean foremost the religious situation of the time, but I think the *actual* core of the woman was relatively uncomplicated. I think she genuinely had fears of sex – I'm sure she had these. We will never know whether she was a virgin or not. I read somewhere that she had a membrane over the hymen which was almost impenetrable, which would have been partly a cause for this fear, as well as all the other elements that we know so well – her mother's death, etc., though I doubt very much if she had any memories of Anne Boleyn. I believe that she imagined that sex, or infidelity, led to death because of Anne. Ultimately, sex killed you. She might have had a jolly time with Leicester! I doubt it, though, but who knows? I believe in spite of this that she was a very sexy, flirtatious woman, who used her sexuality at times, and I tried to bring this out when I played her. Leicester and Elizabeth had an extremely complex relationship – a romantic, sexual friendship – but that doesn't necessarily make *her* a complex woman.

Psychologically, the mother is the most important parent to any child – any therapist will tell you this, even, I suppose, if Henry VIII is your father! But if Henry, as your father, has your mother put to death, whatever the reason for this, the situation is very complicated. Its complication is added to if the reason is adultery, sex, and that is what Elizabeth would have been told, and therefore believed. *When* Elizabeth was told this we will never know, but I suppose it was through gossip. So, already a questionable image is growing up about this woman she cannot remember. Whether Anne Boleyn had the sixth finger or any of those things, we won't know – more than likely the deformities were put upon her because it suited her enemies to represent her as deformed. What we do know is that *she* was a complicated woman who

---

[*] Isabelle Huppert, who played Mary Stuart.

dies in complicated circumstances. All of this would have dripped down to Elizabeth. It is interesting that Henry had such puritanical daughters, though of course in very different ways.

There is a direct link to her mother, though, through the better paintings, images such as the Darnley Portrait – it is the mother's face that stares back at you, even though the colouring may be Henry VIII's. Her fear of sex may also have been a fear that to physically give herself away would take away her power. So that is probably why she remained a virgin – in fact I'm almost certain of it from the research I did. I do think though that the person that got closest to her was Dudley, because he came the closest to understanding her. Also, Christopher Hatton was a great favourite – and there were rumours about him. And I think that Thomas Seymour got pretty intimate too, and she was more vulnerable then, when she was younger. But I feel if she had *not* been a virgin, surely something would have been recorded somewhere. I think her fear would have stopped her every time if she had been tempted. There was a great mystery about her, as well as this great dignity.

And of course there was a tremendous amount of fear then, not only in Elizabeth's personal life, but life in general, especially at court, and the play is dealing with a pretty terrifying time. My agent came to a preview and said to me that she didn't feel that there was enough fear in the court on stage[*]. And Elizabeth did have that frightening quality, I'm sure, that someone like Princess Margaret had, of never quite putting people at their ease if she chose not to, of never letting them forget a curtsey, or that they should call her Ma'am, etc. So, just when the person is feeling relaxed she would say something to upset you, or you would say something to upset her. And I believe Elizabeth had that same, very royal quality. And, for me, it was a lot more fun to play because of elements such as these, as it gave one so many layers. And I think that comes through in some of the paintings too, the very good ones, even now. It's a little like an electric shock is running through them. Of course when the production did increase the fear and respect on stage, for me it became much, much easier to play. It allowed me to have a *steely spine*. It made Elizabeth an intimidating force, respected, and your word was obeyed. It therefore became a stronger base for me to play any of her subtleties and details. Things didn't really change that much – it was more to do with the attitude of the playing. But the result was *electric*. Simply,

---

[*] Massey spoke to the director, Howard Davies, and he agreed that it would be more effective if there was more tension on stage.

Howard told the cast that I was going to up the ante, and that everyone, the court, should be in awe of Elizabeth. Suddenly everybody got straighter spines, really seemed to listen, and the tension was immense, which I'm sure was how it actually was. Before then I had been directed, for instance in the scenes when I was with Leicester, to mentally take off my corset. I don't think Elizabeth ever mentally took off her corset. So with this change in the play, she was much more rigid, and felt much easier to play. Because of this it makes her, in the scenes with Leicester, the highest tease. I think Elizabeth knew the art of flirting phenomenally.

Researching her, I was also fascinated by Whitehall Palace, as it was in her time, and I managed to get hold of the ground plan for the palace, this terribly ramshackle building, built by Henry VIII in instalments. So, using the techniques I always work with* I tried to visualise this building as she would have known it. So I tried to picture where she slept, the rooms she inhabited. The painting of Elizabeth receiving Dutch Emissaries in her Privy

'Elizabeth receiving Dutch Ambassadors', c1585.
This room was replicated in the mini-series *Elizabeth I* starring Helen Mirren
(World History Archive)

---

* Massey created her own technique of learning and creating a part through the use of image memory.

Chamber, actually showing a room how it would have been as she knew it, was invaluable for me. Her bedchamber would have been off that room, and then on the river there was a huge barge-like chamber where all her dresses were kept, which many years later, apparently, all crumbled from attacks by moths. For she was profligate, there is no question about it, certainly in her dress, the sense of her image, and her love of jewels, though many were either handed down or given to her. I certainly believe she liked to receive more than she enjoyed giving!

The paintings, of course, were a huge help to me. Unlike Queen Victoria, who got plainer and plainer as she grew older, Elizabeth's image gets bigger and bigger and more and more adorned and elaborate. I think she rose to the occasion rather fast after her accession to the throne, found very plainly dressed under the oak at Hatfield, and I'm sure the image of Henry VIII did much to influence her in this respect. Also, she cared very much about her popularity of course, and this, then, had much to do with image: popularity equalled safety – just as much as remaining a virgin and playing one suitor off against the other. So even though the jewels might have been added over the years, I do think that from that moment, at Hatfield, it all escalated pretty quickly; it was probably waiting to happen. I think she had that sort of control and foreknowledge.

Going back to the subject of fear, which I tried to create when I played her, it ties up with talking about her accession, as although she gained freedom by becoming Queen, at the same time the fear of assassination became even greater. A modern parallel would be someone like Barack Obama – even though we think of terrorism as a creation very much of our age, in fact it was extremely prevalent in Elizabeth's time as well. For instance, most of her meals were solitary, and her food would have been tasted for fear of poisoning, so even such a mundane act as eating still carried that *fear*.

The positives of Elizabeth in reality (but also within the play *Mary Stuart*, even with all the theatrical licence taken by Schiller – they never met so the play is therefore a fantasy) are very strong. And it has to be remembered, returning again to the theme of fear, that during her lifetime there were several attempts to kill her, by Mary or Mary's sympathisers. So even though nothing is ever black or white, good or bad, with either Queen, the fact that in Schiller's play they do meet, actually makes the decision Elizabeth has to make concerning Mary's imprisonment easier, because she has seen what kind of woman Mary is and it has confirmed her knowledge of what she is capable of. Some of the attempts on Elizabeth's life did come with Mary's approval, after all. But I did research Mary as well, principally from Antonia Fraser's work. For Fraser, Mary is a heroine – I suppose she is a heroine for me as well, it is just that, of the two, Elizabeth is a far more interesting heroine, and certainly more attractive to play. Mary just seems not so interesting a woman – the lovers, the fact that she was influenced by so many people, etc. We also have to remember that Mary was hated just as much as Elizabeth, and they were loved by people in equal measure; that perhaps isn't made as clear in the play as it was in reality.

To begin, when I was first asked to play Elizabeth, I read the Schiller play, which I thought creaked somewhat, but I do think perhaps that Jeremy Sams' version was taken too far into modernity. I say this, though, with the benefit of looking back on it by ten years. I also think the production values were influenced by this as well, and not always successfully. I would have preferred a more muted production. I think the actual interweaving of the characters stands up on its own without all the statements and imagery. The costumes were unnecessarily restricting as well – however accurate one intends to be, effects for the stage can be made which allow the actors to move! In the end it doesn't help you feel the character, it constrains you – these are hurdles that an actor shouldn't be put through. I think I would have felt more on top of it all if the costumes had been more comfortable. I would have liked to have felt freer – I could hardly move my head! The great court dresses I'm sure were very restricting, the ones she was painted in, but mostly, for everyday wear, she would have been in outfits that one could have moved about in. In the privy chamber, for instance, she would have been very at ease. I wanted her to be dressed much more simply, as in the Darnley Portrait, though if that had been the case I don't think I would have played her very differently. I wore one of Miranda Richardson's costumes from *Blackadder* for a charity event – it was as light as a feather but looked tremendously authentic. Really great designers and directors also ask the actor playing the part, 'How do you see the character?' This is perfect as it is a marriage of his or her talent but also takes into account your views as well. The open sets with blinding lights meant that the actors couldn't see each other's faces either, and the whole point of acting, as we know, is reacting. One acts very differently to a look from your fellow actor than you do to a light. It ends up by taking away detail. But then I'm very old-fashioned – give me the footlights: it builds up the fourth wall and gives you something to act within, much better and easier for the actor. I also think there should have been more cuts to the text. Isabelle was very against this and actually wanted more of the original text as well; I didn't agree with this – I felt it was a mistake. I'm not sure that Schiller's play *is* a wonderful play, but I do believe they are two wonderful parts for women. You have to divorce yourself from history and just think of it as a play, set apart from history, although you have to ground your character in history.

I don't think I would want to have another crack at the piece. I believe in onward and upward. I would possibly have another go at Elizabeth in something else, but then I'm the same age as she was when she died. I have enjoyed playing her on the radio, performing the Tilbury speech in particular. But then that is a more intimate medium, and what is sometimes forgotten, especially in some recent work about Elizabeth, is that much of the court, for instance, was very small – they weren't in these big, great cathedral-like rooms – and the costumes in these productions have more to say about our own times than they do about Elizabeth's. Her clothes are chronicled so well by several very great paintings, so one has to ask what are the designers and directors trying to say.

When given a part like Elizabeth one always pretends that one doesn't attempt to see other people's stabs at her, but my only recollection really was growing up seeing Bette Davis play her. I suppose my research came from reading about her, adding to the reading I had already done and doing things like visiting the places she would have known, Richmond Park for example. I did want to bring over the fact that she was phenomenally intelligent and energetic, and at the same time afflicted with a malady that made her at moments extremely indecisive, which is relevant to the play because of her dilemma over having Mary executed. I think her father would have just done it – much less conscience than his daughter – but Elizabeth is a much more complex character than Henry and therefore, returning to an earlier thought, more layered. This crucial decision that she is forced to take is one of the things that makes her so human to us, proving that she wasn't a woman of her time, she was a woman of all time – like the wonderful title of Robert Bolt's *A Man for All Seasons*, I think Elizabeth is a woman for all ages. She had these amazing tussles that we read about today, so they must have been well documented. She was also far more tolerant than any of the Tudors who had gone before – this again makes her more accessible and interesting to us because it is easier for us to relate to – she wasn't a despot. Certainly, as far as religion was concerned, she was happy at times to turn a blind eye. A plot was a different matter, however, though she was always keen to get the evidence rather than instantly make a decision. Another fact that I thought was admirable and wonderful about her was that she surrounded herself with very, very good people, a small group of men, to whom she listened. Margaret Thatcher (but then Mrs Thatcher is mad), Hillary Clinton, strong women of our time, they don't listen – Barack Obama you think *will* listen; going back to Thatcher, though, I don't really see any similarities between the two women: Elizabeth was put into power; Mrs Thatcher was voted into power, in my view because of this fluke second choice win because of Tory rules. Power went to Thatcher's head; it was assumed by Elizabeth, it never overtook her. Mrs Thatcher, and the research I did when I played her,* proves this! She is bananas! People said I overdid it at times, but I don't think so. There is no link at all. Mrs Thatcher never listened, she was dictatorial. Elizabeth had Walsingham, nicknamed 'her Moor'; she had Burghley, 'her Spirit', whom she relied upon phenomenally; and Leicester, on whom she also relied. She was somebody who heard advice; she would then make up her own mind, but she *did* listen and I am sure at times was swayed by the advice of others. But there is *no* link. One is a rather common woman and one is the most dignified person who ever trod this globe! Elizabeth had a purity about her. But Margaret Thatcher – I can't bear her! I always find the walk of the person, a tip from Celia Johnson, and that helped me find her. Mrs Thatcher's walk is that of someone with huge confidence and unbelievable restlessness. Elizabeth wasn't like that, she was hugely intellectual.

Even when I was a girl she was a heroine. Jane Austen and Elizabeth were my two great icons – I suppose quite virginal people. But I'm not sure I want to see people play Jane Austen. She wasn't a public person, whereas Elizabeth was, and I do think that makes a difference where portraying them is concerned. Elizabeth was someone who, for instance, went to Tilbury and made that passionate speech in front of thousands of people, whereas Jane Austen probably never spoke in a room of more than five!

I do believe, though, that often in casting Elizabeth, especially on film, it is the actress of the age playing that part at that particular time, for instance Glenda Jackson in the 1970s and now Cate Blanchett. Character actors will do what I do, which is to try and assume something that you are not, whereas

---

* In *Pinochet's Last Stand*, BBC 2006

a heroine, which someone like Glenda is, or was, as an actress, will try and bring as much of her to the part as she can. The times do the casting. I'm not sure a great deal of intellectual debate went on about who should play the Queen of England: I think it had more to do with who could put as many bums on seats in a cinema at that particular time – although I suppose Cate Blanchett wasn't that well known when she first played her, so perhaps she is an exception? Meryl Streep in the '80s would have been an amazing Elizabeth: she has the strength and vulnerability in equal measure. A lot of actresses wouldn't be able to do it because I'm sure they would have tried to make her sentimental – in trying to understand her, they would have perhaps played her for pity, and there was no self-pity in Elizabeth. Though I do think that Elizabeth is such a vast receptacle of interest for anyone who portrays her that everyone will find something in her that they will identify with. Because she is the queen, the politician, the woman, the child, the old woman, the sexually obsessed woman, the virgin – she is *all* these things, so there is something that you can pull out to suit whichever time in history is representing her. As far as the production that I was involved with, Schiller put Elizabeth into a situation that she would have never put herself into. She would have seen through the plot to bring the two of them together – she was far too intelligent.

She was sexy, she was British, she was formidable, she was tyrannical, she was out of control at times, she was extremely womanly, she threw fits: there were scenes of uncontrolled rages and weeping. And so skilful in her courtships, for if she wanted to go on being Queen and to stay alive she had to play the game that she played. She prevaricated and then left it too late, if she had genuinely wanted a husband and children. But really the chessboard was set and it was preordained: she couldn't have changed the moves. Like our Queen now: she can't give up the throne to Prince Charles, and why should she? She is well and doing a perfectly good job; and Elizabeth was the same, it was *her* job. Even more so for her, because she believed in the Divine Right of Kings, so she was put there by God. Although I don't think that religion was the most important thing to her because otherwise she wouldn't have tolerated the Catholics in the way that she did – and if it had been, I don't think that she would have been blinded by it in the way that Mary Tudor was, bigoted and blinkered. But God would have been part of Elizabeth's armour, there is no doubt about that, and she would have had to believe it. And if she didn't believe it she couldn't have beheaded Mary, but it wasn't an easy decision, hence that wonderful speech in Act IV*: it is at those moments that she is most human. Even though the play doesn't throw up all these questions, if I had been asked all those questions when I had been playing her I should have answered as I do now. You have to be able to answer many, many questions that the play doesn't ask you, to play a rounded character."

---

* A soliloquy in which Elizabeth's dilemma over whether to sign the warrant of execution is explored.

2

The Sentimentalisation of Elizabeth

❧ *Sarah Bernhardt* ☙

'The Divine Sarah'
Les Amours de la Reine Elisabeth 1912

KNOWN IN HER TIME AS 'A WONDER OF THE WORLD', OR 'THE Divine Sarah', as she was dubbed by Oscar Wilde, Sarah Bernhardt was, many might say, past her peak in 1912 and a sad reminder of a style of acting that was rapidly going out of fashion: melodramatic, declamatory and full of grand gestures. Yet, to her credit, Bernhardt, sixty-eight at the time and the right age to play Elizabeth, was keen to embrace the new medium of film. While her contemporaries eyed cinema with suspicion, for Bernhardt, if it could promote her artistry even further around the globe, then she was for it!

On viewing the film today, it is not just the quality of the performances which is striking, but how much screen acting has changed and refined over the years. Bernhardt really was the last of the ostentatious performers, and though her exaggerated style was out of date and theatrical, something she was unaware of, she was astute enough to see that film had a future. Within a very few years there would be other great female stars, like Garbo and Lillian Gish, giving performances in silent film which still stand up to this day.

When some of Bernhardt's contemporaries, Mrs Patrick Campbell for example, took their turn at performing in film, they were usually relegated to supporting roles, and adapted their performances accordingly. Bernhardt does none of this: she is the leading player in all her appearances – who would suppose otherwise?! Although she should be applauded for promoting herself in new media – recordings of her voice also still exist – she in no way tones down her histrionic style to suit a more intimate vehicle.

As Bernhardt's fame grew from the late 1860s, so did her imposing form of performance, and she not only dominated the theatres of Paris, eventually owning her own, becoming an actress-manager, but also those of the world. By the time she played Queen Elizabeth, in 1912, she was out of sync with the developments in acting, and she had no interest in the naturalistic influences of the theatre practitioner Stanislavski which were sweeping Europe. After Bernhardt's death, Lytton Strachey (the author of *Elizabeth and Essex*) wrote: "During her best years, her personality remained an artistic instrument; but eventually it became too much for her. It absorbed both herself and her audience; the artist became submerged in the divinity; and what was genuine, courageous, and original in her character was lost sight of in oceans of highly advertised and quite indiscriminate applause." This was kinder than George Bernard Shaw's remark that "She is no longer an artist, but an international institution". Yet there is a link to the failing Queen Elizabeth in these remarks: as Christopher Hibbert writes in *The Virgin Queen*: "Rising prices, costly wars, continuing troubles in Ireland, trade depression as well as poor harvests had overcast the glory of what had once seemed a golden and triumphant time… good cause to believe that the fulsome praise of Gloriana, Eliza Triumphans as the begetter rather than the patron of these achievements, was a victory of propaganda over reason." So, a perfect casting match one might think? Think again.

Bernhardt would bravely and famously (she was never long out of the newspapers) have her right leg amputated in 1915, having injured herself playing Tosca some years earlier. By 1912 the leg was making movement extremely difficult and painful, and gangrene eventually set in. Therefore Bernhardt's most famous foray into film was badly hampered by the actress's immobility. Still, bringing a whole new meaning to the term 'chewing the scenery', Bernhardt had no fear of the camera lens, and gaily went before it for the fifth time to play the aged Queen, calling the picture "her last chance at immortality".

Queen Elizabeth is shot in four reels and tells the story of the Queen's infatuation with the young Earl of Essex, and his eventual downfall. Cast as the Earl was Bernhardt's then lover, the dashing Lou Tellegen, who would find fame in silent pictures in Hollywood but would end his days a drug addict, committing suicide by stabbing himself repeatedly with a pair of scissors!

Apart from the most general of history lessons (the influence here is Strachey's hugely popular, though not always accurate, study), what do we actually learn from *Queen Elizabeth*? Perhaps more than we would immediately realise. Of course, the obvious things are apparent – Elizabeth is a mother to her people, can be fierce with her ministers and has an eye for a handsome young courtier. Elizabeth was in vogue at the time as the world got ready for war, and Bernhardt wanted to associate herself with this very English image and be seen in a similar light in a medium that would propel her fame further around the globe. It would be over a quarter of a century before another leading actress attempted to play the Queen on film. What is apparent is that little changed from this image of 'Good Queen Bess' until more recent portrayals of Elizabeth questioned, altered and reappraised this notion. Another surprise is that the role of Mary Stuart wasn't chosen for the grande dame. Mary, the tragic heroine with French associations, may have been more suitable. Her passionate and at times melodramatic story, culminating in one of the showiest deaths in history, would surely have better befitted Bernhardt.

Our first glimpse of Queen Elizabeth has Bernhardt smiling graciously to her audience, arms outstretched; she nods her head, bowing slightly, brings her hand to her neck and waves from side to side. She then totters backwards a little, the nods continue and become bows and the hands remain welcoming. For much of the world this was their first glimpse of its proclaimed greatest actress. Like the performance, the costumes have little in common with the Elizabethan period: copious strands of pearls are perhaps the only truly authentic part of the get-up. The ruff is there, as are the skirts over underskirts, but the costumes have more to do with 20th-century interpretation than realism, much as Cate Blanchett's costumes were in *Elizabeth* and *The Golden Age*. The sets are creations based on Victorian painters' ideas of 'Merrie England'. Bernhardt dons a huge fedora hat with a plume; she enters stage right, clasps the back of her chair and is soon seated after walking on Essex's cloak, nimbly slung under her feet.

One scene will be copied and repeated many times in forthcoming Elizabeth interpretations, too romantic to be resisted by future dramatists: that in which the Queen gives Essex a ring and tells him to send it to her if he is ever in need of her assistance and that she will forgive him, "however great his fault may be". She then sends Essex off to quash the rebels in Ireland, before swooning on her throne at the loss of her favourite. On his return Elizabeth welcomes Essex, kissing fluttering fingers to him, something Bernhardt had a habit of doing in real life; she is unaware that he is conducting a flirtation with the Countess of Nottingham and this creates the oft repeated Elizabethan love triangle: the younger man in love with a woman his own age yet playing at being in love with the Queen to further his career. Time and again in representations of Elizabeth's life do we see this show of queenly emotion, stressing Elizabeth's virginity, age, barrenness and jealousy.

On sending Essex to trial (his ambition and popularity having threatened her crown), Elizabeth attempts to persuade the Countess to get Essex to return the ring to her and beg her forgiveness. Bernhardt pulls out all the stops: firstly, we see her watching the procession, with the executioner leading Essex to the Tower, and then, with arms flailing the air, she is assisted by a lady-in-waiting to take a seat as the emotional burden bursts forth in a torrent of overacting. The Countess is victorious but (as with all good tragedy) her husband intervenes and cunningly prevents the ring from being returned to the Queen. The Countess now punished and Elizabeth thinking Essex does not need help or forgiveness, the death warrant is signed.

On visiting the decapitated body, a line on the neck denoting where the executioner has struck, the Queen discovers that the ring is missing from Essex's finger. Dressed in white and ermine and giving her gestures a butterfly effect, Bernhardt registers shock and then mortification and, assisted by her lady-in-waiting for reasons of mobility, the Queen clutches the head of her now dead love. But what is this, as she looks at his dead hand? The finger bears no ring! Arms outstretched, the horror is played out in all its gothic splendour. The audience is later told that the Queen "never had another happy moment". Fade to Elizabeth's presence chamber, the floor slung with cushions, where the Queen dies. Much is made of her insistence on standing (as Glenda Jackson and Anne-Marie Duff will do with greater effect in *Elizabeth R* and *The Virgin Queen*); Bernhardt, surrounded by her ladies propping her up, is allowed to pivot freely, one last moment of independence, and then it is over: she does a tremendous dive, that seems more like a belly flop, into the bank of cushions positioned ready for her fall; the Queen is dead. It is theatre at its grandest level, yet it now all looks faintly ridiculous.

What this film does do, and Bernhardt is to blame as much as the creative team behind it, is to start the trend for sentimentalising the public's perception of Elizabeth, taking minimal historical fact and weaving a film around it. It is the Elizabeth that Hollywood will pick up and bastardise further: the jealous, older, barren, foul-tempered harridan, looks gone, pining for younger courtiers and clashing with her ladies-in-waiting and ministers. She will become a fantasy figure, a Miss Havisham of a monarch, a shell in a vast cake of a costume, until she will have to be pared back and reinterpreted for another generation. The story of *Les Amours de la Reine Elisabeth* will be reworked in *The Private Lives of Elizabeth and Essex*, and its plot formations will appear in *Fire Over England*, both produced in the 1930s, and again in *The Virgin Queen* in 1955. Elements of this type of characterisation will be touchstones for interpretations as recent as Cate Blanchett's double outing as Elizabeth.

Flora Robson will give us the Tilbury speech and win victory over the Spanish, and Bette Davis will show Elizabeth as a shrewd political navigator, but Bernhardt's Elizabeth is all for pleasure, all for love, and this excess, like the sea of embroidered cushions, winds her and us. Bernhardt's performance aside, the film has only a tentative grasp of historical accuracy. The plot is driven by the escapades of Robert Devereux, Earl of Essex, whose actual role in the defeat of the Spanish Armada, where the film starts, was minimal. By the time of the battle, 1588, Essex had become the Queen's favourite (he in fact played a larger role in trying to further England's success against Spain *after* the Armada); and although Elizabeth did not like him going to sea, this would be the first of many times when he went against her wishes, as his stepfather Robert Dudley, Earl of Leicester, had before him. He acted in spite of her, often upon impulse, maddening her, if, for a time, adding to his attraction.

His involvement with the Countess of Nottingham is a plot fabrication that derives from an apocryphal story dating back to the 1600s. Essex's real downfall had less to do with the romance suggested by the film and more to do with his poor performance trying to quash the revolt in Ireland which, to Elizabeth's annoyance, was backed by the Spanish after the defeat of the Armada. Essex returned to England, again defying the Queen's wishes – he had taken little notice of her instruction when in Ireland – and although she might continue to forgive and indulge him, his unpredictable behaviour and arrogance were irritating her and not gaining him friends at court. Whereas Elizabeth had allowed Robert Dudley a seat on her council and had taken advice from him, with his stepson Essex she was less accommodating, which led to his accusation that she did not value him.

He famously burst into Elizabeth's bedchamber before she was dressed on one occasion, to the delight of Victorian painters, and this juxtaposition of young and old, male beauty and the female Queen in decay, continues to inspire dramatists: Glenda Jackson, Anne-Marie Duff and Vanessa Redgrave have all given us versions of this scene. His egotism finally got the better of him and he went too far, staging an open rebellion against the monarchy, imagining himself as a better candidate as ruler than Elizabeth. But the siege, which was little more than Essex and some noblemen marching on the palace of Whitehall and attempting to drum up support on the way, soon fizzled out and Essex was arrested*. Such behaviour has made historians conjecture that he may have been suffering from some mental imbalance or malady. The revolt was a disaster and, even though his conduct was due in some part to the Queen's indulgence, Essex was finally tried and executed in 1601.

Whether her interest in him was maternal (he was, after all, stepson to her beloved Robert Dudley) or whether it had a sexual aspect, as is supposed in *Les Amours de la Reine Elisabeth*, we shall never truly know. We must remember that he was not actually Dudley's son, and therefore did not bear any resemblance to her great love, either in character or appearance (a fact that is often ignored in the retelling when it is implied that when Dudley dies Elizabeth quickly replaces him with a younger model). However, both Dudley and Essex were guilty of arrogance and hot-headedness, and there was obviously some quality of Dudley in Essex's character that reminded Elizabeth of him. Dudley's death soon after the defeat of the Armada neatly coincides with Essex's behaviour beginning to cause complications. The film's message that the Queen never had a happy day after his execution is validated by the eyewitness accounts that after his death she would shut herself away and weep for what she had done. This may have been genuine and similar to the guilt she expressed after signing the death warrant of Mary, Queen of Scots, or it may have been grief at lost love – again, we shall never know. But to let us believe that Elizabeth died for love of a misguided youth damages our understanding of what made her astonishing.

---

*   Many of the men were later involved in the Gunpowder Plot.

3

The Schiller Influence

❦ *Florence Eldridge & Harriet Walter* ❦

Mary of Scotland 1936

FAMED FOR BEING MARRIED TO THE RENOWNED ACTOR FREDERICK March rather more than for her own career, Florence Eldridge was, in spite of this, a respected leading lady on stage and always a proficient performer in supporting roles on screen. Her career was often guided by her husband's choices: they appeared regularly together, most notably in American classics such as *The Skin of Our Teeth* and *Long Day's Journey into Night*. Eventually she only accepted work in productions in which March starred, and so limited her own professional output and prevented herself becoming a leading player in her own right. In 1936, when March was offered the role of Bothwell in *Mary of Scotland*, had he not taken the part it is unlikely Eldridge would have been singled out for first stab at Elizabeth on screen by an American actress.

Other names considered for Elizabeth included Ginger Rogers, under contract to RKO which produced the picture, and Bette Davis. Ludicrous as the casting of Rogers now seems, at the time it was a strong possibility as she was an in-house artist, which would save the studio any loan-out fees to import an actress, always a strong consideration for any studio. In 1936 Rogers was still not as big a star as Katharine Hepburn, who was playing Mary, and she was willing to take a supporting part as she felt it was a change of pace in her career, and she was desperate to be seen as a dramatic actress. However, the powers that be, fortunately, did not see Rogers as Elizabeth, and the only other possible candidate for the part was the Warner Bros star Davis. She was desperate to play Elizabeth, not just in *Mary of Scotland* but in anything. Davis also wanted to work with Hepburn, one of the few actresses in Hollywood she admired, and she had never been directed by John Ford. But obstacles were stacked in the indomitable Miss Davis's way, chiefly Jack Warner, head of her studio, who didn't want to lose his leading female star for the shooting period, especially as she had just won an Oscar, the first woman to do so for the studio. Davis had worked at RKO two years before, when she had begged Warner to loan her out to play the screen's first antiheroine in *Of Human Bondage*, winning rave reviews, an Oscar nomination and catapulting herself to star status, which was embarrassing for Warner as all this went on away from *his* studio. Hepburn had considered the role of Mildred but thought the part too unsympathetic, deeply regretting turning the role down when she saw the effect the part had on Davis's career. Perhaps as a result, she was suspicious of the screen's new serious actress. Davis, less threatened, was happy to take a supporting role. She had read and admired Dudley Nichols' adaptation of Maxwell Anderson's blank-verse 1933 play of the same name, and felt the part was a good one, and was confident that she could hold her own against Hepburn, especially in the confrontation scene set in Fotheringhay Castle. The play, in which Mary Stuart is the chief protagonist, is deeply unsympathetic to Elizabeth, something Davis was unafraid of, and she felt she could use this fearlessness to her advantage. Hepburn, however, wanted no such competition in a film with her name above the title, and so, with Jack Warner adamant that Davis wasn't going to make another hit picture away from his studio, Bette Davis lost the role.

With Davis out of the running, Eldridge was brought in to provide a note of sourness to the saccharine of Hepburn's saintly Stuart Queen. Hepburn herself had little regard for Mary, stating she "thought she was an ass", and would have preferred to play Elizabeth, or indeed both parts (a thought considered and then dismissed), despite having Scottish ancestors who linked her to Mary's love interest in the picture, James Hepburn, Earl of Bothwell. On the film's release Davis should have sent thanks to both Warner and Miss Hepburn for blocking her, as the movie was a monumental flop and only now is gaining some belated interest from film buffs.

Although the plot takes its source from Maxwell Anderson's Pulitzer Prize winning play of the same name, the influence of Schiller's *Mary Stuart* is never far away in its representation of both Queens. The stereotypes are clearly defined: Mary is the woman first and Queen second, and rules with her heart and not her head; Elizabeth is the opposite, a red Queen against Mary's saintly white. Like director Ford's dramatic use of lighting, which washes away any line or expression from Hepburn's face, so the plot removes any of Mary's faults. If Anderson and Schiller are to be believed, Mary was a martyr and the victim of the cruel English Queen's jealousy and neurosis and certainly deserving of the pedestal on which they place her.

Much of the plot will later be re-hashed in Hal Wallis's superior *Mary, Queen of Scots* starring Vanessa Redgrave and Glenda Jackson, a more even battle of talent *and* screen time. But *Mary of Scotland* gave film audiences their first taste of the imaginary meeting between the two monarchs, though Ford keeps the viewers waiting nearly two hours for the rival Queens to have the ultimate dramatic showdown. What we learn along the way is that there is another Elizabeth that that film believes in, aside from 'Good Queen Bess', and this is Elizabeth as a baddie, and Schiller is to blame. In the early 1970s Glenda Jackson had the formidable task of playing both Elizabeth the heroine, in *Elizabeth R*, and the villainess against Vanessa Redgrave's Mary in *Mary, Queen of Scots*. In 1936 the same principles apply when presenting the villain Elizabeth as they will for Jackson several decades later. Visually, she must be formidably and unattractively dressed, though at least with Eldridge's Elizabeth she is more accurately costumed. Walter Plunkett is to be thanked for this: he opts to show the middle-aged Elizabeth as painted by Nicholas Hilliard in the Pelican and the Phoenix Portraits, and the results, although gaudy compared to Hepburn's flawless Mary, are at least more realistic than Bernhardt's dressing-up box approach to the Queen's wardrobe.

But when it comes to characterisation, however, actress, director and writer are way off the mark. Eldridge plays Elizabeth as a schemer, jealous, tyrannical and manipulative, and with questionable virginity, the antithesis of the virtuous Mary. When the foundations of characterisation are set in cardboard by Anderson, heavily influenced by Schiller, and directed by Ford whose chief interest in the picture was Hepburn's face and how to capture it on celluloid, there is little an actress can do but play Elizabeth the pantomime villainess as best she can.

After the opening credits, the screen decorated in tartan (tartan is everywhere in Ford's idea of Scotland, as are bagpipes), we are headed for England: doors are flung open, a sea of courtiers part and Elizabeth marches into the chamber, one hand hitching up her skirts, a fan in the other.

'Queen Elizabeth Discovers She is no Longer Young' by Augustus Egg

Her hips swinging, she heads for her council chamber, calling for Burghley and snapping at anyone else in her way, "Get out, get out!" Both Bette Davis and Flora Robson will make similar entrances in Hollywood movies about Elizabeth: a forthright stride and an angry nature seem prerequisites for establishing the character of Elizabeth. Dramatically filmed in soft black and white, Ford's use of shadow and light throughout the movie is effective if excessive, as is his use of camera angles, all with the aim of presenting Mary as the love object, martyr and, in the trial scenes (where the cameras are placed so low that the court looms ridiculously high, resembling Wonderland rather than England), the victim.

Hollywood has got what it probably always wanted: a chip off the old block, a daughter of whom 'Bluff King Hall', as played by Charles Laughton, could be proud. Eldridge's Queen is therefore brooding, spiteful, temperamental and bitter. She sinks into her chair, one eyebrow raised, plotting her next attack upon the Scottish Queen, her thoughts menacing.

Once the history lesson of Elizabeth's parentage and rumoured illegitimacy is woven into the narrative, and in spite of the blazing fires and painted panels that would look more fitting in New England than Old

England, we are allowed snippets of insight into the Queen's character that are actually based in fact. Already, in Elizabeth's first scene, we are aware that the Queen allows her council to indulge in underhand dealings to do her duty without seeming to order it herself, for instance piracy is condoned but not requested, making Mary's voyage to Scotland precarious. By the time of *Mary, Queen of Scots* in 1971, Glenda Jackson's formidable Elizabeth has no such scruples and forbids Mary safe conduct through England. Eldridge's Queen is no such maverick: she is too sly. We learn that Elizabeth fears war, is bullied by her ministers to have the Scottish Queen executed, is shrewd enough to listen to advice, but that intelligence is tempered by a large dose of cunning. Walt Disney's wicked queen in *Snow White* and her "Mirror, mirror, on the wall" are a direct reference to Eldridge as Elizabeth, jealously eyeing a miniature of her rival as she looks upon her own reflection muttering, "A girl, not a queen". Here we also have a throwback to the Victorians' obsession with presenting historical scenes in romantic portraits. Augustus Leopold Egg's painting 'Elizabeth Discovers She is no Longer Young' is one such image; dramatically effective, it will become a stalwart influence: the Queen is human and must age.

In the 1970 Hal Wallis movie, the relationship between Bothwell and Mary is heroic and romantic, which allows us to make sense of Mary's decision to marry Bothwell so soon after the murder of her second husband, the inept Henry Darnley. The reality is somewhat more muddied, making Mary's actions after the murder questionable to say the least. Darnley was recovering from smallpox (or more probably syphilis), in a residence away from the court, when his house was blown up. It was later discovered that the cause was gunpowder: the house contained two barrels of the stuff, situated in a closet under Darnley's bedchamber. Bothwell, who surely must be one of the few historical figures whose reputation has gone from murderer in his lifetime to romantic hero in the 20th century, was almost certainly the culprit. Mary soon realised she had made a grave mistake in marrying the unstable Darnley, even if it did strengthen her right to the English throne as Darnley was from a family with a claim to England's crown as strong as the Tudors'. The immense physical attraction she once felt for him soon faded, and with Darnley's role in the murder of David Rizzio, Mary's Italian secretary and confidante and the object of Darnley's jealousy, it was soon clear to everyone that the marriage was all but over. Bothwell saw this as a way to the top job of King Consort (although clearly imagining he would be the one in charge) and took advantage of Mary's lethargy after Darnley's murder. Mary made her gravest mistake in pardoning Bothwell at the trial, something Elizabeth would never have done, and her inaction sealed her own fate. Bothwell seized his chance, abducted Mary and, consummating the abduction, left Mary no choice but to marry him. Unlike Hepburn's gallant martyr, the real Mary's actions place her squarely as a contradictory figure, who should have kept focus on keeping her own throne, instead of setting her sights on Elizabeth's as well.

The fact that Hepburn is miscast plays to Eldridge's advantage, even if when trying to show a spark of majesty she refers to "Royal blood in yur veins" after calling it "Ma throne", giving the impression of a Tudor cadence via California, so when the rivals finally meet she ably manages to hold her own with the Hollywood star. Lit beautifully – a single candle burns and smokes like an arrow between them – they come face to face. Inaccurately, first names are used (if they had really met, Sister or Madam would have been the correct term of address). Mary comments on Elizabeth the great monarch, while Elizabeth focuses on Mary the woman, whom men love, each envying what the other possesses. Shot in profile and silhouette, the Queens bicker, Mary the romantic martyr, Elizabeth the calculating pragmatist: Hollywood has reduced these two immortals to chorus girls trading insults. Mary spits out the old chestnut "You're not even a woman!" to her rival. Eldridge, leaning towards Hepburn, the flame dancing under her breath, describes her struggle to survive and what she has lost to secure her life and her crown, in the hope that Mary will admit her guilt and free Elizabeth from the act of ordering her execution. All this has little effect upon Mary, already in love with the idea of her death and her son doing what Elizabeth could never do – uniting England and Scotland – so, with the drama tipped in Mary's favour, Eldridge's petulant prima donna can do little more than flounce from the chamber, and the screen, in the manner she strutted on to it. It isn't really Eldridge's fault: the script gives her few chances to create a character as full-bodied as her acting; though had the movie allowed Elizabeth some brief moments to fill in the gaps of her own history, Mary's character might not appear so irritatingly mawkish and we might be cherishing the film today instead of discarding it in the DVD dustbins.

Elizabeth strongly believed in the Divine Right of Kings and felt appalled at the thought of ending the life of an anointed sovereign. She continually put off the signing of Mary's death warrant, in spite of the pressure put on her by her council, especially Robert Cecil, her chief minister, and Francis Walsingham, her spy master, who had gathered proof that Mary had been part of recent plots to have her assassinated. Yet she still prevaricated over the signing of the warrant. Her famous indecisiveness led her to enquire if Mary could be removed in some secret manner by those who held her under house arrest, but the reply always came back that she must sign the document so that in the eyes of the world it would be seen to be a just act. Finally she signed, on February 1st 1587, and Privy Councillor William Davison, who would witness the signing, was told to put into practice immediately the preparations for the execution. The council was hugely relieved, and the document was dispatched to Fotheringhay Castle. The following day Elizabeth sent for Davison, telling him not to 'lay the warrant before the Lord Chancellor until she had spoken to him', to which Davison replied that the warrant had already left the court – Cecil had taken care of that, knowing his mistress's nature and the fact that she could readily change her mind. This she proceeded to do repeatedly over the next few days, and when the deed was finally carried out, on 8th February, Elizabeth used Davison as a scapegoat, suggesting that she hadn't issued instruction to carry out the execution, even if she had signed the warrant. By this time it was too late; even in the unlikely event that she had really wished to change her mind, Mary was already dead. All omitted from the script.

Future writers and directors will look to this near cameo – Elizabeth's screen time is brief in the context of the two-hour film – and acknowledge this depiction of her by revisiting these same scenarios time and time again. Therefore, Eldridge's brassy performance, combined with Anderson's dialogue and the influence of Schiller, will take decades to shake from the public's idea of what Elizabeth Tudor was really like.

❦ *Harriet Walter* ❦

"The play diminishes Elizabeth"
Mary Stuart 2005 & 2009

THE SENSE OF THE WORLD CHANGING, YET FINALLY STAYING THE same, is the central theme of Phyllida Lloyd's deservedly acclaimed production of Peter Oswald's pared down version of Schiller's classic, which first appeared at London's Donmar Warehouse, before transferring to the West End. The two warring Queens were played with aplomb by Harriet Walter as Elizabeth and Janet McTeer as Mary. With the set stripped bare to the brick walls, the action can flick from Mary's cell to Elizabeth's court in seconds, and the decision to place the women in a close assumption of their 16th-century images against a backdrop of men in contemporary costume creates an eerie isolation in the shifting power of these women amongst the men in suits: "This highlights the similarities between the women, picking up the parallels in their situations. Mary is held prisoner... but Elizabeth too is constricted by the expectations heaped upon her and the machinations of the men around her," observed musicOMH.

Walter – a self-confessed stickler for reading up on her subject – may argue that the piece is a disservice to the role of Elizabeth, yet her playing of the part most certainly is not. Believing the Queen to be a "brilliant politician and absolute poker player", the "prototype English diplomat", when it came to playing one side off against the other and never showing her hand, Walter gives a rich performance that illustrates not only the Queen who wears the crown, but also the 'weak and feeble' woman beneath it. She is no bass-voiced virago: here is a Queen who is vulnerable, haughty and brittle, and she expertly gets across the danger that Elizabeth is in. It is a tough part to pull off, much harder than Mary, with her conflicting emotions and all the audience's sympathy from the very start.

Janet McTeer's Mary serves the piece equally well. Believing that "history is always written by the winners", McTeer plays Mary as Schiller would have wished her to be played. In her final scene, gowned in red, she lifts out her arms in a sign of crucifixion, proclaiming "There is nothing here for me now", before exiting to her execution. McTeer presents Mary as a human being placed in an impossible situation, while in Elizabeth's last scene, Walter, 'ashen and alone', suggests that the power that Elizabeth so freely wielded in Act I may in fact not be as comfortably exercised from now on.

Schiller, although writing about the religious situation of the 16th century, was in fact pouring comment on the state of affairs in Germany in his own lifetime. Here we have the sense of one woman becoming a Catholic icon* and the other becoming a substitute Virgin Mary. The fact that the Protestants were in fact the radicals is often overlooked by modern eyes; here it is perfectly drawn into focus. This was a unique production about two unique women, played by two unique actresses, and it justly won Walter the *Evening Standard* award for Best Actress. When the production transferred to Broadway in 2009 both stars received Tony nominations.

| "History is always written by the winners" |

So said the actress Janet McTeer, when she and Harriet Walter were interviewed during the Broadway run of *Mary Stuart*. On the whole it would be fair to say this statement is true, though in the case of Mary Stuart her history has been rewritten over the centuries, and often distorted, most significantly by Schiller himself, presenting the Scottish Queen as a passionate woman at the mercy of her ruthless cousin. History usually *is* written by the winners, but not here. This was one of the objects that seemed to block Walter when we discussed Elizabeth. Time and again she came up with the problem of separating fact from fiction, fearing that the play distorted Elizabeth in the audience's eye because it didn't give an accurate retelling of her history.

This constant conundrum for Walter (something that other actresses have readily dismissed, opting to simply play what is on the page) proved to be something of an asset in her performance, for Walter's Elizabeth is so multilayered and revealing that she takes Schiller's version of the Queen one step further by playing the lines often against the manner in which they are written. Here, then, is an Elizabeth with a predicament: exposed, and outraged at the quandary with which her ministers and her cousin have

---

* McTeer pulls off a coup de théâtre, as Vanessa Redgrave had in *Mary, Queen of Scots*, when, at her execution, she opens her gown to reveal a scarlet petticoat and bodice, a blaze of colour after all the blacks, browns and greys of designer Anthony Ward's palette.

presented her. Walter's subtle playing is a neat balancing act of ruthless supremacy and hunted animal forced into action. This sits well with what is going on on the other side of the stage. In this production the play no longer seems an outdated version of cat and mouse: here each Queen is flawed, heroic and fighting for her life.

Portraying Elizabeth

Interview with Harriet Walter

Harriet Walter as Elizabeth, with Janet McTeer

"I WAS INFLUENCED, FIRST OF ALL, BY THE FACT THAT SO MANY people had performed her, and that so many portraits exist of her, and that somewhere there was an individual called Elizabeth, who was 5' 4" tall, and was the unique, flesh and blood Elizabeth, and I thought who is *she*? And when I saw Cate Blanchett in *Elizabeth* it was the first time I'd seen a totally believable transition from, not an ordinary girl, because her youth wasn't ordinary, but from somebody who had been isolated and defensive, into somebody who was going to take on a mantle and make a choice about her life that would set the whole of her future upon a train that she would never be able to turn back. I found the final sequence of the film utterly unforgettable. I had never seen Cate Blanchett before, so I didn't think, 'Oh, there's Cate Blanchett' – the unfortunate thing about acting is that we get known as actors, and you don't want to be known – and I got so much out of that performance because I didn't know her. I totally believed in her – certainly in comparison to performances that had gone before, such as Bette

Davis's, which was a different style of acting that was based much more on personality, and you do project onto certain stars an equal force as might have been in Elizabeth. For instance Glenda Jackson, who I watched when I was young, was a forceful actress and I completely believed that that force could exist in this queen, and they matched, even though I didn't think I was seeing Queen Elizabeth – I thought I was seeing a theoretically equal, fire in the blood, lion-hearted woman.

I tried to find what formed this woman, because I realised there was a point at which she *gelled,* something that can't be explained in the history books – how this character formed from zero to twenty years old. That was the period I was interested in, even though I was playing her much later in her life – it was the formative years I really needed to get into, in order to be rooted in the character, so that I wasn't playing a comment or a judgement on the character. I think much of that is dealt with in the play anyway, although Friedrich Schiller is a bigger writer than saying Mary is all good and Elizabeth is all bad – though there is a bias against Elizabeth, the play is slightly stacked against her anyway, therefore I needed to be completely absorbed in the character so that I could defend her position.

I found it very helpful to read the history of the *young* Elizabeth, and how she was thrown into politics from such an early age and on the defensive from that time, and that there were powers out to get her. To combat this she had to play political games from the age of twelve, if not before, and this time was the crucible to creating an extraordinary woman. One could say that of Mary, or any number of Tudor women, and we don't have an equivalent of that now, though I believe that the difference between Mary and Elizabeth – even if there are some that think Mary is political as well – is that Mary is a less political animal, or deliberately quite politically naive. Therefore when Mary threw herself onto Elizabeth's doorstep, by crossing the border seeking help, Elizabeth could not possibly have helped her. There was no way that Elizabeth, with her own particular nature, could have indulged in feelings of sisterliness or cousinliness towards Mary, as she had to defend herself: it was ultimately survival. So, when preparing for the part, I became non-subjectively involved in the character and felt very annoyed by Mary playing the sympathy card. What the hell was Elizabeth supposed to do? Was she meant to say, 'Yes, have my throne' or 'Let your spies come to England, let me be murdered'? It was a completely untenable position for Elizabeth, even if this was naivety on the part of Mary, believing that because they were cousins and both women, Elizabeth would help her, which is what is central to the Schiller play and the human emotion that the audience understands. They agree with Mary, yet for me, responsible for Elizabeth's motives, one has to say, 'No, that isn't that game,' as it's not about sympathy, it's not about flesh and blood: it's about world politics.

I had been asked to play Mary several times in Schiller's play, in different translations, but for various reasons it didn't happen – these are the vagaries of the acting world – but it was interesting that Mary was a part that lots of people saw me as, so when the call came for this production at the Donmar Warehouse I thought I was too old to play her. Then when I found they were offering me Elizabeth, I thought, *Me, Elizabeth?* So that was fascinating for me – though in rehearsals I was very nervous about it, especially for instance in the confrontation scene, which is so difficult for the person playing Elizabeth. It's the pinnacle scene and the one that everyone comments on – the moment when they meet – and it's the hardest thing to rehearse. It did, however, become slightly easier to play, especially with the way it was directed by Phyllida Lloyd, which made it a joy to do. But in rehearsals, when I was doing the groundwork for my performance, I couldn't see my way through it, because quite simply Elizabeth never met Mary, it was never in her interest to meet her; it was a purely dramatic contrivance on the part of the playwright. Most playwrights and film-makers do this. History says that Elizabeth and Mary never met, yet every dramatist wants to make them meet; it's a kind of obvious quest from the audience about that story. Personally, I would have preferred it if they hadn't met in the play, but unless you play the letters, which is dramatically unappealing, I don't see how those two factions can meet.

I understood the dramatic necessity of the scene and the audience's appreciation of the scene, but as a truthful, truth-seeking actress, who got into the skin of the character, who would never allow that meeting, for extremely good and understandable reasons, I had those same reasons for not wanting to play the scene. One doesn't want to meet the woman you are going to have to kill, and you don't want to humanise somebody who has been on paper all your life. Or be seen to do something to somebody which completely compromises you politically, and how you play that publicly. In rehearsal we were very definite about which pieces of that scene were public and which were private, so we got rid of the men, though it was not written into the text, as we felt there were pieces of the text we needed to say as two Queens, which was so electric: two women on the stage alone.

I still feel, however, that as an actress playing Elizabeth, it doesn't hold up logically that the character would allow that meeting, so the hardest piece is the moment when Elizabeth is seduced, rather easily, by Leicester and tricked into having the meeting. That's the moment she makes the decision, and she gets it wrong. So the difficulty is playing the truth of that lead-up to the scene, that she would be seduced just by some kind of vanity into seeing Mary, and believing that you won't be paranoid about that because of her bedraggled appearance at that point in the play, in comparison to Elizabeth's own. Though there must have been in both of them a terrible, magnetic curiosity about seeing the other, and by not meeting the other they obviously grew in each other's imagination, whereas if they had met each would have been confronted by a human being. As an actress, even though one tries to play many different types of women, it is always hard to go out on stage and be disliked.

Having researched Elizabeth so much, I at times was frustrated by being confined by the text, and wanted therefore to say to the audience, "She didn't actually do this." The main thing I felt was that these two women make such good drama because it is the ultimate conflict of power and life and death, and that makes the most extraordinary theatre. It's not good drama for the two of them to compromise. So what I felt strongly and proprietorially about Elizabeth was that, having been on the throne for a considerable amount of time by that point, she had become totally alone, from having her mother beheaded, being proclaimed a bastard, being imprisoned in the Tower and accused of treason, and having her life threatened. Even though she had had figures she had grown attached to, stepmothers and her father, what a crucible to grow up in, and that I stacked in her defence. The other point I wanted to stress was that for thirty years she had kept England, at a period of huge conflict in Europe, on an even keel and at peace; she balanced so many forces. She was not a fanatical pendulum against the work of her half-sister, the Catholic Bloody Mary, and lived much of her life on a knife edge, and was so clever to realise that the strongest card in her pack was the potential that she might marry – but if she had actually done it, it would have been like things won and done. Once she had been won, some of her power would have been lost. Her whole career was a magical balancing act.

When researching her, I tried to read a balanced view of work for and against her, yet kept coming back to the conclusion that she played some extremely clever moves – that it wasn't just politics, it was also very intelligent and what I hope a leader would do, and what today we don't have enough of – people who see the intelligence behind a choice to mediate, compromise and balance. She also had fantastic advisers, but then you get the ones you deserve, and she had great confidence in these people. Yet I think the play, and most dramatisations about her, is about her worst reviews. It seems that history will remember her last twenty years, instead of her first thirty years, because they are more dramatic and they are more interesting to write about, and we remember our history often through drama. So the dramatised version of Elizabeth seems to be the one which we all remember. Fortunately Schiller does give her opportunity for showing glimpses of humanity and sharing her dilemma with the audience.

I also felt it was important that her sexuality was hidden, which arouses more fascination, and I think it a shame that what is missed sometimes by a 21st-century audience is her subtlety, and the mystery of subtlety. And one has to applaud her for surviving in a time when spies were everywhere trying to bring her down because of this. So my journey was very much like the audience's journey, in that I am more of a romantic, more of a Mary by nature than an Elizabeth, and yet sometimes you do your best performances when you are not terribly like the person, because you have to do a bigger journey to get there. And this was so much helped by the director, Phyllida Lloyd, who never allowed me to play for sympathy – even when I felt all Elizabeth was doing was ranting, she said, "No, trust me, don't show it." And fortunately it was right: by the end of the rehearsal I was so plugged in to how Elizabeth was feeling and thinking that I started to get very cross with Mary's manipulation of the people on stage. In the confrontation scene with the long, long speeches that Elizabeth has to listen to, where Mary on her knees begs – and why shouldn't she beg for her life, drenched in rain, and pathetic – and Elizabeth says, 'Stay down there', I felt how do I *find* that woman? But the point is, she made that political decision, she had the forethought and intelligence to rehearse that moment, and she can't give in to it. She has to make that terrible decision to authorise the death warrant, which is comical in the manner in which she prevaricates and blames the minion for taking it, very ignoble of her – it is a terrible thing for a woman to feel that she has condemned her own cousin to death. A terrible thing to ask of someone.

Whether the key to the *woman* Elizabeth is the death of her mother is hard to say. I'm not sure if just one thing is ever the beginning of all of us, though I do think it must be the key to her not being like anyone else we shall ever meet. And her sublimating the mother and glorying in the father, because it was the political thing to do, also interested me. The fact that she gloried in her father, even when she was Queen, I find frankly quite bizarre, even Thatcheresque. By this I mean the way that Mrs Thatcher is reputedly more devoted to the male members of her family than the female ones, emulates men, and doesn't seem to like women, certainly not promoting them in her cabinet, and the fact that she wants to show herself as good as men, and to put men down in a competitive sense, that says to other females, 'If I can do it, you can, but I'm not going to support you'. And I think there is a strand of that in Elizabeth, certainly in Schiller's play and this production. But the crucible that formed her, you could put at three years old, ten years old or any of the other milestones that she passed while growing up – these things are what formed the woman who couldn't go back on her past, and she stuck to this for the next forty plus years. Whereas you and I have the luxury of change throughout our lives, she had none of that, and that was where the transition scene in the film *Elizabeth* was absolutely crucial to me – the scene in which Cate Blanchett as Elizabeth 'becomes' a virgin again. And I agree wholeheartedly with Bette Davis that in playing her one wanted to be understood and not necessarily liked.

The other piece of information that I wanted very much to tell people, and I only had a line in the play to get this across, was that there was a fatwa out on her. The Pope said to all British Catholics, "Your loyalty is to your faith and not to your Queen." So basically, 'you will be doing us a favour if you kill her'. And I wanted to almost flag that up all the time to the audience: Mary may be crying, in the rain, but try running a country under those circumstances! But also understanding that, just as I, as an actress, couldn't show those things and beg for sympathy, nor could Elizabeth. And that rooted me in her even more.

When we first performed the piece in 2005, I felt there was an atmosphere in the world and in the country that would understand the phrase 'sympathy for the overdog'. Because I had always had sympathy for the underdog, which is the fashionable thing, but in 2005 there seemed to be a feeling that tough decisions *do* have to be made. And I believe it's as relevant now as then, in that Elizabeth has to make this impossible decision. Not that one is begging for sympathy: as an actor you want people to understand you; and my enemy, both in life and on stage, is judgement – and inevitably people judge. But I want to keep people confused for as long as possible and keep their minds open for as long as possible, both in life and on stage, and it is terribly hard, because in the media everything is geared towards judgement. For me, though, my aim is towards openness and fluidity. And sometimes I would leave the theatre, after the performance, and some people would congratulate or comment, and some would say, "You were a right bitch!" And I would think, have I wasted my whole evening, is that all you can draw from this complex play? And that is when the comparisons with Thatcher often arise.

Originally Phyllida Lloyd wanted the production to be in contemporary dress, and I was very concerned about this when we were originally discussing the production, before I took the job, because I didn't want to play a power-shouldered Condoleezza Rice/Margaret Thatcher head of a corporation type. Because none of those women actually come close to what Elizabeth had to deal with; her situation was unique. Fortunately, by the time rehearsals began, it had been decided that the two Queens would remain with their iconic silhouettes, while other members of the company wore modern dress, though I didn't, for instance, have red hair. What we were saying was that this was Schiller's Elizabeth, because I was definitely playing his interpretation of her, even though I needed to root myself in all the history that formed her. And through that discovery – although as an actress one always wants to be open and flexible – I felt that, after the age of about twenty, Elizabeth had to close various doors that would otherwise have been open to women of that time with a less extraordinary background. Certainly this becomes paramount when she is faced with running a country, something that very few women had had to deal with before. But going back to my earlier point, it isn't the same as being, for instance, Margaret Thatcher: the situation is vastly different. Therefore the costuming of the two women helped present Elizabeth's situation even more because it showed her isolation to a greater degree against all the men in suits, something that women have had to deal with down the years, but especially women in that position, in a society that was still fairly primitive, where the topic of the day in Parliament could be whether the Queen had had a miscarriage or not, whether her bed had blood in it, whether she was still a virgin – totally humiliating for a woman; this was the stuff of her reign, the ongoing discussion amongst the *men* in suits about her position.

Because of the research I do for the women I play, I did have to make a token gesture and I did rinse my hair in a dark red colour, but this was an instance where a designer was crucial because I was not playing the historical Elizabeth, and because of this it in a way got one off the hook of all the things you might wish to say about her and all the things that weren't quite true about her, or were rather biased against her – not that I am saying Schiller got anything wrong, but he was very selective in what he chose to say about her, as well as the glaring fact that she and Mary never met and that Leicester was not lover to both of them. What Schiller was showing was a piece of dramatised history, to make a point about German enlightenment. So, for me, I was playing an image that wasn't totally like her, more of a hybrid Balenciaga/Chanel/1950s/Bette Davis influenced image of her. I know that Anthony Ward, the designer, was keen to create an iconic, '50s, Bette Davis, nipped-in waisted, high-collared image. And these choices helped tell the story of where the play was placed in terms of history or theory or dramatic licence, and this relieved me from having to make apologies for that.

Another element that helped me amazingly was an account I read of her in her early years going on a walkabout on her way to London, when she is first told she is to inherit the throne, and it describes her walking through the crowds and talking with this silvery, light, beautiful, piping voice, and through the writing I got this incredible, vivid sense of the actual woman, Elizabeth. Fortunately, with the many images of Elizabeth, you can find a common denominator of what she looked like: high forehead, long, thin nose, heavy lids; and these images, coupled with that piece of writing, made me terribly aware that there *was* this individual called Elizabeth. However, I did choose to lower my voice for the role, to have the authority, in 21st-century dramatic and political terms, and that perhaps could be interpreted as a 'Thatcherism', but going back to the earlier point, there any similarities end. I had felt as an actress, because I have quite a light voice, even though it has lowered with age, that I didn't know if the play would support me in being the opposite of Janet McTeer, who has, when she chooses, a very big, deep voice, yet there was something in what we are taught at drama school to root your voice deeper so that it has more authority and power. In this play you are competing with male voices – I'm sure in Tudor England she didn't have any worry about being heard, but once again this was a 21st-century production and this element had to be taken into account. I feel that if I had played her on television or film, then I would have wanted to create, to a greater degree, something much more revealing of a human person, which *Mary Stuart* perhaps denies one as an actress. Though I did feel that the play did operate on quite an operatic level and that there was equivalence in the style of the production as a whole that did lend itself to the extraordinariness of both these women. I do believe, though, that narrowing the story of Elizabeth, by saying this is not her life in its entirety, makes it slightly easier for a performer. Of course, there had to be masses that I had to leave out about her, however much I wanted to convey it, which frustrated me because I was feeling like a guardian of her image, but at the same time the brief was so different that it didn't allow me to. On television that might have been different.

The difficulty in playing Elizabeth in a piece such as this lay in the fact that I felt I was a guardian for her, as she was very sensitive concerning public opinion about herself, and I believe she deeply cared about her popularity, and the need to be loved. So, to play, she was a wonderful balancing act between somebody who had emotions and sensitivities that I and we could all relate to but due to her position was forbidden to act on those instincts. It didn't, though, mean she didn't have them, and that interested me."

4

The Queen's Head: In the Image of Elizabeth

❧ *Flora Robson* ❧

> *"I'm best remembered for my Elizabeth I"*
> **Fire Over England** 1937

NEVER A BEAUTY, DAME FLORA ROBSON TOLD THE ACTRESS Joanna Lumley, in a rare television interview, that she was unbothered by this because it meant she could carry on working as she aged, whereas the beauties lost their looks *and* their careers. In a career spanning six decades she was never afraid to tackle unsympathetic characters and murderesses, stating that they had "more meat". Of her contemporaries, she perhaps most resembles Bette Davis. They share the same attitude to their careers, happy to take a supporting part if the part is a good one, delighted to tackle a villainess. They also share a no-nonsense approach to their craft and an understanding that it is talent, not looks, that brings success. Unlike Davis, though, Robson didn't photograph well on camera; Davis's sour prettiness can, when necessary, give the impression of beauty, something Robson's plainer features never achieved.

She made her screen debut in 1931, and by 1933 was acting opposite the temperamental star Elisabeth Bergner in the historically inaccurate film *Catherine the Great*. After playing Mary Tudor on stage in 1935, she landed the part of Mary's half-sister Elizabeth in *Fire Over England*, which led to Hollywood and another stab at the Virgin Queen, making her the first actress to play the part twice*. She didn't stay long in Hollywood though: "The further I went in films, the more disappointments, until I steeled myself not to expect much… It's just a diversion, really. I always prefer the stage." Robson did, however, enjoy the result of *Fire Over England*, if not the actual process of making it. Released in March 1937 by United Artists the film is a piece of historical froth weighted chiefly through the speeches of Elizabeth herself. Set in 1588, the year of the Spanish Armada, relations between England and Spain are at breaking point due to the looting of Spanish vessels by English seamen, led by Francis Drake. Drake's exploits cause a sea battle, and the English Richard Ingolby is captured by the Spanish. Ingolby's son Michael, played by Laurence Olivier, manages to escape and, injured, washes ashore on the land of the Spanish Don Miguel, the head of the Spanish fleet. The young Ingolby is nursed back to health by Don Miguel's daughter, and before long love appears to bloom, at least on her part. Back at the English court, Vivien Leigh's young and beautiful Cynthia, granddaughter of Lord Burghley and a lady-in-waiting to the Queen, pines for her lover Michael, while avoiding the wrath of the jealous, ageing Queen (Robson is a perfect foil for Leigh's vivacious loveliness). On learning of his father's execution by the Spanish, Michael escapes to England, where he pleads with Queen Elizabeth to fight Spain. Moved by his words she agrees to let Michael travel back to Spain as a spy, to get hold of the letters that plot her assassination (this theme runs throughout Elizabeth's time on stage and screen and becomes particularly topical in the 2000s). Armed with the documents, Michael returns to England, though during his voyage the Spanish Armada has set forth to do battle and the Queen has addressed her troops at Tilbury (this sequence would have a similar effect on the pre-war English public as Olivier would achieve with his rousing speeches in *Henry V* six years later). Michael is knighted by the Queen (as an act of atonement) and, on a perilous undertaking to beat the Spanish, uses lighted ships, the 'Fire' of the title, to strike their Armada by night, thus destroying it. The rest is history, and the English, led by Michael, are victorious. The lonely and vain Elizabeth, after banishing all mirrors from the palace (again the influence of Victorian paintings), agrees to the marriage of Michael and Cynthia and resumes her role as mother of her kingdom and people.

---

*   She would also go on to play her in Maxwell Anderson's *Elizabeth the Queen*.

To some degree Robson would become synonymous with Elizabeth: "People were happier when I donned my red wig, pearls and gowns as the Virgin Queen." As recently as 1970 (Robson died in 1984) she was reprising the role in a new play, *Elizabeth Tudor*, but it is her first outing as Elizabeth for which she is best remembered.

Like most of the actresses selected to play Elizabeth on screen, Robson was the only choice for the part. She had been under contract with Korda since 1931 (he was impressed with her work on the historical *Catherine the Great*) and he wanted her for the third lead in his new film. It seems, though, as with her previous screen work, that this picture would also prove problematic for Robson. The box office appeal of the picture, as far as Korda was concerned, lay not with the Queen but with the story of Michael and Cynthia, along with the action scenes involving the English fleet and the Spanish Armada. A character triangle emerges – but not a love triangle, there is no romance between Elizabeth and Michael – which places Robson at a dramatic disadvantage. Her relationship with Michael is that of gracious Queen and loyal subject, yet with Cynthia it is that of an ageing monarch jealous of her beautiful, young lady-in-waiting.

Robson felt uncomfortable in the costumes, and the false nose she was given to wear also proved a challenge. This disguised her rather bulbous nose with a graceful slope, that looks more natural than many a prosthetic of the time. She was further hampered by finding motion pictures a trial and being 'inserted' into scenes somewhat alien, as well as missing the camaraderie that comes with being part of a theatrical company. Due to the weight of the costumes, which often left her breathless and in pain, especially the headgear, and the time it took for the wardrobe department to dress her, she was unable to change for meals, and for some reason Denham Studios, where Korda had made *The Private Life of Henry VIII*, hadn't thought to create a special chair for her, so, as she was not capable of sitting on an ordinary chair, she was relegated to managing on a stool for the entire shoot!

Robson was learning film acting as she went along, and wisely insisted on watching her rushes each day. She tried to quickly correct any mistakes or mannerisms that she thought inappropriate and became something of her own director, in the face of little interest from William K. Howard. The nearest he gave Robson to a note was to tick her off after one scene, in which she had to cry, telling her not to behave as if she were at a premiere! However, he seems to have trusted Robson to know what she was doing, so focused his energies on the action and love interest of the film. This was perhaps unfortunate when one considers that in two years' time the country would be at war and looking for all the morale British leadership and sovereignty could give. Robson learnt that she often gazed down when in thought, forgetting that the key to cinema acting is through the eyes; this she soon righted, but she was concerned that she was often photographed in profile – the cinematographer was keen to accentuate the famous Elizabeth silhouette, but Robson felt that instead it only drew attention to her false nose.

She had been surprised to be cast in the role, feeling that she looked so unlike Elizabeth that it would prove a problem on camera, yet in fact she would triumph with her 'unusual' interpretation. Robson's physical unsuitability for the part was not to be the last implausible casting decision with regards to the Queen. When a major reinterpretation of Elizabeth is needed, the actress chosen is more often than not an established star (Cate Blanchett, in *Elizabeth* 1998, and Robson to some degree, are exceptions to this rule), and because of this few attempts have been made to reinterpret her exact appearance; Robson's choice is to settle for a middle ground: her hairline remains, and a heavy wig is added, the costumes are fairly accurate, and she got used to the putty nose. Yet she still doesn't really look like the Elizabeth of portraits, especially the more naturalistic images, such as the Darnley Portrait, perhaps the most authentic likeness we may have. Robson, Davis, Jackson and Judi Dench all have rounder, fuller faces that just aren't the angular template that we know to be Elizabeth's. The bewitching oval, inherited from Anne Boleyn, later to become the hooked crag, 'long and thin' in Elizabeth's decay, and the eyes that range from being described as black, beautiful or beady, have no similarity to the features of Robson or the other actresses mentioned. Helen Mirren in *Elizabeth I* and Anne-Marie Duff in *The Virgin Queen* are also not natural Elizabeth lookalikes, yet they, and those before them, were deemed appropriate casting. Jackson, in the latter of her two incarnations, was pitted against Vanessa Redgrave, an actress with features more like Elizabeth's, who had been a persuasive and hypnotic Anne Boleyn in a cameo performance in *A Man for All Seasons*, yet because of her 'type' and box office record she was cast as Mary. Elizabeth is cast according not only to which actress is in vogue at the time, but also to her *type*. Most of these women have a personality in the public's imagination, and are often remembered or recognised less for their weaknesses than for their screen – and often off screen – strength. So it comes as no surprise that, after playing Elizabeth, Robson's film work was peppered with formidable, sometimes sinister characters: her Queen of Hearts in *Alice in Wonderland* has much that is recognisable in Robson's Queen of England.

When Robson nervously went under the lights, she should not have worried: she was merely one of the first in a long line of unlikely looking actresses to wear Elizabeth's crown. Elizabeth has such a strong visual image in our memory that to a degree the costumes speak for themselves and the face doesn't have to be a carbon copy. As the novelist Hugh Walpole wrote, "a head of hair loaded with crowns and powdered with diamonds, a vast ruff, vaster skirt and a load of pearls are the features by which everyone knows at once the pictures of Queen Elizabeth."

Fortunately for Robson, by mid-production the director had grown interested in her scenes and began to pay her more attention, probably because her 'Mother of England' interpretation of the Queen seemed to be walking away with the film's acting honours. The interior court drama often required Robson to learn many pages of dialogue; she was always terrified of forgetting lines, and Howard grew more respectful of the diligent actress when she appeared word perfect for each take. She was often required to conduct her own rehearsals with fellow actors, but although she was flattered to be trusted in such a manner it also increased the alienation she felt at acting in this relatively new medium. Matters weren't helped when Olivier insisted on doing all his own dangerous stunts; this irritated the producer, Erich Pommer, who was anxious not to have a costly injured actor on his hands. Robson defended Olivier, telling Pommer that "He would feel a fraud to be praised for a scene he did not do himself." Pommer's succinct reply was, "All film acting is fraud." But in time matters improved, so much so that, when it came to filming the pivotal Tilbury speech, she felt confident enough to express her view that the four lines of Elizabeth's in the scene were not enough for such an important moment in the picture. At first she went to the writer Clemence Dane, but it appeared that she too thought the speech lacking. The decision to keep the Queen's famous speech to the minimum was made by Pommer, who wanted *Fire Over England* to be an action film (hence the director's focus on Olivier) and particularly accessible to the American market, rather than historically accurate. Robson spoke to her friend Charles Laughton, with whom she had worked at the Old Vic, and he advised learning the famous speech by heart and then merely suggesting it to Howard as an alternative.

This was not to be the last time an actress would feel so strongly about

Elizabeth that she would be forced to intervene on behalf of her character. It might have appeared to some that Robson was just beefing up her role and enlarging her screen time, but this was not in her nature: she truly believed that her heroine, Elizabeth, justified such treatment; and the film is all the better today for her intervention. We will see several more cracks at the Tilbury speech over the decades, although in many ways Robson's, the first screen attempt, is possibly the finest due to its honesty and simplicity.

In the film, Tilbury is an elaborate mass of tents that perhaps inspired the Agincourt sequence in Olivier's *Henry V*. Filmed on location at Bulstrode Park in Buckinghamshire, Robson, putty nose melting in the sun, though majestic in a breastplate and plumed hat, had to contend with her understudy's horse as her own mount was lame. Robson was not experienced at riding side-saddle and the horse didn't react well to crowds, but in spite of this she plucked up courage and asked if she could leave the text and give a condensed version of the Tilbury speech. Despite the temperamental horse, Robson gamely ploughs on with a firm, modulated delivery: she makes no attempt to cook up an Elizabeth voice other than her own rich, warm tones*. Her right hand tightly clutching the reins, she raises her left in a half salute before anticipating a "famous victory!" Technicians knelt to stroke the horse's legs to calm the animal, out of sight, while others tried to hold the tail to still it. "Cut!" was finally called and the actress had her way: the speech was kept in. Clemence Dane, the writer, agreed that the scene was the better for using Elizabeth's own words. Dane was then asked to quickly write another scene for Elizabeth showing the celebrations for victory over the Armada at Old St Paul's. But it is the Tilbury scene that remains in the imagination after the film is over; even if the famous "I know I have but the body of a weak and feeble woman" speech is shortened and altered (for example, "heart and stomach of a king" becomes "heart and valour"), it is Elizabeth's own words and intention that resonate still. She was genuinely moved by the warmth with which she was greeted by her troops and shed tears as she declared "God bless you all" to the cries of "Lord preserve our Queen". Affected by the emotion of the situation, she stated that she felt "in the midst of the heat of the battle" and wanted to ride out to meet the invasion should it occur, much to the distress of her ministers. But the intention was genuine, and the effect of her rousing

---

* Elizabeth's own voice was reported as 'high and shrill', a description that bears little similarity to most of the actresses who have attempted the role.

words, later published, have become as synonymous with her as the ruff round her neck or the colour of her hair.

Does the film stand up today? Yes, though because of the circumstances of the Olivier/Leigh courtship the quality of the movie is often overlooked in favour of what was going on behind the scenes: both Leigh and Olivier were unproven on film, yet their love affair is now one of the picture's chief claims to fame. But in spite of all the fuss made of the liaison, the core of the film remains the Queen, and she is the thread that holds the drama together, all credit going to Robson for this. Often when Elizabeth is in a movie, even if she isn't the chief player on screen, she can, through sheer force of personality, appear to dominate the proceedings, as for instance Judi Dench's performance in *Shakespeare in Love*. So, do we believe in Robson's playing of the Queen very much as the history books of the 1930s would have shown her? The film doubles as a piece of propaganda due to the onset of the Second World War, therefore Elizabeth is a mother, a nurturer, Good Queen Bess the heroine rather than villain; we admire and want to emulate her stoic sense of duty and desire to serve her nation, for isn't she married to her country and England her husband? Hasn't she made the greatest sacrifice of all? Robson portrays all this with aplomb and gives us a Queen that is often overlooked by showier performances.

In her first appearance, under a coat of arms inaccurately bearing the motto *Dieu et Mon Droit* (*Semper Eadem* – Always/Ever the Same – was Elizabeth's motto), and in a court that bears no resemblance to any English court of the period, the Queen sits, glittering in a gown that Elizabeth would never have worn. Yet somehow it works. Robson, her large lips powdered over and her false nose in place, is so committed to the role that when she tells us, in one of the most beautiful voices to grace either the English stage or screen, "*I am England,*" the inaccuracies seem trivial and inconsequential, and within moments the audience is won over. Her Queen is concerned and tender, sometimes snappy; she talks of her fear of invasion, and we really believe that her fear is genuine (as, at the time, was England's fear of war with Germany). Worry follows Elizabeth like a shadow. When Cate Blanchett in *The Golden Age* discusses the same anxieties, we get a sense not only of her desperate concern for the nation but of what it will mean for her *own* future, perhaps a similar fate to that of her mother? The image of the setting sun, implying the Queen's age and in time her death, whether that is by murder or natural causes, haunts the Queen on stage and screen, and the threat of assassination isn't a plot device to tie in with recent historical events. In *Fire Over England* a supporter of the Catholic cause will try and murder Elizabeth, but Elizabeth graciously pardons the woman and appears only momentarily shaken by the incident, soon regaining her composure – as Great Britain must if it is to go to war – the illusion being that the Queen is divine in her mercy, her image taking on religious heights. Later in the picture she reflects on her actions towards Mary Stuart and contemplates her own good fortune not to have been killed. The monarch is plucky and inspirational: this is Elizabeth as heroine. Absent for most of the middle section of the film, when the drama moves to the court of Raymond Massey's Philip II of Spain, Robson's Elizabeth talks of springtime being over for her and Robert Dudley, but it is done with warmth and understanding, so much so that we feel the Queen has accepted her advancing years, something we know in reality to be false, yet despite this she continues to insist on trying to look young. She is touching in her dealings with her aged chief minister Burghley, her 'Spirit' (Elizabeth had a fondness for bestowing pet names on favourites), feeding him broth – something the Queen did in real life.

How close does Robson get to the Queen and the woman? There are some who have felt that she is too tempered, too middle class, too much of an English schoolmistress to be a complete representation of so dynamic a character, but this is the nature of the film and what it was trying to say at that time in history.

On the film's release, Robson speedily grew in status as a character actress in the cinema. She would never become a movie star and would always state that her face was the chief reason for this. However, *Fire Over England* did her career no harm at all, and the critics raved about her "magnificent portrait". *The Morning Post* stated that "no one who saw the film was likely to forget the sensitive, but forceful and sympathetic, performance of Flora Robson as the Queen, whom she succeeded in investing with real life." The film went on to win the Gold Medal in Paris and was a resounding box office hit. No one was more surprised than Robson herself.

❦ *Bette Davis* ❦

The Queen of the Lot
The Private Lives of Elizabeth and Essex 1939

THOUGH THE WARNER BROS 1939 HIT *THE PRIVATE LIVES OF Elizabeth and Essex* was shot in Technicolor, our first glimpse of Bette Davis's bravura portrayal of the sixty-year-old monarch is chillingly filmed in dark silhouette. Always thinking of new ways to introduce their top stars, Hollywood studios concocted business, often silent, that would set up the character on screen. Davis had recently won her second Oscar for playing a Southern belle who enters the film on a defiant, tricky colt, the implication being that she, like the colt, is tricky and defiant but can be mastered. These are signals of Hollywood's 'Star Acting'. And no star was a more superior actress with a capital A than Davis, no actress more of a star. She flouted the star system, challenging the many who thought you could only have a leading career if you were a recognised beauty, and refused to follow the traditional Hollywood pattern that women should be accommodating, eventually changing the face of the female on the screen.

By 1939, Davis was at the peak of her powers and Queen of the Warner Bros back lot, with two Oscars and three nominations behind her (she would acquire another eight) and a string of four hits back to back. In Hollywood's greatest year, she would gain her fourth nomination (missing out to Vivien Leigh as Scarlett O'Hara), receive the best reviews of her career for *Dark Victory* and give another three performances all worthy of Oscar nominations. Although *Dark Victory* and *The Old Maid* proved the bigger pulls at the box office, *Elizabeth and Essex* probably gave her the greatest challenge as an actress and would remain one of the handful of her favourite roles. By the time she played the Queen she had gained a reputation for forcefulness and fearlessness, going head to head with her studio bosses as she fought for better scripts, better parts and equal pay for women, which resulted in a court case with Warner Bros in 1937.

Davis had a lifelong fascination with Elizabeth, finding similarities in their character, and was keen to stress her jealousy of Elizabeth's power to "Roll heads!" In the first of her autobiographies, *The Lonely Life*, published in 1962, Davis called Elizabeth 'My tankard of tea', and it is not surprising that in the next sentence she mentions Charles Laughton. The 'difficult' Laughton, a sobriquet frequently attributed to Davis herself, was visiting the set of *Elizabeth and Essex* when he gave Davis a piece of advice she took with her to the grave: "Never not dare to hang yourself for your art." This fierce belief in her 'art', this dedication to her career and the playing of the character over merely playing oneself, made Davis unique amongst film actresses of her time, and this was made brazenly clear to Laughton when he viewed the shaved scalp and missing eyebrows that Davis insisted on in her journey towards artistic truth. It now seems unsurprising that she received this advice from Laughton as there is a direct link between his performance of Henry VIII and her Elizabeth. Although *The Private Life of Henry VIII* is a history lesson with its tongue firmly in its cheek, with the King as a drumstick-hurling old lecher doing the same degree of damage to Henry as Shakespeare's interpretation of Richard III would do for that king, Laughton's Henry and Davis's first attempt at Elizabeth are both created with a tremendously broad brush stroke, Davis creating a performance as vibrant as the wig she donned for the part. Neither was famed for underplaying, and when portraying monarchy both decided that all the stops should be pulled out. Laughton won an Oscar for playing Henry VIII, and Davis would have been nominated had she not gained a nod from the Academy for *Dark Victory*.

The fact that the director was one of Davis's least favourite, the bullying Michael Curtiz, seems not to have worried her before filming began; she was now known as 'The Fourth Warner Brother', such was her status at the studio. Much had changed since Curtiz spat out insults at her from behind the camera: "No-good, sexless, son of a bitch!" Davis was, however, concerned by the picture's proposed title; before *The Private Lives of Elizabeth and Essex* was picked, various titles had been considered. The script had been adapted from Maxwell Anderson's *Elizabeth the Queen*[*]; Lytton Strachey's *Elizabeth and Essex* was still a bestseller; and these two works combined had set a precedent for playing up the romantic elements of the relationship between Elizabeth and Robert Devereux, stepson of her long-time favourite Robert Dudley. Warner Bros was no different from any other studio and was

---

[*] Anderson had a penchant for Tudor women: not only would he write about Elizabeth and Mary but also Anne Boleyn in *Anne of the Thousand Days*, later to be made into a film starring Geneviève Bujold.

more interested in creating a story that would appeal to an audience made up of women, Davis's core fan base, with some action scenes to keep the men happy, than in the historical facts. The combination of Davis and Flynn seemed like a sure-fire hit.

Davis of course favoured Anderson's title. Warner wanted a title that would include the other star of the picture, Flynn, and came up with *The Knight & The Lady*. Davis refused this, stating that it held the wrong connotations, and *The Private Lives of Elizabeth and Essex*, a throwback to Laughton's film, with her character gaining top billing, was finally agreed upon; such is the business of Hollywood; but Warner knew there was nobody else in the studio who could play Elizabeth, nor any major actress in Hollywood either, and Davis was well aware of this.

However, when it came to the casting of the Earl of Essex she was less fortunate. William Wyler had recently completed filming *Wuthering Heights* with Merle Oberon and the young Laurence Olivier, who had found international fame as Heathcliff thanks to Wyler's taskmaster direction, and it made him realise the power of the film medium and to give it the respect it deserved. Davis didn't need to be taught this lesson, a skilled stage actress, with successes in material as diverse as Ibsen and light comedy, she had already switched allegiance from stage to screen. She had been told of Olivier's new commitment to celluloid by Wyler, who had worked with her on *Jezebel*, Davis's second Oscar-winning role, and had conducted an affair with her during the movie's shoot. Davis would rank him as her greatest director and, at his suggestion, she decided she wanted Laurence Olivier as Essex. No hogging the limelight for Davis, a frequent accusation, she wanted the finest actors, directors and technicians. These, she believed, would 'up her game' and produce a better picture. Instead, she got Errol Flynn, whom she (politely) summed up as a "fly in the ointment". It is a pity, for seeing the film today one can only imagine that the pairing of Olivier and Davis would have made the picture, great as it is, even better. Flynn is hopelessly outclassed by Davis. In spite of this, due to the off-screen tension between the two stars, the film crackles with energy, and Davis, overcompensating for Flynn's light playing, produces an Elizabeth who is at times heavy duty but nonetheless a truly magnificent spectacle. Davis was the first actress to play Elizabeth on screen who would really search to make the Queen's image as lifelike as she possibly could. With her rather round face, huge eyes and short nose, Davis is very far from the Elizabeth of portraiture, but in terms of personality, it makes sense to cast this inferno of intensity.

With eyebrows plucked and her face heavily painted and powdered, to give the impression of egg white, alum, borax, poppy seeds and lead, which Elizabeth favoured, her eyelashes also powdered, to make the eyes appear smaller, and her lips, fairly small like Elizabeth's, painted to fit their contours, rather than the generous helping of lipstick we normally associate with Davis, the actress makes a startlingly convincing queen. Davis weighted her exhausted frame in historical detail*. Though she incorrectly stated that she studied many of Hans Holbein's portraits of Elizabeth in her research (Holbein never painted the Queen), she knew she would be up against difficulties if she wanted to create an authentic likeness. So she test shot her costumes, hair and make-up with those acceptable to the studio, which presented Elizabeth in a softer, more romantic light, while having another set of costumes, make-up and wigs prepared for the actual shooting. When the time came to start filming, Davis donned her preferred garb, chalked up her face, and nobody questioned her choices when they viewed the rushes. She certainly wasn't beautiful, but neither was she the "Frankenstein" (sic) that they feared. Whereas other actresses wanted to appear attractive on screen, Davis cares nothing for this: "I don't give a fuzzy rat's ass what I look like!" she was fond of exclaiming. With Elizabeth she goes one step further and transcends herself almost unrecognisably, forcing her own distinctive features into those of Elizabeth's.

The palace of Davis's Elizabeth is a lavish spectacle. Painted backdrops mix with supposed 'real' sets, and the soft tonal quality gives the piece a storybook feel. The sets take on mammoth proportions, something all Hollywood interpretations of Elizabeth inaccurately create. Shekhar Kapur's 1998 *Elizabeth* will also feature operatically scaled interiors. In actual fact the courts of Elizabeth were a warren of small chambers, each leading off the next. The use of colour in the Tudor court *is*, however, correct. In the last few years the restoration of paintings of the period have found that Tudor England was brighter and more decadent than had originally been supposed. Warner Bros' creative team goes for impact, and this matches some of Davis's own choices when portraying Elizabeth. She had always wanted to play her and had been particularly influenced by *Elizabeth the Queen* starring Lynn Fontanne at the Guild Theatre in 1930, the production co-starring Fontanne's husband, Alfred Lunt, as Essex. This play set a precedent

---

* Warner kept their top star extremely busy and Davis was near collapse from overwork and stress. She had recently become divorced and weighed only eighty pounds at the time of shooting.

for Davis to view other productions on Broadway before having them made into movies for herself, much to the annoyance of actresses who had created the parts on stage.

Davis's Elizabeth is a very different creation from Fontanne's: less poetic, more gutsy*. We already know that the Queen is 'difficult' – Robert Cecil tells us so as the court awaits Essex's return after a great victory. We hear Davis's voice, lower than usual to give the effect of age, spouting a Hollywood form of English, commanding and clipped – the use of 'me' rather than 'my' tells us that we are in the 'Merrie England' of Shakespeare, as a costumed silhouette (hooped skirt, enormous ruff) quivers and twitches behind a screen as she finishes her toilet, assisted by her waiting women having difficulty getting a shoe onto the fidgeting Royal Foot. In fact the Queen would have been dressed by ladies-in-waiting of rank, not serving wenches, but we are not here for the historical accuracy. We want to see Queen Bette play Queen Bess, and Curtiz keeps us tantalisingly waiting. Elizabeth is only revealed when the court is assembled; the camera focuses on the shoe, now in place, before it pans up the skirts, across a bodice swathed in ropes of pearls, before settling on the face of the Queen. One can only imagine the original audience reaction. Respect at her bravery? Or the feeling that she was again going too far, as she had recently aged up to star in an adaptation of Edith Wharton's *The Old Maid*?

The film won Davis some of the finest reviews of her career†, and in one scene allows us an insight into what it is to be not only a female ruler but also at the top of your profession, and female, in Hollywood: "To be a queen is to be less than human. To put pride before desire. To search men's hearts for tenderness, to find only ambition. To cry out in the dark for one unselfish voice, to hear only the dry rustle of the papers of state, to turn to one's beloved with stars for eyes, and have him see behind them only the shadow of the executioner's block. A queen has no hour for love: time presses, events crowd upon her. She is a shell, an empty glittering husk; she must give up all that a woman holds most dear." The scene is played with a taut numbness, not with overt bitterness or any form of self-indulgence.

---

* If her interpretation could be compared to any other Elizabeth, Glenda Jackson's would come closest.

† In *The New York Times*, Frank S. Nugent wrote, "Bette Davis is a strong, resolute, glamour-skimping characterisation against which Mr Flynn has about as much chance as a bean shooter against a tank."

'Elizabeth with Time & Death' by an unknown artist

It is Davis at her finest and simplest. The hand twitches a little, a familiar mannerism, but the gaze into her future, knowing very well what she can expect, is focused and dead, the mark of a truly great performer and exponent of the female dilemma.

Flynn, as the Earl of Essex, returning to court having defeated the Spanish at Cadiz, is rather less memorable. Instead of the warm welcome from the Queen he anticipates, Elizabeth reprimands him for not obtaining the Spanish treasure fleet. Infuriated, his ego puffed up by his increasing popularity with Elizabeth's subjects, he leaves her presence, turning his back on the Queen. He could be Robin Hood or any of the other romantic rogues he was playing at the time. "You dare turn your back on Elizabeth of England? You dare?" she snaps, striding from her dais, and we see for the first time Davis take on Elizabeth's walk, which by the time of *The Virgin Queen* (1955) will begin to look, as one reviewer put it, as if she had "a third leg"! She imbues Elizabeth with a mannish sashay/stride that zigzags its way across the floor, before she plants a hearty slap on Flynn's head. The assault was for real, no doubt tempered by their mutual dislike. Flynn was continually late on the set and unfamiliar with his lines, but had Davis known that he had a condition that could make a blow to the head fatal would she have eased off? In his autobiography, Flynn tells of trying to ask Davis to go easy on him: "Joe Louis himself couldn't give a right hook better than Bette… My jaw went out, I felt a click behind the ear and I saw all these comets… I felt as if I were deaf… 'If you want a little slap, that is just too bad!'" Davis reportedly told him.

After Essex's stormy departure, Elizabeth places Walter Raleigh in a higher position at court, something that she knows will infuriate Essex, and even though she regrets her harsh words she is forced to send Essex to Ireland to quash the rebels there. During his absence, their letters are intercepted, the Queen's displeasure with Essex thaws and in time he will return triumphant. This is all the brainchild of Anderson. There is no history of any letters being intercepted between Elizabeth and Essex, and although the love between the two is chaste it is also clear that there *is* a love between them. Anderson, ably assisted by Lytton Strachey in his dual biography *Elizabeth and Essex*, cooks up a romance between the two that never actually occurred. Essex was a favourite of the Queen but that had much to do with him being the stepson of Elizabeth's real love, Robert Dudley. Her interest in him was maternal, not sexual. When her fondness for him was returned with ingratitude and greed, it was clear to Elizabeth and her council that Essex's interest was for his own advancement and not to serve his monarch.

The chief culprit of the interceptions is a lady-in-waiting* (Olivia de Havilland), a rival to the Queen in Essex's affection. Again we have a love triangle similar to *Fire Over England* – in fact we have an identical scene in which Elizabeth comes out of the shadows of the court to discover the lovers. She dismisses the younger woman and steps aside for her, in a sarcastic bit of majesty that only Bette Davis could pull off. We also see Elizabeth, once again at her mirror, cruelly reminding herself of her ageing looks, while her lady-in-waiting, this time de Havilland, looks on.

Essex returns to Ireland again and is now defeated, but he still returns to London as if victorious, to a triumphant welcome, even though the Queen

---

* At this point in her reign Elizabeth had very strained relations with her young ladies-in-waiting, many of them having affairs, marriages and even pregnancies in secret, for fear of upsetting the irritable and embittered monarch. Her treatment of Olivia de Havilland's Lady Penelope is relatively accurate; as well as being a great Queen, Elizabeth was also petty, jealous and spiteful towards younger women whom she saw as a threat.

and he are at odds due to the situation over the letters. Essex threatens to overshadow her, more popular with her people than ever, and the Queen has him sent to the Tower. Once again, we have Elizabeth as the captor and Essex, a figure of romance, a male Mary Stuart, more attractive, popular and, most importantly, younger than Elizabeth, at the Queen's mercy. Even if the plot of the film and some of the dialogue can be traced to historical sources, the actual idea of the emotional tragedy played out between these two characters is a fantasy.

The film's story is only loosely based on historical fact, and it is interesting to analyse the Queen's character, given that at last we have a fully rounded performance rather than a cameo or character turn. So, how like Elizabeth is Bette Davis's Elizabeth? Though Davis was dubbed the 'wide-eyed Sarah Bernhardt' of her generation, and could be a scenery chewer herself, only three decades separate the two performances, yet Davis's can still be appreciated, whereas Bernhardt's is a period piece. But playing "my favourite woman in history" doesn't necessarily make for a truthful and accurate performance and, as with all her characters, there is much of Davis in the finished article; for instance, her arsenal of nervous tics are channelled to become the Queen's nervous countenance. Davis's Elizabeth is over thirty years into her reign, with a wealth of emotional baggage, and the main playing choice that Davis makes is to show the embittered character that now wears the heavy crown of England: ever distrustful, desperate for personal affection yet suspicious of it when it is offered. She is very much the Elizabeth of the 'Time & Death' portrait, painted in the reign of Elizabeth's successor James I, the weary burden of state soon to be lifted by the great leveller, death. Elizabeth is reflective, despondent, lonely and bitter. Davis's fidgety body, not just the hands but every part of Davis, jigs with a pent-up energy that can't seem to find an outlet. Her creaking gait and the frozen expression all make for an Elizabeth emotionally tortured, desperate for this one last stab at happiness, yet knowing herself well enough to realise that this will never happen. In many ways it should be a perfect fit between actress and role; Elizabeth was Queen of England and Davis was Queen of Hollywood: both were bossy, prone to emotional fits, famously difficult, unpredictable and moody, grumpy, loyal, strong, inspiring, resolute and determined. Until Glenda Jackson's momentous performance in *Elizabeth R*, for over three decades Davis's Elizabeth wasn't to be challenged.

An interesting postscript to *The Private Lives of Elizabeth and Essex* is that it is now, when on sale or shown in cinemas or on television, often re-titled *Elizabeth the Queen*, Maxwell Anderson's original title: Davis, no doubt, would have approved.

5

Are You a Mary or an Elizabeth?

❧ *Helen Mirren* ❧

"As you get older, you get asked to play Queens"
Elizabeth I 2005

ENGLAND 1579, AND QUEEN ELIZABETH HAS SO FAR REFUSED TO marry. Familiar territory, though this interpretation of Elizabeth is not. Our first shot of her is being disrobed (in the style of Stephen Frears' *Dangerous Liaisons*, where the two leads, Glenn Close and John Malkovich, are seen being dressed by their large assembly of servants as the credits roll). In *Elizabeth I*, we have Elizabeth unmasked, an attempt to strip away all previous incarnations of her, though we have seen behind that mask before, so the opening sequence of the Queen having a fertility check, as in *Elizabeth R*, is again familiar to us.

This Queen is flesh and blood, and the production instils the idea that the audience wants to know what makes the woman, not the monarch, tick. Though as viewers we should take stock, for we wanted that back in the 1970s, and got it in *Elizabeth R*. *Elizabeth I* is dressed up as a modern analysis that will be revealing to a modern audience, but...

In the role of Elizabeth we have a leading actress of great acclaim, giving a fresh spin on the Queen by casting her slightly against type: Harriet Walter, Mirren, and to a degree Cate Blanchett, are all actresses who initially might be thought of as inhabiting the role of the more emotional Mary Stuart. Which begs the question: are we now less accepting of tough female protagonists? Are the ball-breaking heroines of the '30s and '40s – Bette Davis, Joan Crawford, Margaret Lockwood and Barbara Stanwyck – a thing of the past? Certainly over recent years Elizabeth has been sexualised and made more passive with varying degrees of success.

For all its excellence of production – putting to shame the more ham-fisted theatrical efforts of *Elizabeth R* – *Elizabeth I* emerges as modern, somewhat suburban in its casualness and its effort to make Elizabeth a creature of the people. As Mirren disappears in the labyrinth of dark court chambers and corridors, adding layer upon layer of fabric to the cacophony of clothes that adorn the Queen's sacred body[*], she doesn't seem to be the woman who saved her neck during the turbulent years of Bloody Mary, or fought Spain's Armada; Mirren's Elizabeth almost fades away. This is a miscalculation on the part of both actress and director Tom Hooper: Elizabeth must be of the people, not be just one of them. The decision of where to pitch the performance results in ordinariness, and ordinary was something Elizabeth never was: she was *extra*ordinary. And unlike Blanchett's Queen (a fresh and exciting interpretation – but not the final word on the subject), Mirren's Elizabeth bears none of the incredible, hypnotic amalgam of emotions and intelligence that the Queen so obviously possessed.

Elizabeth might be Mirren's "ideal role, with big dresses and loads of jewellery", but her performance is too 21st century to truly convince. She is neither heroine, to be ranked in the annals with Blanchett and even Jean Simmons, nor decisive enough to cross over and become an anti-heroine to be grouped with Schiller's villainess or Florence Eldridge. Mirren in this interpretation, unlike Jackson and Davis, is a very unstarry star – and Elizabeth was a star. When she is not the central theme of the drama[†], as in Mary Stuart inspired productions, Elizabeth is required to be a 'star turn', a showy performance given by a character actress of ability, that can distort the focus of the entire drama; while if she is the main player, the actress tackling the part must sustain a virtuoso scope, keeping all the plates spinning in

---

[*] Mirren chose not to embark on any extreme form of ageing process for the piece.
[†] Glenda Jackson is the only actress to have played Elizabeth in these two different contexts: star vehicle – *Elizabeth R* (1970), and star turn – *Mary, Queen of Scots* (1971). The problem with the latter performance is that, once again, she is so convincing and entertaining at playing Elizabeth, even in this less superior production, that she upsets the balance of the piece and we long for her to be equal to Vanessa Redgrave.

the air, which must surely challenge even the most proficient of performers. Mirren, a favourite with critics, the public and award judges, would go on to win an Emmy, Golden Globe and Screen Actors Guild Award for her efforts and some of the best reviews of her career (though Alesandra Stanley wrote in *The New York Times*: "the interpretation, like so many others, wallows in the painful self-pity of a powerful, ageing woman who craves true love").

For all that might dissatisfy in *Elizabeth I*, it is an assured creation, which a lesser actress might not have managed: it has an emotional arc, even if it is a very moderate one, lacking many of the undulations that should typify the multilayered Queen; and there *are* moments of magic, which can only make one wish for more. Mirren delivers brilliantly in *The Queen*[*] and in so much of her work – but here unfortunately she does not. It seems that when playing one of our two Queen Elizabeths, she is better suited to the one famed for keeping her emotional identity in check.

The drama, written by Nigel Williamson[†], was shot in Lithuania, where Whitehall Palace was reconstructed using original plans for the building which was burnt down in 1698. This is both accurate and marvellous to the eye, presenting the court in a far more extensive and colourful light than had previously ever been seen. Mirren enjoyed the recreation immensely: "You suddenly start to feel you live here." But though the script often pulls in Elizabeth's own words, the drama relies too heavily on familiarity – "What's the news, old friend?" Elizabeth asks, hands outstretched to her lover, Robert Dudley. Mirren's appearance (more Restoration maiden than Elizabethan monarch) and casual demeanour set the tone for the rest of the production. "She's raising her last chance of presenting herself as a catch," stated Mirren at the time of shooting this "very personal story", and this theme, along with Elizabeth's infatuation with Dudley and then Essex, dominates the film. Mirren suggested that the piece would benefit from some added text, focusing more on the political situation: the politics are here, but this is a private story, one that places too much of a present-day spin on a 16th-century dilemma. By modernising Elizabeth in such a way, yet presenting the production authentically, the audience are confused into believing this was what Elizabeth and her life

---

[*] Due to shooting schedules, Mirren only had six weeks between the two productions.
[†] Mirren accepted the part before reading the script, stating: "I think it's an age thing: as you get older, you get asked to play Queens." As well as Elizabeth II, she has also played Charlotte of Mecklenburg-Strelitz, wife of George III, and a television drama about Catherine the Great of Russia has just been released.

were like, that she was like us, and that Elizabeth and Dudley were cosy lovers. With phrases such as "Kiss me, Bess", we are back at the court of Bette Davis's Queen, which at least acknowledged that the presentation was a fairy tale. Elizabeth was human, but she was also a shrewd stateswoman during one of history's deadliest times. Mirren's Queen is emotional, fallible, vulnerable, a mass of "extremes", as Mirren pointed out, but these we rarely see. 'Elizabeth I is still Queen of the Screen' proclaimed *The Daily Telegraph*, but for all the pomp and the 'big dresses' she isn't *Queen* enough. The historian David Starkey would argue that, as Shakespeare did, it is acceptable to play "fast and loose" with the facts, but people will think, because of the appearance of the production, that this is real. Elizabeth never met Mary Stuart, or Mary's son, James I. And there are more general discrepancies, usually in the presentation of how the court reacts to the Queen – courtiers sit in her presence, and do not remove hats or kneel when speaking to her. Though these may seem small details, they do not create a sense of who Elizabeth truly is, undermining her, making her less impressive, and ultimately less powerful.

Speaking at the time, Mirren said that her main inspiration for playing Elizabeth was Miranda Richardson's Queenie in *Blackadder II*: "Her Elizabeth is genius. It's just fabulous and, in its comedic, excessive way, there is a lot of accuracy there." Mirren has a point here. Glenda Jackson states that Elizabeth must have been "impossible", and there is much that is genuinely based on fact in Richardson's performance – if only Mirren had brought some of those extreme flashes of impossibility to *her* characterisation. Hooper misjudged his initial concept for the film: "It's going to be *The West Wing* with ruffs," before going on to say that he wanted to focus on an older love affair (between Elizabeth and Leicester) and the latter part of the reign which he felt was less normally covered. But in fact the fate of Mary Stuart, the Spanish Armada and Elizabeth's relationship with the Earl of Essex are all presented with common recurrence; it is the middle years which are so often ignored.

The production's main themes therefore, the Queen's lifelong love affairs with Dudley* and then his stepson, and the threat to Elizabeth and her crown at the hand of various assassination attempts, driven by Mary Stuart and the Catholic cause, create a heady mix of love and danger. Thrown into this

---

* Mirren believed that Elizabeth, as she always stated, "lived and died a virgin". Though in the production, after an attempt upon her life, Elizabeth contemplates spending the night with Dudley. "You mustn't be alone tonight," he soothes. "Nor shall I, my Lord," replies Elizabeth. Then she decides against it and leaves his chamber.

conundrum is that Elizabeth is still seeking a husband, or playing at seeking one, and that this is her last chance in the game of matrimony. The Duke of Anjou and his manservant make their comic appearance, and Elizabeth and a jealous Dudley bicker over his suitability as her spouse: she wants to go forward with the match, he, and most of the court, think she should not. Elizabeth is torn: whom can she marry to please everyone, and does she not have a say in the matter? The attempt to present Elizabeth's emotional reaction to such a predicament in this modern light is a mistake: it implies again that she is like us, and misses the fact that our interest in her is that she wasn't.

With the return of Anjou to France and the discovery that Dudley has married without the Queen's consent, matters take a darker turn. Another attempt is made upon the Queen's life, and the problem of the captive Queen of Scots comes to the fore. With a tone similar to the final meeting between the cousins in Hal Wallis's *Mary, Queen of Scots*, Mary[*] states that she does not want Elizabeth dead and Elizabeth replies that "I am the only thing that stands between you and destruction." With news of Mary's death, Mirren's rage and guilty repentance is one of the magnificent moments of the series, as she flails about the corridors of Whitehall in search of her ministers and Dudley, before she slaps him about the face and threatens execution on the poor messenger Davison (see Chapter 3). With the death of Mary, the threat from Spain intensifies and war is declared. Mirren, accurately donning a breastplate in the style of Robson, Jackson and Duff, meets her troops at Tilbury. Breaking with convention, she dismounts from her horse and speaks to the soldiers at eye level, with an intimacy which further widens the gulf between the real Elizabeth and this progressive version of her. With victory over Spain, and the death of Dudley (Mirren adds a white powder to her face to show the passing of time), part one closes.

It is strongly implied by Dudley on his deathbed that Elizabeth and his stepson, the Earl of Essex (Hugh Dancy), must care for each other in the coming years. Dudley, knowing the Queen's fancy for younger men, plays matchmaker from beyond the grave. Many had thought *him* an unsuitable

---

[*] An excellent turn from Barbara Flynn, who had played the part in the Greenwich Theatre production of *Vivat! Vivat Regina!* opposite Janet McTeer. Greenwich had also produced *Mary Stuart*, with Fiona Shaw as Mary and Paola Dionisotti as Elizabeth. The production, directed by Tim Albery and designed by Antony McDonald, combined period and modern dress in a similar fashion to Phyllida Lloyd's 2005 production.

romantic partner, but Essex is more so, and Elizabeth, with Dudley dead, is shown as a fool in love. This modern take on the situation makes something of a joke of Elizabeth, only in reality this could have happened, had she not kept control of the state of affairs and acted to rid herself of Essex when matters got out of hand. Dudley, it is implied, kept Elizabeth sailing in the right direction, which is not an accurate interpretation of the part he played in her life, and makes the roles of Cecil and Walsingham less integral to her reign than in fact they were.

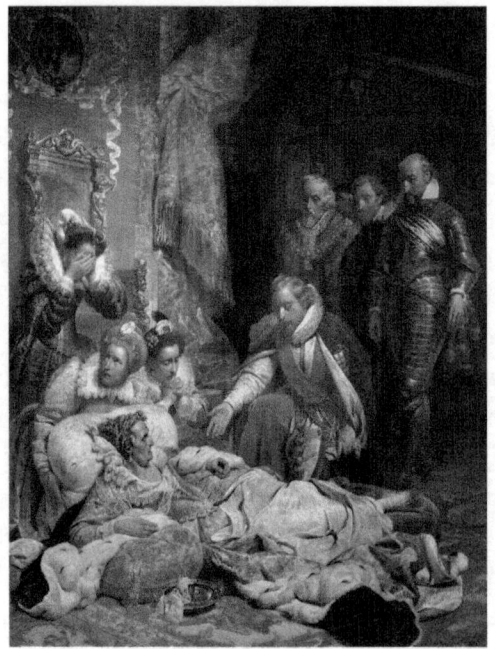

Delaroche's 1828 interpretation of Elizabeth's death
(Peter Horree)

Part two opens with Elizabeth 'the saviour of her country' and asks who will succeed her. The Queen, where once she was unwrapped as the credits roll, is now, in the manner of Cate Blanchett's Elizabeth, dressed and painted into a more familiar rendering of the image we know of her later years. Essex's troublesome influence dominates much of this second half, as does the shifting of power between Walsingham, Cecil and Cecil's son Robert. Suspecting that Essex is plotting with James VI of Scotland (here presented as older than he would have been in reality, and his homosexuality heavily implied), Elizabeth describes James as "that creature in the hat", as she secretly meets him to tick him off for "making overtures to the nobility of [her] court". The Queen gives her last speech to Parliament ('The Golden Speech'*), taking refuge in the words (though Mirren doesn't utter them): "For it is my desire to live nor reign no longer than my life and reign shall be for your good." Elizabeth takes to her cushion-scattered floor, sucks her finger – something the Queen did as she neared death, and first used by Glenda Jackson in *Sweet England's Pride* – and contemplates death. Writers, as well as painters like Paul Delaroche, have become obsessed with the drama of Elizabeth's death. Now visibly older, she banishes those about her, raises herself to her bed and dies, as she had lived, alone.

When *Elizabeth I* was released, a *Daily Mail* magazine article asked, 'Are you a Mary or an Elizabeth?' urging women to define their personalities by characteristics of the rival Queens. To illustrate the article, certain celebrities and actresses were categorised as being either like the English or Scottish Queen. Generalising the Queens' personalities, the article suggested that a typical Mary was best summed up by Princess Diana, Elizabeth Taylor and Sarah Jessica Parker in *Sex and the City*, while Elizabeth was defined by Mrs Thatcher, Madonna and Cynthia Nixon in *Sex and the City*. Cate Blanchett was in the 'Elizabeth' list, the only actress who had actually played the Queen. The article went on to describe Elizabeth as "an intellectual and a pragmatist... Her qualities are admired by Mrs Thatcher, who tried to mould herself in Elizabeth's image and saw the Falklands campaign as her own Armada", while Madonna is, like Elizabeth, "imperious and focused". Mary on the other hand is a "reckless romantic but by no means a fool".

Taking all this into consideration, the actresses who have made any impact in the part might be either Marys or Elizabeths in their personal lives, but in their public personae they have often very definite personality traits that make them highly suitable to play Elizabeth. The most obvious of these are two of the most famous Elizabeths: Bette Davis and Glenda Jackson, who combined stardom with character work; both often took roles on the merit of the film and part rather than its size, both famously shunning glamour, and possessing a no-nonsense fearlessness towards their craft and

---

* 'The Golden Speech', so called because it was said the words should be printed in gold, contained the famous passage: "And though you have had, and may have, many princes more mighty and wise sitting in this seat, yet you never had, nor shall have, any that will be more careful and loving."

the business of acting. It is unsurprising that Davis believed Jackson her natural successor and one of the few actresses she genuinely admired. Other casting decisions have been less straightforward. Cate Blanchett has played the gamut of difficult, complicated women and, although she has a more glamorous image than Jackson or Davis, she scored a personal triumph as the Queen on two occasions. It would not be impossible, however, for her to be cast as Mary. Both Greta Scacchi and Harriet Walter expressed surprise that they were cast as Elizabeth rather than Mary. Janet McTeer was Tony nominated for her Mary in *Mary Stuart*, but wasn't as convincing when she played Elizabeth some years earlier. Eileen Atkins wouldn't have been an obvious casting choice as Mary, and in the same way Anna Massey also probably wouldn't have persuaded as the Scottish Queen. And would Vanessa Redgrave have won over critics if she had played Elizabeth at an earlier point in her career? Probably not: the success of her Virgin Queen was that she played the aged, vulnerable Elizabeth, dealing with the complexities of her diminishing mental health. Anne-Marie Duff is another instance of an actress who twenty years ago would have been a definite casting choice for Mary, but now that Elizabeth is being reinterpreted as softer and more passionate, she joins the list of Redgrave, Mirren and others who find themselves in the part.

Helen Mirren might seem a clear example: to many she may appear an unlikely Elizabeth, yet she scored a triumph in the part, as she did as Elizabeth II. So is Elizabeth the modern-day Mrs Thatcher the article suggests? It seems it will take more than Mirren to truly shift any preconceived ideas about the Queen away from such generalisations. The storybook idea of Elizabeth created by Florence Eldridge and Dudley Nichols' script, based on Maxwell Anderson's play, continues to stick, but what does seem clear, from Mirren's performance, is that we are now keen to cast actresses better suited to playing Mary in the guise of Elizabeth, creating a more vulnerable, passionate and human Queen.

6

Elizabeth: Heroine or Villainess?

❦ *Jean Simmons* ❦

"*She loves life, she loves fun, she loves England!*"*
Young Bess 1953

Y*OUNG BESS*, RELEASED IN 1953†, HAD STARTED LIFE AS A ROMANTIC novel by Margaret Irwin, published in 1944, and was the first part of her 'Elizabeth' trilogy. The other two titles focused on Elizabeth's time in captivity and her relationship with her brother-in-law, Philip of Spain. The book was well received by the public and critics alike, the latter praising Irwin for her research and ability to weave historical accuracy with romantic fiction, so MGM decided that it would be a suitable Technicolor vehicle for British star Jean Simmons, now a resident in Hollywood, and bought the film rights.

It would be easy to write off *Young Bess*, as some critics did back in 1953, as a star vehicle, a piece of froth, grossly sentimental and bearing little resemblance to the hard, historical truth. But what the film does do is present Elizabeth for the very first time as a fully-fledged heroine in her own drama.

---
* Part of MGM's campaign for the movie.
† Coronation year, which is significant as the film emphasises the journey from Princess to sovereign, unlike Benjamin Britten's opera *Gloriana*, which debuted during the coronation celebrations, telling the story of Elizabeth and Essex and presenting Elizabeth as an aged, vain and weary monarch; unsurprisingly the production didn't meet with royal approval.

Before 1953 she had either played second fiddle to Mary Stuart, or shared her screen time with a love interest, the Earl of Essex (in both the Bernhardt and Davis renderings of that particular story). Here, in *Young Bess*, however broad a brush stroke Elizabeth may be painted with – and some moments of screen time are unbearable in their mawkishness – she is a heroine, presented in a positive light, who paves the way for performances such as those given by Cate Blanchett. It is barely credible that Elizabeth had to wait so long for such an interpretation on film, and it is a pity that the end result is so sadly lacking.

With the news of Mary Tudor's death, Kat Ashley (Kay Walsh) and Thomas Parry (Cecil Kellaway)[*], who are servants to Elizabeth, narrate the story of the Princess's journey from cradle to throne. To the oft-repeated singing of the ballad 'Here we go up, up, up!' when something positive happens in the Princess's life, and "Here we go down, down, down" when the opposite occurs, the early years of Elizabeth are neatly recorded as her mother is swiftly eliminated and followed by a succession of stepmothers. Anne Boleyn's neck (Elaine Stewart) comes into sharp focus as Henry VIII (Charles Laughton) roughly caresses it. By the next scene she is, incorrectly (as Anne was executed by a swordsman in the French manner), resting her neck on the executioner's block. Taking the words of the song to extremes, even the road which Elizabeth and Kat Ashley take in their carriage to and from court heads uphill towards London and downhill back to Hatfield, where the Princess was banished after Anne Boleyn's execution. There is nothing terribly inaccurate about the telling of her story in such a manner: her parents *were* "a dangerous mixture", Ashley and Parry *must* have been happy to learn of Mary Tudor's death[†], and it is true that for a while Henry "couldn't bear the sight"

---

[*] Kat Ashley was Elizabeth's governess in her formative years and even spent time in the Tower when Elizabeth was arrested during Mary Tudor's reign. Along with Blanche Parry, who cared for both Elizabeth and Edward VI, she became, to some degree, a mother substitute for Elizabeth as she matured. Both women stayed in her service until their deaths. Thomas Parry was Comptroller of the Queen's household, and he too had been in Elizabeth's employ before she took the throne. All three were rewarded and valued for their loyalty above all things.

[†] After a series of phantom pregnancies (it was said that the Queen's stomach had swollen, probably a result of uterine cancer, which was the suspected cause of her death), Mary deteriorated from the start of 1558. Elizabeth would have been made aware of her half-sister's health on a regular basis and must have felt that it was only a matter of time before she would be crowned. It was now obvious that Mary would never bear a child – in fact Philip had abandoned his wife and returned to his native Spain. Mary died in November and was interred in Westminster Abbey: a small plaque marks her resting place under the colossal monument and effigy that bear the body of Elizabeth.

of his daughter. Snippets of information are cleverly woven into the narrative: Elizabeth's attire, in this case her shoes, are sadly worn, as indeed they were – Ashley had to request funds to aid her charge, as after Anne's death little consideration was given to her upbringing. Such regard for historical detail is all at odds with the generally light-hearted nature of the piece. However appealing such comic turns as Laughton hamming it up as Henry may be, the overall effect is too Hollywood, too gloss, too sugary and too slapstick. Matters deteriorate with the introduction of the adult Elizabeth in the form of Jean Simmons, wearing a puritan-inspired costume of the drabbest shade Hollywood could find. Yet her initial 'pilgrim' appearance tricks the audience, for take another look and see how the fabric clings to the actress's ample body, accentuating her bust and waist. Elizabeth is Cinderella, to be whisked off her feet by Prince Charming, who is just outside the door (a door which Elizabeth has locked) and who is knocking to come in. Chances to redeem itself from such froth are further smashed with the entrance of Stewart Granger as Thomas Seymour (Hollywood was keen to promote husband and wife as a double act). For the type of film that *Young Bess* is, Granger is perfect casting; he bears no resemblance to the real Seymour, any more than Simmons does to Elizabeth, but he does have a suave, roguish air and looks impressive in his Tudoresque britches. Little knowledge or understanding of Elizabeth seems to have been gained in the fourteen years since *The Private Lives of Elizabeth and Essex*. Granger is as unsuitable to play Seymour as Errol Flynn was to play the Earl of Essex, and Simmons is no match for Bette Davis.

Young Bess eventually unlocks the door to Seymour. Refusing to go to court to meet her latest stepmother, who would no doubt soon be replaced by another*, she had locked herself in her chamber, standing with her arms crossed, legs spread, and feet firmly planted, reminiscent of her father, something Seymour recognises as he spies on her. Yet only on Henry's death had the King acknowledged Elizabeth's character as very much his own: "Keep an eye on her," he tells those at his bedside, as if he has finally met his match.

Until now everything has been pretty much true to fact about Elizabeth's formative years, "heads were falling around [Elizabeth] like cabbage stalks"†,

---

* Elizabeth was particularly fond of Katherine Howard, Henry's fifth wife and Elizabeth's third stepmother. Howard was executed for adultery at the age of seventeen.

† An exception is the suggestion that Henry was happy with the birth of Elizabeth. Although he made the best of it, to save face, it was the beginning of the end for Anne, such was his displeasure at being presented with another daughter.

and the rarely mentioned event of Katherine Parr acting as Regent while Henry was on his final campaign in France is also brought to light[*]. So, too, are Parr's religious beliefs, which caused Henry much consternation, for although he had broken with the Catholic faith he was not an extreme a Protestant as Anne Boleyn had become, or as Katherine now was. Parr's views very nearly brought about her execution, but she was quick-witted and managed to win the King over, much to the annoyance of those who opposed her ideas and thought them heretical. Psychological insights are attempted as Elizabeth watches, horrified, as Henry berates Katherine and then warns of how heretics are punished, by deftly stroking the Queen's neck. Elizabeth screams, the significance of the gesture clear.

With the introduction of Deborah Kerr's[†] Katherine Parr, more saccharine is poured into the pot, and the film loses any chance it has of being taken seriously, which is one of the reasons it is often dismissed as an inferior telling of Elizabeth's early story. The other major fault is Simmons herself. Her Elizabeth is too confident, brash and fearless of the perilous situations she finds herself in. She gives the part few emotional layers and relies too heavily, as does the script, on Elizabeth being a replica of Henry, making Laughton the true star of the film, for even when dead his performance is feminised by Simmons' own.

A love story now unfolds: Henry VIII dies, Edward becomes Edward VI, and Elizabeth admits she is in love with Seymour, even visiting him on the night of Henry's death. But evil influences operate at court and Thomas Seymour, the late King's choice as Lord Protector of the Realm, is overlooked in favour of his less charismatic brother Edward (the Duke of Somerset), whose shrewish wife Ann (the excellent Kathleen Byron) sniffs out the romance and has Elizabeth banished to Hatfield: "Down, down, down" we hear the familiar lament once again, as the carriage heads downhill. "I shall love him till I die," she confesses to the worried Kat Ashley, only to discover that Seymour already has a lover: Katherine Parr. In reality, it seems that Thomas Seymour had been on the lookout to make an advantageous match for some time. Elizabeth would have been too young at that point, though for the sake of dramatic licence she is older here; Princess Mary did not suit, due

---

[*] Katherine was successful as Regent, as was Henry's first wife Catherine of Aragon, and her time in power, even if only by marriage, was said to have been an inspiration to Elizabeth.

[†] Kerr had initially been the choice to play Elizabeth.

to her religion; and even Henry's fourth wife, Anne of Cleves, the 'Flanders Mare', was considered. In the end Seymour set his sights on the Dowager Queen, and Katherine, three times married herself, and never really out of love with her old flame, fell once again for the magnetic Seymour, and six months after Henry's death they married. The film suggests that Seymour's ambition to take a wife of high rank and his attraction towards Elizabeth reveal a man in love with two women at the same time. The reality was probably less romantic: Seymour was an ambitious adventurer, impatient to get his own way and, like his brother, advance to the highest possible rank at court. He wouldn't have considered Elizabeth as a future bride, a child at the time of Henry's death – he was far too hasty to think that far ahead – but the Dowager Queen could be and, as the film includes, on Katherine's part it seems to have been a love match still after several years. Seymour's character is also misinterpreted: Granger is jovial, the friend of the people and the young King, to whom he gives money, as the Lord Protector keeps his young charge out of pocket. He is a hero as an admiral on sea crusades, while his brother and his wife play the villains of the piece to such a degree that Lady Anne is dressed like a pantomime wicked Queen. Edward actually mistrusted both his Seymour uncles, and was far from the pouting imp of *Young Bess*, who thinks he can exert some authority at court by posturing as a caricature of his father; so when Thomas Seymour tried to break into his nephew's apartments (possibly to steal control of the King away from his brother) and shot one of the King's spaniels because it barked, Edward, with Edward Seymour's sanction, had him arrested and taken to the Tower.

In *Young Bess* the historical facts of Elizabeth's departure from the Parr household are glossed over: Katherine realises that Elizabeth and Seymour are in love, a chaste infatuation, but, of the two women, she says she needs his love the most, she is not strong… fast forward and Katherine is dead. The famous encounter in the gardens at Chelsea, in which Katherine held Elizabeth while Thomas tickled her and cut her gown "into a hundred pieces", and Thomas entering Elizabeth's bedchamber to wake her each morning, are ignored by Hollywood. The closest the film gets to these incidents is Granger passionately kissing Simmons or slapping her as she laughs in the style of Anne Boleyn: coquettishly, hysterically. Simmons' Elizabeth actually considers marriage to a foreign prince – something the real one played at but would never seriously contemplate – her logic being to make Seymour jealous. In reality, Elizabeth distanced herself from Seymour quickly, even before his arrest. She was attracted to rogues, but on her terms: even at such a young age she was aware of the trouble that might come from such an attachment.

It is only with the replacement of Elizabeth's servants (Ashley and Parry fared poorly under questioning and were removed to the Tower) and her return to court that director George Sidney brilliantly captures Simmons in silhouette as she exits from discussing Seymour's fortunes and their future together with the King, and the film finally picks up the sense of menace that it so often lacks. Simmons is excellent as she hears creaking and footsteps as she lies awake in her bed, only to discover that Seymour has broken into her chamber. The encounter ends with Elizabeth suggesting that they may meet again "perhaps never" – but such moments are few, and not enough to redeem what could have been an interesting exploration of the young Elizabeth's journey to the throne.

Talk that the young King "will not make old bones" sets the story up for Edward's ending, making Elizabeth one step closer to the crown. Yet it is surprising that there is so much talk speculating the ascent of Elizabeth to the throne. Although it was discussed, it would never have been an accepted conclusion: a female ruler was still the last choice when deliberating the succession. With Seymour's arrest, Elizabeth is plunged into greater danger and is questioned by Edward Seymour about her relationship with his brother and their supposed plot to overthrow the King. At first Elizabeth cracks, then, regaining her stamina, she fights her case and ends by striking Edward across the face with a horse whip, threatening that one day he will hang. She faints on quitting the chamber. But such heroic gestures are too late, as is the letter she and the King begin to write – once she is allowed to see her brother – to save Seymour. The drum rolls off, she presses her face to the leaded windowpane; Sidney beautifully captures Simmons' features, a study of despair and resignation, in the soft blacks and greys of her costume and the casement. Edward Seymour has won over his brother Tom, bad has conquered over good, and the gunshot to signify Tom's death confirms this. Elizabeth departs, almost floating, impressively shot as a large silhouette exiting the frame.

Fast forward again, Elizabeth is released, and the story reverts to "Up, up, up!" as Ashley and Parry sing on the eve of Elizabeth's coronation. Elizabeth is dressed more like Mary, Queen of Scots, in black velvet and pearls, a sign of her loss of Seymour or perhaps the death of her hardly mentioned half-sister Mary, or, like Kapur's *Elizabeth*, a tribute to her virginity? Earlier she claims that she would "rather die than be lonely all my life" and this sums up the misconception of the Queen's character and the vehicle: Elizabeth chose to live alone – and she did just that. Perhaps this is why the picture doesn't work: Elizabeth isn't really Hollywood's idea of a heroine.

The film did reasonably well at the box office, with Oscar nominations going to Art Direction and Costume, though both are sometimes outrageously inaccurate, the latter seeming to be heavily influenced by LadyBird books. It also earned its star a National Board of Review award for Best Actress. Simmons was a leading lady in Hollywood by this time, and there had been talk of an Oscar nomination, which did not materialise. The movie has not gone down in history as either a popular favourite or a stand-out performance in the annals of film Elizabeths. What Queen Elizabeth II and her naval husband thought of it, back in coronation year, is not recorded.

❦ *Cate Blanchett* ❦

"The challenge of Elizabeth was enormous"
Elizabeth 1998

IT WAS FIVE MONTHS INTO HIS SEARCH FOR AN ACTRESS TO PLAY Elizabeth, in his forthcoming film of the same name, when director Shekhar Kapur found himself watching a promotional copy of *Oscar & Lucinda*, the 1997 adaptation of Peter Carey's Booker Prize winning novel, and he became transfixed by the unknown Australian actress playing the part of Lucinda Leplastrier. Kapur says, "There was a certain ethereal quality. I was totally fascinated because that's how I saw Elizabeth at the end, very ethereal. And there was a certain fire in the eyes." Knowledge of Blanchett, who had been gaining rave reviews on the Sydney stage since 1992, seemed to have eluded the director, but one viewing of her first motion picture was all he needed[*].

With another two films under her belt Blanchett now found herself on the most gruelling shoot of her career. *Elizabeth* took three months to film and was said to be "the most demanding shoot" Kapur had ever put a cast and crew through. Blanchett would rise at four each morning, and then spend three hours in make-up, before working until eight pm. She insisted on having her hairline shaved to achieve Elizabeth's high forehead, along with bleaching her eyebrows[†]. Twenty-seven costume changes, and locations in Britain's unpredictable climate, found cast and crew travelling all over the country, taking in Bamburgh Castle, Durham Castle, York Minster, Haddon Hall and Durham Cathedral (doubling for Whitehall Palace), to name but a few, all adding to the pressure on Blanchett in the biggest role of her career so far. Blanchett rose to the challenge, magnificently giving us an Elizabeth that ranks as one of the finest. Her "respect for the history" and Elizabeth's character are laudable. *Elizabeth* evolves as a marriage between Kapur's visionary retelling and interpretation of English history and his placing within that world an

---

[*] Before then the red-headed Nicole Kidman's name was frequently mentioned as lead runner for the part.

[†] The demands on Blanchett's hair were particularly gruelling: at one point the dye turned it pink!

actress of luminous beauty and ability, not seen since Greta Garbo graced the lens of director Clarence Brown.

Not breaking with Hollywood tradition, *Elizabeth* begins with a history lesson on cards: "England 1554... The country is divided... Catholic against Protestant... The Catholics' greatest fear is the succession of Mary's Protestant half-sister ELIZABETH". Opening with some disturbingly gruesome scenes of Protestant martyrs burning at the stake, Kapur places his leading figures in colour camps, as he will again in *The Golden Age* – the court of Mary Tudor is dark, dungeon-like and dangerous: a sinister dwarf bustles about the ailing Queen, while foreign-looking ministers plot, surrounded by grey statues of the Virgin Mary; all early imagery of the Princess Elizabeth guides us into a blinding white light.

Using a cinematic trick, also employed in the BBC series *The Virgin Queen*, to introduce the title character to the audience, Kapur keeps us guessing as to whether one of the dancing ladies or the girl riding into the scene on horseback with Robert Dudley is actually Elizabeth. The setting is the grounds of Hatfield House, the Princess's residence, the situation: Dudley (Joseph Fiennes), who has come to court Elizabeth. She carries on dancing as the other women depart the frame. The sexual tension intense, this is a new Elizabeth: haunting, mysterious and vulnerable. While the court of Mary implodes, along with her marriage to the restless Philip of Spain, Elizabeth dances with her handsome suitor.

This is our first cinematic youthful, romantic Elizabeth since Jean Simmons was cast in *Young Bess*. Audiences must adjust their expectations: gone are the white-masked harridans of Davis, Robson and Eldridge; Blanchett's Elizabeth is a beguiling enigma who – it is clearly suggested – can never earn the epithet 'Virgin Queen'. The character of 'Sweet Robin' is of paramount importance to the film, as he was in the Queen's life, and though here, as with the entire film, the lines between fact and fiction are blurred, the sense of attraction and comradeship is genuine and effective. In reality it is highly unlikely that Elizabeth and Dudley did consummate their attraction for each other, but of all the many suitors in her life Dudley was the one who got closest to any form of intimacy. Nearly the same age, and both prisoners in the Tower at the same time, this bloody start bound Queen and favourite in an understanding of the other for life[*].

---

[*] Dudley was imprisoned when his family, who had backed Lady Jane Grey as Queen, fell from royal favour at the start of Mary Tudor's reign. Dudley had been condemned to death in 1554, pardoned, but had had to see his father face the executioner the year before.

With Elizabeth's accession to the throne, Dudley's fortune soared*, although over the forthcoming years it wasn't always a harmonious relationship: Elizabeth was continually jealous of his flirtatious nature, though she herself was renowned for being a prize flirt. In 1559, only a year into Elizabeth's reign, Dudley's first marriage ended when his wife was found at the foot of a staircase with a broken neck. It was common knowledge that the marriage was not a happy one: Lady Dudley, Amy Robsart, stayed away from court, leading a reclusive existence as a semi invalid, tortured with jealousy over the conduct of her husband and his supposed relationship with the Queen. At Amy's death the finger of suspicion pointed towards Dudley, and even the Queen was incriminated, while some thought it suicide, others that the death was caused by an accidental fall; many, however, thought it was murder†. Dudley was sent from court, but after careful investigation nothing could be proved and he was quickly returned to favour.

The relationship was further tested when Elizabeth decided that she would offer him as a second husband to Mary, Queen of Scots. The latter was freshly landed in Scotland and on the lookout for an alliance through marriage, probably a foreign one, that might threaten the safety of England still further. If Mary were to accept Dudley, then Elizabeth would have lost the man to whom she was probably closest but at the same time acquired a secure future for England while Mary lived, and inside information on the goings on at the Scottish court. Mary refused to marry one of Elizabeth's cast-offs, favouring the unstable Henry, Lord Darnley, a decision that signalled the beginning of the end for the ill-fated Scots Queen. Dudley returned to the English court and continued to woo Elizabeth, in the hope that she would make him her consort. This was not to be, and Dudley, after a string of intrigues with court ladies, prompting the Queen's jealousy, married Lettice Knollys, Elizabeth's cousin, whom she famously loathed. So worried was Dudley about telling the Queen that the marriage remained a secret for nine months. When the matter was disclosed, Elizabeth's wrath knew no bounds. In time, once again, he was forgiven – after all, he was the man to whom she had bequeathed her beloved country, when it was feared

---

* Being the Queen's favourite – she would call him her 'Little Dog', whether as a term of endearment or diminishment – led to jealousy from other courtiers, and this, coupled with Dudley's famed arrogance, made him unpopular with many.

† Amy was actually suffering from cancer, and suicide is now the supposed means of death.

she would not survive smallpox, shortly after she became Queen – and his return to favour marked a mellowing in their stormy relationship. Although she remained deeply hurt by this second marriage (in fact she was against any of her inner circle marrying), and belittled him in public about it, she continued to rely heavily upon him for guidance in matters political and personal, and was devastated by his death in 1588, after which it was noted that her spirit deteriorated and became more melancholic. For this was the one man who had, until his marriage to Lettice, never really given up hope of being Elizabeth's consort, and had made such effort to achieve this: hadn't he, after all, laid out a garden – overnight – so that she might wake, look out and find the view from her bedchamber window changed as if by a miracle?! On Dudley's death, the Queen made no provision for his burial or any form of commemoration for the man presumed to be the love of her life. She also claimed back all the properties she had leased him over the years. The motive: Elizabeth's famous miserliness, revenge against Lettice, or was there another reason?

The film *Elizabeth* doesn't solve that mystery or deal with any of the later facts, but instead imagines what might have happened had the two become lovers, though, if one looks at the facts, Dudley's behaviour in the film is completely out of character: he was far too shrewd a social climber to risk his position as the Queen's chief suitor. *Elizabeth* also throws up the question that remains one of the biggest in English history: was Elizabeth a virgin as she stated she would remain when she told Parliament in 1559, only a year into her reign? "And in the end this shall be for me sufficient, that a marble stone shall declare that a Queen, having reigned such a time, lived and died a virgin," she famously declared. At the time it was dismissed by Elizabeth's ministers, sure she would take a husband, bear children and secure the Tudor dynasty and the safety of her country, as any Queen should. Others feel that it is interesting that the remark was made at the start of her reign, and her later behaviour remains open to conjecture. The film chooses to dramatise conjecture about Elizabeth, her myths as well as her history. We will never know if her statement was adhered to, but it is extremely unlikely that it was not, from the standpoint of her psychological make-up and her views about marriage and where it can lead – sometimes to the executioner's block – as well as her concern for national security. By neither naming her successor, nor producing one through marriage, there was less opportunity for her overthrow. She was arguably the greatest sovereign the country has known, and she did leave England safe and prosperous, just not in the way others intended her to.

It is almost immediately shown that Elizabeth and Dudley are lovers, that he is the most important man in her life. "Remember who you are," he instructs her, as she is arrested, terrified, and sent to the Tower, incriminated in the plot by Thomas Wyatt to overthrow Mary and place Elizabeth on the throne. Eventually she is permitted an audience with Mary (entering through a door bearing a tapestry of the Virgin breastfeeding her child), who is willing to forgive her if Elizabeth declares her allegiance to the Catholic faith. Elizabeth's reaction, that she must be guided by her conscience where her religious beliefs lie, is historically accurate and justified. Did the real Elizabeth, as Blanchett's does, state, "Madam, you are not well," and guess that Mary might not be long for this world, such was her physical condition at the meeting? Mary, who can only see the 'whore' Anne Boleyn in her half-sister, doesn't sentence Elizabeth, but leaves her with the feeling that: "Tonight, I think I die." "Feed her to the wolves," declares Mary, as she instructs Elizabeth not to leave, as she had entered her presence chamber secretly but in full view of the court. The phrase grows in meaning in the light of Hilary Mantel's novel about the Tudor court in the reign of Henry VIII[*].

With the death of Mary, those who had fled the Catholic reign returned to England from exile in Europe. Walsingham (Geoffrey Rush), who will play a far greater part in the fortunes and history of Elizabeth, as far as the film is concerned, than William Cecil (Richard Attenborough, twice Blanchett's age, whereas in reality Cecil was only thirteen years Elizabeth's senior), takes up office as her chief minister. Mary's coronation ring is removed, with some effort, and, under an oak tree, bathed in more blinding light, Elizabeth is proclaimed Queen by her council.

Kapur then recreates the coronation exceptionally, and the famous coronation portrait of Elizabeth[†]: in the robes worn by her sister, taken in to fit her slimmer frame, Blanchett stares back at us, as Elizabeth does from the canvas, short-sighted, oval-faced, frighteningly pale, with the face of her mother and the colouring of her father, and exultantly aware of the burden of the office she now takes up.

---

[*]   *Wolf Hall*, a reference to the seat of the Seymour family, but also used to give the image of the court as a place of danger, full of wolves.

[†]   The most famous of which is a copy of the – now lost – original, painted at the close of Elizabeth's reign, and hanging in the National Portrait Gallery.

Kapur explores Blanchett's emotional journey as Elizabeth more accurately than he does her historical story. One can only speculate as to how the real Elizabeth dealt with her first sessions of council with her ministers, as there must have been some period of apprenticeship before she became the seasoned political player that the world feared and admired in equal measure. The threats of the Catholic Norfolk (who bullies her in council), and Mary of Guise, in Scotland, may not be historically correct, but they do give an urgent sense of the treacherous world Elizabeth inhabited, and the poor state of the country she inherited. It is only when Walsingham steps into the frame that Elizabeth can achieve the guidance she needs and become the ruler she desires to be. Elizabeth, now Queen, still takes Dudley to her bed, though its hangings bear eyes and ears, taking inspiration from the Rainbow Portrait: in the painting the Queen hears and sees everything, but her bed hangings imply that the court sees and hears all that Elizabeth says and does. Her body is now the property of the country, her sheets are checked, her hand in marriage is sought, yet she continues to take Dudley as her lover. The balance and order that Elizabeth craves, and will become famous for, seem an impossibility when the English are defeated on the border by the Scots, with their breast-plated Queen Regent (Fanny Ardent) instructing Elizabeth "not to send children to fight Mary of Guise"*. The result of the battle is an embarrassment, to say the least, for Elizabeth, and she seeks solace at the foot of a vast painting of Henry VIII, stashed away in a dusty storage chamber. Elizabeth, hair plaited about her head, face puffy from weeping, is a far cry from the nymph-like Princess who danced with her ladies: Blanchett appears very nearly ugly, in a foretaste of the Elizabeth she will become at the close of the picture. Once again Walsingham steps out of the shadows: Elizabeth believes her council and people think her "unfit to rule!" Walsingham's comment, that the bishops, who speak out against Elizabeth, do not expect her to survive, prompts the first decisive action of her career: she has found the correct path and agrees to consider Mary of Guise's nephew as a possible husband. She further distances herself from Dudley – having already informed him archly that "I am Queen now" – in a scene bordering on domestic argument, as Cecil comments that Dudley's head will end up on a spike rather than on the Queen's pillow. Although

---

* Mary of Guise's appearance makes a welcome change to that of her daughter, in dramas about Elizabeth.

the facts are far from accurate, Blanchett* marvellously gives a sense of the weight that has fallen on Elizabeth's shoulders and the colossal pressure she is now under, far more than perhaps she imagined. *Elizabeth* is about the apprenticeship as Queen and the ability to reign in her own right. Not even in *Elizabeth R*, given a much larger timescale, was it suggested that Elizabeth appear so exposed, so human: Elizabeth has travelled a huge distance from Florence Eldridge's carping autocrat.

The scene in which Elizabeth prepares to speak to the bishops on the Act of Uniformity perhaps takes this modern approach and re-examination too far, the delivery too contemporary, though her handling of the bishops has weight, femininity, wit and a calculated sense that she, with the help of Walsingham, holds the upper hand: "I have no desire to make windows into men's souls," she informs them, as Elizabeth in reality said upon the sensitive issue of belief, and her idea of the Church of England is formed.

The film gains impact as we see just how exposed to danger Elizabeth is. She survives an attack on her barge at night, and the attempt to murder her with the use of a poison dress (put on in secret by a lady-in-waiting, the Queen escapes a most horrific death), along with the threat of a dark assassin from Rome, in the form of Daniel Craig, out to murder Elizabeth with the blessing of the Pope. She must become her father's daughter: she has the "heart of a man" she declares. She retires Cecil, Lord Burghley, and Walsingham becomes the man to trust and advise her; she sharpens her wit and hardens her heart. She acts with rapid surety, much faster than the real Elizabeth would have done, always keen to hedge her bets, and divests England of her enemies (the suggestion that there was as much bloodshed at the start of her reign as Mary had in hers is an exaggeration); even Norfolk is got rid of: "I am Norfolk!" he declares. "You were Norfolk," Walsingham retorts succinctly. Norfolk goes the way of all the others who "had not the courage to be faithful". All this might be enough to make Elizabeth the great ruler she so wishes to be, delivering her people to the 'Golden Age' she dreams of, but the emotional tug on the heartstrings still persists, and as suitors are refused Dudley remains. Kapur invents a misrepresentation, that Dudley was in fact a traitor (privy to a plot to murder Elizabeth), and gets him out of the way for any future film he may make about Elizabeth; this also allows him to fully justify the sacrifice that Blanchett's Elizabeth must

---

*   Blanchett would earn herself a deserved Oscar nomination as Best Actress for her work in *Elizabeth*, along with numerous other awards and nominations.

now wholly make. Looking like Glenda Jackson at the close of *Mary, Queen of Scots*, hair up, wearing a severe ruff and riding habit, she confronts the broken Dudley and spares him his life, "to always remind me how close I came to danger". It is a clever stroke on writer Michael Hirst's part for, even if historically incorrect, it cements in Elizabeth's mind the sacrifice she must make and allows a modern audience a way in to understanding the motive behind her decision to remain – or in this case become – a virgin.

Praying before the Virgin Mary, Walsingham – again there to advise and guide, giving the impression that it is he who governs the country – informs Elizabeth that "they have found nothing to replace her". The idea takes: Elizabeth will become a living Madonna. Cut to the process of Elizabeth converting to the virgin: tresses are cut, as Kat Ashley weeps, the paste, that we associate with the later images of the Queen's reign, is applied to her face and hands, the body is sacrificed for the sake of the country: the image is complete. Elizabeth once more appears through a blinding light, and addresses Cecil, Lord Burghley, and begs him observe that she is married to England. Her courtiers kneel, someone kisses her gown, and Walsingham looks on, with tears in his eyes, at the creation of artifice, statue like, before him. Blanchett, voice lowered, eyes dead, face a painted mask, takes her place on her throne. At blackout a card reads that Elizabeth reigned for another forty years. By the end of the film there is never any doubt that she could. It will be work that Kapur must undo to transport Blanchett to *Elizabeth: The Golden Age*, but for now Elizabeth's journey is complete. Of course, the real transformation of Elizabeth from Queen to Icon was far more subtle, but Kapur cleverly substitutes art for history in a way that sits perfectly in a medium concerned with visuals. Elizabeth was obsessed with image and the role it plays. The iconography that shaped her later image was created for her by portrait painters, writers and her own idea of theatre. If *Elizabeth* the movie were a painting it would be the Rainbow Portrait by Federigo Zuccaro, full of hidden meaning and messages, and presenting the Queen as ever young, her ladies forming a backdrop that heightens the cult of Gloriana, divine, fantastic and goddess-like. The film is a breathtaking, visionary retelling of Elizabeth's later years as Princess and early years as Queen, and Blanchett is luminous in its centre.

❦ *Greta Scacchi* ❦

"We need more Scacchis, more Schillers"
Mary Stuart 2008

GRETA SCACCHI EARNED HERSELF A SYDNEY THEATRE AWARD nomination for Best Actress and left her audience in no doubt of her readiness to present herself in an unglamorous and unflattering light when she stepped onto the stage at Sydney's Ensemble Theatre to deliver a tour-de-force as Elizabeth I in Peter Oswald's version of Schiller's *Mary Stuart*.

Director Mark Kilmurry assembled a larger company of actors than is usual for Ensemble. They all enter at the start of the play, staring out at the audience (placed on three sides); flares blaze on the remaining single slate wall, producing a rare show of colour in the otherwise darkened space. Scacchi's Elizabeth received rave reviews, the Australian Stage calling it a "masterful job in imbuing the somewhat ambivalent characterisation with believability and emotional texture. She is not an outright villain, mind you, and like her cousin it is clear she is constantly the object of other people's agendas and is in a thoroughly difficult position when it comes to trusting the motivations of the Lords who constantly drown her with advice. Anyone expecting a more customarily romantic or heroic depiction of Elizabeth is in for an intriguing surprise."

It is a twitchy, nervous performance, one moment still, thinking, cunningly preparing her next move like a chess piece, fingers to her lips as she bites her nails and flesh, deep in thought, then flighty, anxious, pedantic and impossible as she rustles about the confined space like a dark, trapped insect, her brilliantly orange wig resembling the lighted torches.

Many critics picked up on the element of spoilt infant that Scacchi brought to the role, *The Spectator* calling the performance that of an "autocratic child star", going on to be "wowed" by the actress's "unhinged energy… This is the Virgin Queen as an aging, monstrous baby doll. Scacchi sways, she lilts, she shuts her eyes and coos, she screeches like a fury", and concluding "We need more Scacchis, more Schillers: more big old plays new-minted, and more actors with the equipment to do them."

As with the production at the National Theatre in the early '90s, the design of the play as a whole has been shifted to the Renaissance, making comment on the time in which the play was written, one of European "political turmoil, intrigue and treachery"*. The rest of the cast are by and large effective – a weak link is Kate Raison as Mary, who simply lacks the grace and range to tackle a character who demands the heights that Schiller's heroine does. This unbalances the drama, such is the strength and commitment Scacchi brings to Elizabeth, and forces one to wish for a performer of equal assurance to be cast as Mary, as had been the case in London in 2005, when Harriet Walter and Janet McTeer were the first to play in Peter Oswald's excellent new version.

It is a tense, dark, sometimes alarming, sometimes moving and humorous evening in the theatre. After an initially tentative start, the overwrought energy rises on stage and a thrilling retelling and reinventing of history unfolds. Scacchi keeps the emotional plates spinning and makes the role that of a manipulative Queen Bee, around whom all circle like planets circling the sun, her own.

> "When you play Elizabeth you have to ask yourself: 'Who am I?'"

Whatever one's view might be of Schiller's *Mary Stuart* it must be applauded for containing powerhouse roles for two leading actresses. If cast with performers at the top of their game, the result can be explosive. Unfortunately the Sydney production is lopsided and at times this unbalances the play. Scacchi's Elizabeth is the jewel of the production, changing the original concept of Elizabeth (villainess) and Mary (heroine). Her performance blends the traditional with a questioning undercurrent that threatens to unsettle what is usually a conventional reading of the Queen. This Elizabeth bridges a gap between Florence Eldridge's 'fire and brimstone' posturing and a deep-rooted understanding of the perilous nature of the play and Elizabeth's dilemma. She unsettles the audience by showing an Elizabeth they instantly recognise, then pulls the rug from under their feet and gradually peels away the Tudor mask, revealing a disturbing terrain of often monumental monstrosity that hides, at its core, a frightened child.

What it did for Scacchi and her career was to present to the public a side of the actress that had been bubbling and threatening to explode for so long. It showed an inner maturity and a fearlessness in scaling the heights and

---

* *The Spectator*

depths of the human condition and finding that inner turmoil. Both she and her heroine Bette Davis were unflinching in their relentless presentation of Elizabeth's physical grotesqueness. By doing this Davis is declaring: I am a serious actress, I don't care how I look, unlike other actresses in Hollywood today. Scacchi says: I am not the Hollywood actress you tried to make me; I am a serious actress and look what I can do.

In *Mary Stuart* she has the ball at her feet; it is thrilling to see how far she kicks it.

Portraying Elizabeth

Interview with Greta Scacchi

Greta Scacchi as Elizabeth
(With thanks to The Ensemble Theatre)

"WHEN I STARTED READING THE PLAY – I HADN'T SEEN A PRODUCTION before – I soon realised that Elizabeth was portrayed in a pretty unforgiving and negative light. It was a shock to discover there were no heroic speeches (for example the Tilbury Speech), no 'Good Queen Bess' – there was none of that, and it was difficult to understand that what Schiller had created was the same Elizabeth as we know her. I thought, *Oh no, why have they asked me to play her? I'd rather play Mary*, because Mary is presented as a heroine. I thought Elizabeth was presented as one-dimensional: evil and possessing no virtue. Mary, I thought on that first read, had layers of vulnerability, and I couldn't find the emotion in Elizabeth. And then, on closer scrutiny, I started to find that there was a lot of humour to her, there was more depth, and suddenly I began to be drawn in; my appetite was whetted.

There is a psychotic quality about Schiller's Elizabeth, and perhaps the real Elizabeth possessed this also, and I tend to always like – particularly in something that has got emotional dimensions that are founded in reality – the absurdity of human nature. So I found Schiller's very negative slant – because he has chosen this bloody time of British history as a metaphor for what had recently happened in European history* – appealing. And maybe, because he was a Shakespearian scholar, and was inspired by him, it seems to me that Schiller sees himself as writing the play Shakespeare could have written, had he still been alive – almost a missing play, where if Shakespeare had to make any political comment he would refer to the Romans or something of a previous time, and make a statement about what was happening now. Didn't Elizabeth herself, for instance, recognise the political parallels in *Richard II* when she remarked "I *am* Richard II"?

Therefore, at first, I felt that Elizabeth's character was merely a tool to frame the plight of Mary. But by the second reading I thought there is so much in her that is actually wilful, arch, violent, disturbed and paranoid. Elizabeth contains elements of despotism, and is an immature and frightened person, who has been given power, but that power brings with it enormous cost. One of the most important things to remember with her, whether playing Schiller's Elizabeth or the real Elizabeth, was that this was a child whose father had her mother executed when she was two and a half. So that would scar you, even if you had no memory, or very little memory, of your mother. Even though she had received guidance from Katherine Parr, who I believe was quite an intellectual, even with that influence, sobriety of reason and strategy, even with all of that, the effect of her mother's death is monumental.

Despite all this, we know, because we can see in the context of the history of this country – even though that was not what Schiller was interested in when he wrote *Mary Stuart* – that this was overall a great ruler, a ruler of courage and stature. You can't get away from that. She was popular, mostly, but particularly early on was coming through a decidedly difficult period, after Mary Tudor's reign, and negotiated this efficiently and cleverly to reunite England. So, she is one of, if not *the* greatest ruler in British history. It's funny how the women did so well!

Yet, if you didn't have some knowledge of this, you might mistakenly see her as a despot because, to a degree, that is how Schiller portrays her – and also Burghley, her chief minister – as scheming and self-serving, interested

---

*   The French Revolution had just ended.

in keeping their heads on their shoulders. That is the feeling in the play, to a degree, and probably what Schiller wanted: he wanted the audience to have sympathy with Mary. Dudley, I think, is also self-serving in the play: there is no genuine love for Elizabeth – she is sentimental about him – as there obviously was in real life; here, he enjoys the comforts of being a favourite, but in a very ruthless manner.

But I did find there were many more layers when I explored it further and inhabited her. Schiller does actually give Elizabeth complexities: chiefly, she doubts what she is doing and thinks, *Shit! Why have I been placed in this dangerous position? I've got to cut off other people's heads before they cut off mine!* And Mary has been across the border for a very long time, the cousins creating a menacing duo, a feeling of checkmate – 'This town isn't big enough for both of us!' Which also suggests historically that Elizabeth had a resistance to doing the deed – she prevaricated.

Going back to the beginning, knowing what I knew of Elizabeth and Mary, I did think I was personally more of a Mary than an Elizabeth. Especially as I had just had a success playing in Rattigan's *Deep Blue Sea* and felt that I had gained a reputation for showing vulnerability. But then I had a sea change, and wanted to play this monster character, a psycho character, and have a chance to branch out and explore new territory.

Also there was a lot of comedy to be played, and as I get very few comic parts I decided that this could be brought out as well – that was one of the key elements in accepting the role. Though the main thing that seduced me into playing her was – and this is in reality as well as in the text – that this woman didn't have anyone to answer to. And she believes in her own status: she talks, again as she did in life, of the Divine Right of Kings. Key to this is the scene when she signs Mary's death warrant: Elizabeth's only monologue is a great study of her doubt; she is so troubled and there is an 'angel/devil' element to what is going on in her mind. For the production it was staged in such a way that Elizabeth is holding the quill, about to sign, moving around a lectern on which the document is positioned – is she going to sign or not? The scene begins:

> "What slavery it is to serve the people,
> What ignominious drudgery, to flatter
> This idol I despise with all my heart!"

There is a Webster-like, dark quality about the writing, similar to the Duchess of Malfi saying: "The misery of us that are born great!" For Elizabeth is in an impossible situation in so many areas at this point: "Do I have to kill somebody to save myself? … I can't woo a man, but a man can't woo me." And bringing in another point: it clearly comes down on the side of the view that she is a virgin, she really is – she can play at having a dalliance with Dudley, but she would never go further because the stakes are too high, the male is too dominant.

When you play Elizabeth you really have to ask yourself: "Who am I in this?" And at this moment in the drama Elizabeth is asking, "Oh, when shall I possess my throne in freedom?" Meaning when shall she be free from this stress? Elizabeth must defer to the situation, but her inner self fights against it, something she has known from birth. She is born into a thankless, precarious situation – including a period in the Tower – a constant fight for survival. She has power now, without autonomy, but in many ways nothing has changed for her, she is still trapped. She is paranoid: it's a paranoid age and it has been all her life.

I did feel, which is perhaps a contradiction, that she had an unselfconsciousness of behaviour: because of her power she was uninhibited – again this links in with her belief in the Divine Right of Kings. She was wilful, she could have tantrums, she didn't have to guard her behaviour amongst that group of men, her ministers, that immediate circle, who although on her side, or at least the side of the Crown, were putting her under enormous pressure. She had an upper hand, but only to a degree, and Schiller does allow the audience to see this, even if it isn't all strictly historically accurate. It makes for a strange conflict within her. She has extreme vanity: by staying young – or young looking – she can remain powerful, because she can still bargain herself in the marriage market; along with reminding people she will live and die a virgin, she also lets people know how dispensable they are to her.

She obviously has great conscience – "Only to tie my hands for the first inevitable act of violence" – but along with this has a mass of contradictory emotions, that seem to fly about inside her, making her impossible to pin down, and that essence, I believe, Schiller has portrayed correctly. So, of course, she naturally doesn't want to condemn Mary, it isn't in her nature, but she would be quite happy to be woken "one morning with the words: She's dead; Your enemy, Mary Stuart, died last night." For, as Burghley reminds her, "Her life is death to you, her death your life." She doesn't want to have to be the one, and it shows how constrained she is by her role as monarch.

In this scene her argument and her dilemma as ruler are quite clear –

although when the play was first produced it might have been played in a more one-dimensional way, so as to favour the Mary character, strengthening their differing roles as villain and heroine – but this insight into Elizabeth's inner thoughts is not something explored often in the play, and this brief glimpse of her inner turmoil could come across as monstrous and bloodthirsty. But my job is to understand her point of view, and her position is pretty claustrophobic.

I did do a lot of research – and did have some prior knowledge of the subject – as I felt it was important to try to understand this group of people, not just Elizabeth but all of them. One of the strongest feelings I gained was that the period Elizabeth spent with Katherine Parr, even though it ended rather messily* – another of the hazards of being a woman at that time – was a period of some calm for her and was hugely influential on her later character: Thomas Seymour (Parr's husband) and Parr were an anchor for her.

So, with what I knew about her, and with what I was later to research, I did have one recurring thought about the casting of myself as Elizabeth, in that I felt, not only because of the types of parts I had played up to that time but because of my more European nationality†, I actually had more in common, in terms of upbringing, with Mary. And although that might seem trivial now, these things often matter when you are finding your way into a part that at first seems daunting and so far away from you – you want to find whatever you can as a lead-in‡. But this Websteresque quality to the writing – a writer that I've always wanted to do and never had a chance to – completely drew me in to Elizabeth and the play as a whole. So, this quality

---

*   After the death of Henry VIII, Elizabeth lived with her final stepmother, often at Parr's residence in Chelsea. Scacchi felt that Elizabeth obviously "looked up to Seymour, was influenced by him, and felt safe – something of huge importance to Elizabeth, though it probably didn't often happen – and she was an interesting, remarkable teenage girl, that he found himself attracted to." Tracy Borman believes that "Katherine may have known full well that Seymour's attentions towards Elizabeth were motivated by lust, not fatherly affection as he claimed." In time, the situation got out of hand and Elizabeth left Katherine's household with dowager and stepdaughter "barely on speaking terms". Soon after, Katherine died in childbirth, another reminder to Elizabeth of the dangers of matrimony.

†   Scacchi's father is Italian.

‡   Scacchi commented on the difference between the upbringings of Elizabeth and Mary: "Mary grew up cultivated, sophisticated, well groomed, in the French court: there was nothing more civilised than this at the time – it put any culture, or society, in England to shame. Whereas Elizabeth, although probably more intelligent than Mary, was raised in the mayhem of Henry VIII's hedonistic lifestyle, which the rest of Europe was criticising, no doubt finding Elizabeth somewhat crude."

of being angry, sick and tired of the rest of Europe thinking her to be a fake because they believe her parents weren't properly married in the eyes of God, is wonderful to play. It was staged as an 'inner voice' moment: the lighting changed, I was alone on stage; some of the scene I played at a frantic pace, some very slow, and the real Elizabeth – frustrated, angry, under pressure – is allowed out of the box. It could be played in an evil manner, but her argument is a good one, and valid. And it is all there in the text – Schiller directs her actions. She is terrified of what she has done, and she drops the pen after signing very quickly – it's a moment of high drama, Elizabeth's big moment within the context of the play. I tried to create an air of tension throughout in the way she moved and gestured – I bit my nails and fingers, and kept my hands from being still, even if the rest of my body was.

In terms of her appearance we obviously studied the huge wealth of visual research there is available. I had one costume, with a removal ruff, and 'kinky' patent, black leather boots. We created a Vivienne Westwood theme to the costume, with the fabric, a waterproof material, black – the orange in the costume, and the wig, were the only colour on the stage – printed with a design with slashes of orange through the skirt, and sprayed to create a crumpled bin bag effect – the "frilled neck lizard"[*] reviews were justified as there was a reptilian intention by the designers. The skirt had the front panel cut away so my boots (non-period) were revealed, giving the impression of power – in the riding scene a crop was added, which was used at one point to threaten Mary. That's the scene where Elizabeth and Mary first meet, and a little black veil was added: as I see her across the stage, I gradually pull back the veil (made of black chiffon, giving a funereal effect), which accentuated the idea of fantasy – this didn't really happen, but we are going to make it happen, and they are going to meet face to face, underlying this enigmatic moment of invention and vulnerability of these two women: Mary, beautiful (although historically was she? Probably not), and I, as Elizabeth, look a horror! And I loved that! (Incidentally, there was another play I did, my favourite part, in which I played Bette Davis – another Elizabeth – and at points during the play looked a horror and undid people's preconceptions about me.) I was very keen, though, on the idea of a white face, almost a blank canvas of paste and powder, contrasting against the dark not only of the costume, but also the stage, and exploring how it accentuates the eyes,

---

[*]   Several reviews picked up on Scacchi's resemblance to Australia's frill-necked lizard.

and features, creating a kabuki skull effect. The director, Mark Kilmurry, urged me to go further in the way Elizabeth looked and behaved, and I sometimes felt that everything was getting too big, and I was being over the top, though at the same time, perhaps somewhat perversely, I did relish undoing the glamorous image I'm labelled with sometimes. It was scary, though, pulling out all the stops, and Elizabeth did mark a change for me in my attitude towards how I presented myself. Elizabeth might have thought, as she looked at herself in the mirror, resenting her wrinkles, that she was under pressure to look a certain way, stay young for her public image, but as *we* presented her she has been misguided and she is a sight! It is a very precarious thing for a woman to get older. Of course, from a distance, as most people would have seen her, she could probably still get away with it. It's all about power, keeping yourself young so you can stay in the marriage market, and manipulate events and people. But I didn't have any concerns about my appearance as her until much later on in the rehearsal process – to start with I was more interested in her core, and what made her tick. As far as the make-up went, I probably practised that two days before. I had a wig fitting – I didn't have to shave my forehead, though I would have, as I naturally have a very high hairline, which suits playing Elizabeth – and then somebody showed me how to use the white wax I had on my face, which took a very long time to learn how to apply – everything was covered, even the eyebrows – for as you rub it in, it comes away, so you have to apply and powder over it. (I used the same technique for the Bette Davis[*] play I did a few years later, where I had to dress up as Baby Jane from *Whatever Happened to Baby Jane?*) The Ensemble Theatre is very small, and backstage there are only two small dressing rooms, so I was sharing a dressing room with Mary Stuart and Hannah, her servant, and the joke was that once the wig went on I became appallingly bossy, forthright and rude! Something clicked inside me, and then I would come back, offstage, and they would say, "*Get it off!*" Elizabeth had taken over in some way! And I believe that she was all those things, in real life as well, and this is multiplied because she is so stressed. I really felt confident playing her and felt that I could tap into the monster side of myself, that we all have and don't usually show. This role allowed me to

---

[*] Scacchi also stated: "I was very aware and pleased that Bette Davis, whom I admire greatly, had played Elizabeth: the fact that she and I look similar made me feel that I could play someone whose face is so recognisable, yet very different from my own. Bette and I share the same 'poached egg eyes'! I liked her performances as Elizabeth very much.

let go of a lot of the baggage I carried. If audiences expected her to be noble, dignified, poised and grand, as I have been in other parts, especially on screen, then they were going to be disappointed as they saw me: monstrous, fierce, hysterical and violent. I wasn't restrained. Elizabeth has to take the steering wheel, drive things, she has to have steel, and I relished that. After Bette Davis, in *Bette and Joan*, she is certainly my favourite part."

7

The Body of the Queen: The Playing of Elizabeth & Other Tudor Women

❧ *Vanessa Redgrave & Joely Richardson* ☙

"Divorced from and engaged with reality"
Anonymous 2011

An "extraordinary creature... in a black hole with shafts of sunlight" is how Vanessa Redgrave viewed the elderly Elizabeth she played in Roland Emmerich's *Anonymous*. Redgrave was no stranger to playing Tudor Queens, and Elizabeth rounds off a hat trick of performances that include Anne Boleyn in *A Man for all Seasons*[*] and Mary Stuart in *Mary, Queen of Scots*. Perhaps Redgrave's Elizabeth is the crowning glory of all three: Eileen Atkins (Redgrave's friend, and author of the screenplay for *Mrs Dalloway* in which Redgrave took the starring role) stated that Redgrave's was probably the most "convincing" Elizabeth brought to the screen. Atkins went on to express doubts over the rest of the film, a view shared by many, but Elizabeth emerges as a touching and illuminating Queen, giving new insight into the state of her ageing mind and body. This Elizabeth may dress like Gloriana, but her faculties are far from immortal.

---

[*] In 1988 the film was remade, and Redgrave took the part of Moore's wife, Alice.

In her earlier triumph as Anne Boleyn in the original film version of Robert Bolt's award-winning *A Man for all Seasons*, Redgrave's brief cameo remains one of the picture's most haunting moments, and leaves us with an Anne few can match, even when given hours of screen time. We believe in her as the woman whom Henry will go to such enormous lengths to marry, the woman who will bring about Thomas Moore's downfall*.

While Redgrave's exquisite bone structure is admirably suited to Anne's dark looks, it also lent itself well to those of Mary Stuart some four years later. Redgrave, at the peak of her box office power, found the doomed romanticism of this other beheaded Queen similarly attractive, and the resulting performance garnered her an Oscar nomination, some of the best reviews of her career, and a Mary that hasn't been equalled in her beguiling plausibility by the host of actresses who followed in her footsteps.

The timeline of Redgrave's Elizabeth picks up where Glenda Jackson's, in *Mary, Queen of Scots*, leaves off. This Elizabeth is far from the alabaster virgin Cate Blanchett becomes in *Elizabeth*: she is very much flesh and blood. The fact that Elizabeth is played by an actress of the same age as the character in the film brings a greater resonance and truthfulness to the importance of the Queen's body to the country, and the problem of its frailty and eventual decline. It makes for a touching understanding of the woman, making her all the more human.

If Emmerich had concentrated on Elizabeth (Redgrave was singled out as giving a significant performance in a poor film) and made a movie about the acceptance of mortality, he might have produced a film of greater critical acclaim. Instead, *Anonymous* is a sprawling, disjointed affair, that questions the assumption that Shakespeare was the author of his work. If Emmerich had kept his focus on this plot instead of introducing Elizabeth, then once again he might have made a better picture. But by continually shifting the

---

* The plot of Bolt's play covers what became known as the 'King's Great Matter', a period lasting from 1525, when Henry became enamoured of Anne Boleyn, to 1533, when she was eventually crowned Queen and gave birth to Elizabeth. Such was the certainty that she would be a boy that documentation announcing the birth of the prince can clearly be seen to have later added 'ss' for princess. Thomas Moore, one of the King's most learned and trusted friends, strongly opposed the match, and he was executed in 1535. Some argue that Moore has been presented in a more accurate light by Hilary Mantel in her novel trilogy *Wolf Hall*.

spotlight onto Elizabeth's imagined romantic affairs and resulting bastards*, the movie sinks into incomprehensibility, skidding from touching realism to Monty Pythonesque escapades, in an attempt to follow Shakespeare's tradition and bring in a set of secondary comic characters from time to time. This lack of focus was one of the main criticisms upon its release; some went further and called the movie a "disaster".

It begins with Derek Jacobi, as a present-day actor, rushing to a theatre to perform in New York, where he gives an impressive speech questioning Shakespeare's authorship and suggesting the writer is a fraud. We are transported back to Tudor London, a vast panoramic city dominated by the River Thames (one of the high points of the film is the recreation, by cinematic wizardry, of the city of London). Here, Edward de Vere, 17th Earl of Oxford (Rhys Ifans) is in an unhappy marriage to the daughter of William Cecil, Elizabeth's chief minister – it is suggested de Vere was blackmailed into marrying Anne after committing a Hamletesque-type murder, resulting in the death of a spying servant. Because of this de Vere was forced to marry Anne and, the Cecils being puritanical Protestants, they have made him give up life as a playwright and renounce his genius as a writer, something which has been established in flashback, showing de Vere entertaining the Queen with his penmanship, wooing her with his verse, and later bedding her.

Not to be defeated, de Vere finds himself a channel for his brilliance in the guise of an actor, William Shakespeare (played as a comic buffoon by Rafe Spall), and his work is then produced under Shakespeare's name, making the actor the toast of London. This is the hypothesis of the aptly named J. Thomas Looney, founder of the Oxfordian theory. If that was all, it might have been enough, but there is more, much more. Along with the battle for power in the Cecil family, as father William clashes with son Robert (the Queen's next chief minister), Elizabeth herself has her own story, some of it presented in flashback, with Joely Richardson (Redgrave's real-life daughter) as the young Queen, and then with Redgrave as the aged Elizabeth looking back on her affair with de Vere, which resulted in a bastard son (one of many bastards that the council knows about and hides with extraordinary success).

But despite all these sons, the elderly Queen will not name one as her

---

* At one point Cecil (David Thewlis) states to de Vere: "You're not the first or the last of her lovers."

heir. Instead of a feisty refusal, as we have been accustomed to, here the Queen is weary, tired and in the grip of dementia – the Queen's body, a time bomb waiting for the last tick, as court and council endlessly speculate on the question of the succession, ready to begin afresh with a new monarch. All eyes are turning to the future. Everything will change with her last breath, which surely must be soon. But will he who bears the crown be a bastard of Elizabeth's flesh?

Redgrave's Elizabeth is movingly authentic: bad teeth, most of the costumes inspired by paintings – in particular the Ditchley and Sieve Portraits – with an emphasis on black and white, her hair often in long tresses (the sign of virginity, in this case faux) as was Elizabeth's wont, ringlets surrounding her chalky white face. She has trouble dressing; her lady-in-waiting fumbles as she tries to put on the Queen's wig. The essence of Redgrave's Elizabeth is a worn-out body: the care and fatigue of governing her nation have finally taken their toll; the Queen's famous energy is sapped[*]. She admires the writings of 'Anonymous' (de Vere's early pseudonym) and is a lover of the arts (this premise is set up early as the Queen delights in a dwarf performer). Elizabeth's mind, not as lucid as it once was, begins to wander… Flashback forty years and Joely Richardson's Elizabeth watches the same play. If it were not mother and daughter playing the same character, Richardson's Elizabeth could hardly be more different from Redgrave's impressive creation. When interviewed, they spoke of an "osmosis" or "wavelength" that tunes in when they work together, so that one knows how the other might play a particular scene or emotion. In the case of Elizabeth, the technique hasn't come off. In her defence, Richardson (here dressed more like a medieval lady than the Tudor Queen) is poorly served from the start, as the script just doesn't aid her character or justify her actions.

There is much that is good about the picture; Emmerich's eye for detail cannot be faulted when the older Elizabeth is the focus of his lens. We see her watching a private performance of *Hamlet* at court. Engrossed in the drama, and needing to breathe with greater ease, unconscious of those around her she sits back in her chair, legs lightly spread, and casually unpins her bodice, casting about her the pins that keep it secure, as members of her court watch

---

[*] Elizabeth's vitality was prodigious: riding, dancing, walks upon waking, in her private gardens, sometimes still in her nightgown – she left others flagging. Not an early riser (she seems to have been up and about by eight o'clock), she instead could work through the night, draining her ministers, who often complained, wishing for their beds.

uncertainly*. The ravages of her mind have taken their toll, and those around her can only look on with horror or bemusement. This marks one of the few links between the performances of Redgrave and Richardson – a spoilt childishness that must be at the heart of many people in power; the elderly Elizabeth feels she can behave as she pleases, while Richardson's Queen splutters out her passion for de Vere, or points to her breast petulantly when confronted about her amorous actions and declares, "I can do what *I* want!" Thrown into the bevy of storylines is the oft-told tale of the Earl of Essex trying to overthrow the Queen and his calamitous downfall. Redgrave's Elizabeth is less well informed than Bette Davis's suspicious monarch in the same situation, her mind a disjointed puzzle. Even her wig doesn't seem to fit anymore, as strands of grey are visible about her neck. We are privy to Essex barging into the Queen's chamber: surrounded by ladies, she seems momentarily paralysed as she gathers her thoughts, touchingly trying to fathom how to deal with the situation. Her hand flutters to cover her face, her tresses straggly, white and loose about her shoulders, and her 'wasp-waisted' corset undone. "Get out," she hisses. In an instant a lady-in-waiting jumps into action, "Get out!" and the doors are hastily closed on a scene even Elizabeth cannot control†.

Next, Elizabeth at first seems back in command of her faculties as she rages at Robert Cecil, demonstrating how Essex burst in on her. Yes, she wants him arrested, then she doesn't. Then she doesn't know. It isn't that Elizabeth faces the dilemma of her romantic attachment to Essex overriding

---

* The inspiration for this piece of business is the recollections of the French ambassador, André Hurault, Sieur de Maisse, when the Queen was sixty-seven: "She was strangely attired in a dress of silver cloth, white and crimson ... [with] slashed sleeves lined in red taffeta, and was girt about with other little sleeves that hung down to the ground, which she was constantly twisting and untwisting. She kept the front of her dress open, and you could see the whole of her bosom... and often, she would open the front of her dress with her hands, as if she were too hot... On her head she wore a garland of rubies and pearls, and beneath it a great reddish-coloured wig, with a great number of pearls, not of great worth. On either side of her ears hung two great curls of hair, almost down to her shoulders and within the collar of her robe, spangled like the top of her head. Her bosom is rather wrinkled... As for her face it is... long and thin, and her teeth are very yellow and irregular... on the left side less than on the right. Many... are missing, so that you cannot understand her easily when she speaks."

† In reality the Queen "astonished by the sudden appearance of a man she had supposed to be still in Ireland and unsure as to whether or not he had brought an army with him, received him with guarded pleasantries and in so reassuring a manner that... he confessed his relief... thanking God he had 'found a sweet calm at home'... When next he saw the Queen her behaviour was not so pleasant." In under eighteen months he would be executed.

any logical reason, but rather she really is paralysed as to know what to do; her mind begins to unravel. Sitting, childlike, on the steps of her dais, she taps her knees and asks simply, "Has he gone mad?" The response from Cecil, that Essex believes himself to be the Queen's equal*, doesn't bring about the expected fury of other Elizabeths: her tongue licks her lips and she gives a look of confused regret.

Creating stunning backdrops to frame Redgrave, Emmerich plays with the concept of the Queen's famous vanity: she catches herself in reflections, mirrors, and, pleased with her appearance as she prepares to meet de Vere, she dances a step, in front of her glass and her ladies, singing the nursery rhyme 'Mary, Mary, Quite Contrary'. It is a touching image, a harking back to Elizabeth's past glory: we can see she was once beautiful, once great, and her ladies-in-waiting sense there will be few more occasions such as this. It is a representation of the Queen, well researched and hauntingly beautiful. The idea of Elizabeth having one last romantic hurrah with de Vere is short-lived, as Essex (aided by the Earl of Southampton, Elizabeth and de Vere's son) storms the Palace – "Fireworks!" she exclaims at first, before panic seizes her: Essex is threatening Elizabeth's life, and the reunion between the Queen and de Vere must be postponed.

When they finally do meet, de Vere pleads with Elizabeth to save their son (Essex has paid for his sins with the loss of his head), but, instead of a playful mistress who danced before her mirror, Elizabeth is sunk, both physically (she sits hunched on her throne, in a confection of a costume, with huge puff sleeves) and mentally: the siege has left her weary, but aware of whom she can trust. She is bitter about what has been attempted and speaks of the value of loyalty, which she has received only from the Cecils, father and son. No one had thought Elizabeth "very important at all" except William Cecil, and because of them she has survived. A pact between the old lovers is formed, but the price de Vere must pay is that no work of his shall ever bear his name. Redgrave holds out her hand to be kissed, just as Elizabeth would have done to conclude a meeting, and it is all over, and Shakespeare remains the author of the *Complete Works*.

---

* It is ludicrously suggested that Essex is another of the Queen's many bastards. At one point Elizabeth declares that "No son of hers [meaning Mary Stuart] will ever rule [England]," the supposition being that Elizabeth has plenty of her own to fill the throne. She reads from *Venus and Adonis*: "And so in spite of death I shall survive. In that my likeness is left alive." Then, as she gazes at her reflection in the window pane, the scene fades.

All that is now left for Elizabeth is to name her successor and die. As Elizabeth contemplates her life, sitting on cushions, sucking on her index finger (as she was reported to do), Robert Cecil shows her the Act of Succession. Redgrave's dark eyes dart across the document before she hurls it from her.

The Queen now dead, Emmerich creates a magnificent spectacle of a snow-clad London in deepest mourning. The funeral procession parades across the frozen Thames, the black and white (a theme of Elizabeth's later costumes) of mourners against snow appearing at first as small as stitches on cambric, before the camera pans in. The image is brilliant. In reality, after the Queen died one of her ladies-in-waiting, Lady Scrope, removed a ring from the Queen's finger and gave it to Robert Carey, a cousin of Elizabeth's on her mother's side, who proceeded to ride to Scotland to report the Queen's death to the impatient James VI.

When the accession of James was proclaimed, the people did not rejoice, "so sorry for Her Majesty's departure was so deep in many hearts, they could not so suddenly show any great joy." Elizabeth had died at Richmond on March 24th 1603, so the court returned to London, leaving three of her ladies to embalm the body (though some argue that Elizabeth had forbidden this), and after five days the coffin was taken by barge at night to Whitehall, the main seat of the monarch at that time*.

She was buried on 28th April, in the North Chapel of Westminster Abbey. James VI erected a vast monument to her, with a life-size effigy, copied from the funeral effigy. Thousands of mourners lined the procession path to pay their respects, and it wasn't long before James VI's rule soon confirmed to them what they had lost.

---

* It is uncertain what Elizabeth actually died of, as she had forbidden a post-mortem to be carried out. She had been in fine health in January of that year but had refused the advice of her ladies and gone out walking wearing clothes more suited to summer, and this had resulted in her catching a chill. She seems to have developed pneumonia or bronchitis and complained of sore throats, aggravated by abscesses and ulcers. These eventually burst, making breathing easier. Never having much of an appetite – surviving clothes from the time show her to have been painfully thin – she stopped eating altogether and began to waste away. She was also severely depressed: by her late sixties Elizabeth had very few contemporaries alive, having recently experienced a series of deaths of those she loved, and this, combined with the nervous disposition she obviously possessed, made her deeply melancholic. The combination of this with her ailments seems the logical cause which terminated the life of Gloriana. However, there is one school of thought that believes Elizabeth died of lead poisoning, brought on from the lead that was a staple ingredient of the cosmetics she applied daily.

Overall, *Anonymous* is a flawed film. Emmerich once said, "I do the movies I want to do. I'm not a favourite of the critics." But Redgrave's performance is worthy of great praise; accurate, nuanced, fine-grained, it was singled out as one of the best of her career.

8

The Portrait as Cameo: Elizabeth as a Supporting Role

❧ *Judi Dench* ☙

'With a crack in her voice'
Shakespeare in Love 1998

IN THE SPRING OF 1999 JUDI DENCH DID WHAT NO OTHER ACTRESS playing Elizabeth has done before or since: she won herself an Oscar. Dench, who came late to film, always preferring stage and television, had never been afraid to take on cameo parts, and like many British leading stage actresses, Flora Robson for example, had often been seen in supporting roles when working in film. All this changed with her first leading part as Queen Victoria in *Mrs Brown**, garnering the actress her first Oscar nomination; from then on Dench has been seen taking leading as well as supporting parts in films as diverse as the James Bond series and *Iris*.

In just eight minutes of screen time, and four scenes, Dench delivers an Elizabeth that could have been just a comic turn, but instead she instils her Elizabeth with a weight and conviction that illuminates a side of the Queen rarely seen on screen: it shows her possessing the common touch,

---

* The film was originally to be made as a TV film, before getting backing for cinema release.

and the ability to interact with her people, a quality that she had and most definitely enjoyed. Dench once confessed, when faced with the role of Cleopatra, to being given the advice not to play the whole character in one go but to gradually show parts of the character's personality with each scene, eventually building up a cohesive whole. With Elizabeth, Dench isn't given the luxury of time; instead the whole character has to be produced instantly, and we see an interpretation of her that is selective, though none the less compelling.

Dench is nothing like the real Elizabeth, either in appearance or vocally (judging by contemporary sources Elizabeth didn't have a low, husky voice, with a famous "crack in it", as described by Jonathan Miller, but a higher pitched, lilting quality), and to overcome her height (Elizabeth was approximately 5' 7") she had to wear immense heels to give an impression of the Queen's stature. So Dench belongs to the large group of actresses who have been cast for their abilities rather than any physical resemblance to Elizabeth. In Dench's case, her casting was dictated by the need for a leading and popular actress to play a minor but immensely showy and influential part, and however meagre her screen time Elizabeth remains the core of the picture. The film, visually, musically and in its depiction of Tudor England, owes much, as does Dench's performance, to *The Virgin Queen*, the Hollywood romp that starred Bette Davis. Dench's Elizabeth delights in being hearty, carping, capricious, very human and extremely robust. There is no hint of the vulnerable, neurotic, fragile side that Elizabeth undoubtedly had. Dench plays her as an old sea dog of a monarch and most assuredly her father's daughter. She gives Elizabeth the power that she certainly possessed; there is also a sense of the loneliness the Queen knew, when she tells Gwyneth Paltrow's Viola, "I know something of a woman in a man's profession, yes, by God, I do know about that." The camera remains on Dench's still face, with its knowing, beady, dark eyes, and the sentence is delivered with such conviction that for a moment we really do feel as if we are seeing into the heart, and mind, of the real Elizabeth. The moment is fleeting: within seconds, the Queen is addressing the Globe theatre audience once again. The weary, wise and humorous Elizabeth returns, acting as a learned general turning disorder to order, a common theme in Shakespeare's work and in the film.

Costumes by Sandy Powell create a strangely metallic Elizabeth, giving the effect that she really is a divine being on earth, almost from another world, as she gleams brilliantly in her more muted surroundings. Choosing to dress her this way continues the habit, since *The Virgin Queen*, of deliberately creating an image of the Queen that gives a sense of the woman, while not actually copying costumes from her portraits. This allows interpretation to be stamped on the ever-malleable Elizabeth and makes the presentation of her more representative of *our* time, rather than her own.

The film, a smash hit winning seven Oscars, including Best Picture and Dench as Best Supporting Actress, deals with a fictional relationship between William Shakespeare, then a struggling writer in 1593, and Viola de Lesseps, a woman pretending to be a man, who impresses him when she auditions for the part of Romeo, before her true identity is discovered and the couple fall in love. Viola is then summoned to the court of Elizabeth, and Shakespeare, now disguised as a woman, pretending to be Viola's cousin, makes a wager which the Queen witnesses: that a play cannot capture the nature of true love. Viola is to be betrothed to Wessex (Colin Firth), who bets against Shakespeare: Wessex loses the bet and the Queen commissions *Twelfth Night*, one of Shakespeare's cross-gender comedies and an obvious inspiration for the film. Viola takes over from a boy actor whose voice has broken and who therefore cannot play Juliet anymore; this feat of a woman pretending to be a man pretending to be a woman is only pulled off because the Queen doesn't give the game away about Viola's true identity, a fact she never doubted, emphasising Elizabeth's intellect and perspicacity as the only character in the film to see the truth.

Along with *Twelfth Night*, another of the film's inspirations is a painting by David Scott which shows 'Queen Elizabeth viewing the performance of *The Merry Wives of Windsor*, at the Globe in Merrie England', as imagined by the 19th-century painter. The play was supposedly commissioned by the Queen because she had enjoyed the character of Sir John Falstaff so much in *Henry IV Parts I & II* and wished to see him in another play. Legend has it that Shakespeare wrote *Merry Wives* especially for her, but there is no proof of this – in fact there is no evidence that Shakespeare and the Queen ever actually met, and the likelihood of the Queen donning a cloak and visiting the theatre with only her ladies-in-waiting in tow is highly implausible[*]; at court the Queen would have sat distanced from the other audience members, as befitted her status. Like the meeting of Elizabeth and her cousin Mary, the

---

[*] Dench's Elizabeth is served by the same two actresses who were her ladies-in-waiting in *Mrs Brown*.

meeting of Elizabeth and Shakespeare is so often imagined because people want it to have happened. They want to see these two great minds encounter each other, and in some cases it has been proposed that Elizabeth was not just his patron but his mother or, more bizarre still, that Shakespeare and the Queen were in fact one and the same: experts have transposed images of Elizabeth, chiefly the Darnley Portrait, with the famous engraving of Shakespeare that appears in most copies of the *Complete Works*, only to find that it is evidently one and the same likeness!

Much blame lies once more at the feet of Victorian artists and writers, such as Sir Walter Scott in his *Kenilworth* series, who create a comfortable and comforting view of Tudor England as romantic, bawdy and to a degree safe, a sort of harking back to Victorian values. At the core of all this is the Queen herself, loved by the people, and most definitely amongst them and one of them. It will come as no surprise that just as images such as these were being circulated, Victoria sat on the British throne and there was much hype about the creation of a new Elizabethan age, just as there is every time Elizabeth II has a Jubilee. Perhaps they wished to show *their* Queen, who by the 1860s had removed herself from public life and would remain a recluse for a number of years, mourning the loss of her beloved husband Prince Albert, that she should come amongst them once again and be seen as part of the national identity in view as well as in thought. But the Queen did not, and to a degree Elizabeth did not either. Although she was famous for her progresses that took her about the safer regions of her nation, the Queen didn't journey very far north in all the forty-four years of her reign. These progresses allowed Elizabeth to escape London in the summer months when fear of the plague was rife, and to meet her people and show herself off to them. These subjects only knew of Elizabeth by word of mouth, on their currency, and by mass-produced portraits of her generated by the schools of the many artists who painted her: Elizabeth kept a beady eye on which likenesses actually made it into wide circulation. But although the image of the Queen on horseback stopping and chatting to her subjects is a popular one, we must also remember that her status was impenetrable, her word unquestioned, and her body that of God's on Earth. The Divine Right of Kings wouldn't be questioned for nearly another half a century after her death, and the washing of the feet of the poor by the English monarch went on for another century, in the belief that the ritual had healing powers, such was the conviction that the sovereign was above mere mortals. So Elizabeth as

Queen frequenting the theatre, even in disguise, is a long way from the truth of how the Elizabethans themselves viewed their Queen. She answered to no man, not even the Pope, thanks to Anne Boleyn and Henry's break from the Church of Rome: she only had to answer to God. This the people believed and this Elizabeth believed herself, hence her exclaiming, on learning of the death of her half-sister, Bloody Mary, and her own ascension to the throne, "This is the Lord's doing, and it is marvellous in our eyes."

Shakespeare in Love is Merrie England for the American market, and casting Dench, a national treasure on both sides of the Atlantic, validates Elizabeth's importance, not only in the film but in our consciousness, then as well as now. It takes someone of Dench's stature to pull this off: the world knows her as another Queen, *Mrs Brown*, and as 'M' who runs the SIS and is therefore hugely powerful, so anyone else but Dench, in such a set-up as *Shakespeare in Love*, just will not do. And when she serves up such a deliciously droll, world-weary and quick-witted Queen, one recognises that this is the right actress in the right part at the right time. In the reworking of the Sir Walter Raleigh gag, in which the courtier drapes his cloak over a puddle to enable the Queen to continue her walk, here no cloak is produced in time and Dench's Elizabeth is forced to hitch up her skirts and tramp through the muddy puddle herself, muttering, "Too late, too late." This is Elizabeth Tudor screen magic: in our imaginations, this is just how we should like her to have behaved.

❧ *Lalla Ward* ☙

'An Honourable, not a Lady'
The Prince and the Pauper 1977

THE CHOICE TO INCLUDE *THE PRINCE AND THE PAUPER**, THE 1977 Warner Bros picture, might appear to be, at first, a strange addition to the list of Elizabeth's portraits on screen. Certainly the movie as a whole has very little insight into her real life, and her screen time, as in *Shakespeare in Love*, is minimal. The famous story by Mark Twain of a pauper, Tom Canty, from Pudding Lane, and Prince Edward, later Edward VI, and their experiment in switching roles for a short time, is well known and has been dramatised on numerous occasions. The switch backfires on the two boys as their resemblance to each other is so uncanny that everyone believes Tom to be Edward and Edward, Tom. Only after the death of Henry VIII, and at the eleventh hour, at Edward's coronation, is the substitution revealed and the real Prince crowned King, the 'short' time being much lengthier than either had imagined!

The film, with an all-star cast including Oliver Reed, Raquel Welch, Rex Harrison, George C. Scott, and Charlton Heston as Henry VIII, did poorly at the box office and was critically panned, ending Mark Lester's (Edward/Tom) career as a child actor. But in her cameo part as the Princess Elizabeth, spanning the period of Henry's final years and the accession of Edward, Lalla Ward is something of a revelation. Most famous for playing Lady Romana in *Doctor Who* opposite Tom Baker, Ward is, by birth, an 'Honourable'. When asked in the 1990s if she was, she replied in the affirmative, but stated that she was not a 'Lady', a frequent mistake about her. She has since retired from acting, preferring art, illustrating and writing, yet, despite being hampered by a blithe script and caricature characterisations, Ward brings to the young Princess such gravitas that one can clearly see the ruler that she will become. The role could have been dismissed as merely that of a bossy blue stocking, scolding the pauper (when he is meant to be the Prince) for not behaving in a regal manner, and steadfastly retaining an icy exterior when her father takes

---

* The US title was *Crossed Swords*.

a fancy to a movie idea of a Tudor strumpet. Instead Elizabeth is played with an air of future majesty. She is dismissive of Lady Jane Grey (Felicity Dean), who she sees not as a rival in any form but as a being beneath her, a view Elizabeth seems to have often held about women herself. Ward's Elizabeth bears the mark of the Divine Right of Kings without question, and she has the belief that she too could one day rule England, even though her only knowledge of a female ruler at this stage would have been the Empress Matilda's attempt in the 12th century. Ward's chief scene involves her outburst towards Edward (a particularly wooden Lester) about what she sees as his mismanagement of state affairs now that he is King, not knowing that this is actually not her brother. Ward plays the scene at one moment an angry spitfire, the next a coaxing mother, trying to make sense of her brother's behaviour and persuade him to take the kingship seriously. The argument terminates with Edward telling his sister that he doesn't need her "advice, or her fish-wife tongue!" He is "King here, and I'll do as I like, and I'll rule as I please! If the day ever comes when you're on the throne, then you can take care of England!" Elizabeth turns at the door, pauses and then belts the line back at 'Edward': "By God I will!" She turns, opens the doors, hitches up her skirts, and we see her retreating figure angrily heading down a vast Tudor corridor. It might not be authentic, it may appear silly, but here Ward conveys an essence of the Princess who would be Queen.

At the Prince's coronation, it is Elizabeth who looks more regal than Edward, even with her implausible crown and her fake ermine[*]. And it is fitting that the last image we see in the entire film is a repeat of Elizabeth's exit from the King's presence, only this time she leaves in a stately fashion, as Rex Harrison narrates, "Princess Elizabeth… became Queen in her own right, when she was twenty-five; as she had promised, she took good care of England…"

---

[*]   Elizabeth wears Anne Boleyn's famous 'B' pendant in the movie.

❦ *Quentin Crisp* ❦

'A Droll Turn'
Orlando 1992

"DO NOT FADE. DO NOT WITHER. DO NOT GROW OLD," WARNS Quentin Crisp as the aged Queen Elizabeth, in Sally Potter's 1992 release *Orlando*, Virginia Woolf's time traveller, who changes identity, and sex, through his/her travels over the centuries. On paper it seemed impossible to film, but Potter, after years of trying to get the project off the ground, created a sumptuous movie that does justice to Woolf's imagination, and the picture was lauded on its release, gaining Academy Award nominations for Art Direction and Costume Design. Tilda Swinton, as the hero/heroine (based on Woolf's friend and lover Vita Sackville-West), had been on board from the beginning, as had Quentin Crisp[*] as the aged Elizabeth I. Potter felt Crisp was "The Queen of Queens… particularly in the context of [the film's] gender-bending qualities", and the idea of a man playing a woman works in a context that shifts from Elizabethan England to the present day, and encompasses music as diverse as Handel and Jimmy Somerville. But this is a fantasy Elizabeth: if you want the historical accuracy of *Vivat! Vivat Regina!* or *Elizabeth R*, shield your eyes, for it could be argued that this and other representations of the Queen at this time (for example, Miranda Richardson in the *Blackadder* series) do Elizabeth a disservice. The spectacle of a man playing Elizabeth invites the audience to remember all the rumours of the time, and beyond, that Elizabeth was in fact a man, since surely a female couldn't rule with such efficiency and brilliance! The most famous of these theories became known as 'The Bisley Boy Mystery'. It dates from 1543/4, and the story goes that Princess Elizabeth was sent from court to the Cotswolds, to avoid the plague, and then died of the fever while there. Elizabeth's governess (supposedly Lady Bryan or Blanche Parry) was obviously distraught and searched the community for a child of the Princess's colouring and looks. None could she find, so she replaced the dead Princess with a boy who did fit Elizabeth's description, and returned

---

[*] A volume of his autobiography is entitled *How to Become a Virgin*.

to court with the decoy. Of course it is a preposterous story, especially when Elizabeth from cradle to grave hardly had a moment alone, either when dressing, disrobing or sleeping, and surely, if substituting males for females was so easy to pull off, Catherine of Aragon or Anne Boleyn, both of whom had a succession of male stillbirths, might have been tempted to swap one baby for another*.

Crisp's portrayal, described as "a droll turn", by CinemaSource, was shot chiefly at Hatfield House and covers Elizabeth's final years and death. Orlando, her favourite (of questionable gender – perhaps Elizabeth sees something of herself in the youth?), is bequeathed a castle and fortune, so long as Orlando heeds the Queen's advice not to fade and age, as she has done. After this Orlando moves through time, but the image of Crisp's Queen is one of the most haunting in the film: its success based on the androgyny of Elizabeth and Orlando and their understanding of each other, Orlando becoming an Earl of Essex figure for the Queen, a bittersweet reminder of her lost youth, an Estella for her warped Miss Havisham.

---

* Other significant rumours concern Elizabeth's parentage: was she the incestuous daughter of Anne and her brother George Boleyn? Or, as Mary Tudor always felt, the bastard daughter of Marc Smeaton, a court musician and favourite of Anne? Elizabeth's colouring would come to her rescue to quash such tittle-tattle, but the fact that she resembled her mother so strongly and not her father caused speculation throughout her reign.

❦ *Jenny Runacre* ❦

'Elizabeth & the Queen of the Anarchists'
Jubilee 1978

IT IS HARD TO IMAGINE ELIZABETH I IN A LESS LIKELY CONTEXT THAN a punk film, directed by the late Derek Jarman, and set after the Silver Jubilee of Queen Elizabeth II, before the 'Winter of Discontent' of 1979. In *Jubilee* Elizabeth is a time-travelling observer of the state of her country in the reign of her namesake. Dressed in a costume resembling the Ditchley Portrait, played by the actress Jenny Runacre, with a cast of punk stars including Adam Ant and Toyah, Jarman creates the impossible, in a depressing, sideways look at how society has turned out. Elizabeth II is dead and Elizabeth I watches with the aid of Dr Dee, Richard O'Brien – who has conjured up Ariel to guide her on her journey; "Reveal the shadow of his time," he exclaims about the antics of a group of anarchists, representative of the punk and nihilist scene of the era. Elizabeth as time traveller is a novel context, and at times an unsettling one, for her as well as the viewer, as she is shocked by the state of her England.

Runacre has the dual role of Bod, the Queen of the said Anarchists, who violently does away with Queen Elizabeth II, pinches her crown and spends the remainder of her screen time wearing it. But with the loss of our Queen, with the benefit of hindsight, we can see that perhaps a new Elizabeth was on the horizon and, if the Virgin Queen does not have the means to right the wrongs of the centuries that followed her reign, the grocer's daughter will no doubt think she can in her place. Runacre isn't a particularly effective Elizabeth, and the darkness of her settings, the mysterious Dr Dee, the skull on the fireplace, her black-gowned dwarf, all create a seriousness not really matched by the actress. What the film does, however, is plug into a new wave of interest in the first Elizabeth, that sees her not so much in her historical context, but how her image can be placed in fantasy settings. Other pieces to use this technique include Dario Fo's *Elizabeth, Almost by Chance a Woman*; Liz Lochhead's *Mary, Queen of Scots Got Her Head Chopped Off*; Boublil and Schonberg's *The Pirate Queen*; and Timothy Findley's *Elizabeth Rex*.

❦ *Eileen Atkins* ❦

"The life of the play comes with her"
Vivat! Vivat Regina! 1970 & 1972

EILEEN ATKINS' ROLE IN *VIVAT! VIVAT REGINA!* SHOULD NOT BE included in this section, for in reality it is far from a cameo, the part of Elizabeth sharing the above title billing with Mary Stuart. But in Robert Bolt's initial conception of the character, the stage time designated to Elizabeth was considerably smaller than presented on the Chichester Festival Theatre stage in the spring of 1970, and certainly less than the revised script that played in the West End later that year, and on Broadway two years after. Yet by this shift in stage time for Elizabeth, Bolt achieved what no other writer on the subject has done: he presented both Mary and Elizabeth in equal measure and created a play that is not biased towards either Queen. This was achieved by default rather than intention. The piece was written as a starring vehicle for his wife, Sarah Miles, as Mary, to showcase her talents as a beautiful and emotional leading lady, and Elizabeth, rather like Glenda Jackson's part in *Mary, Queen of Scots*, was intended to be a supporting role. The play is also historically accurate, proving that often truth creates a better fiction.

What happened was a fusion of writer (Bolt) creating a fine part, and actress (Atkins) fitting that role like a glove. And although Miles would regard the part of Mary as fitting *her* like a glove (she would even attend the Academy Awards ceremony, in the spring of 1971, in a Mary Stuart themed black evening dress, complete with fur trim and a large crucifix), it would seem she actually wasn't comfortable in the guise of Mary or with the material, and there were problems from the outset. Bolt was thrown into the tricky situation of rewriting some of his material, and as he did so the part of Elizabeth grew in size. Surprisingly, the one person who wasn't so keen on the changes to the play's structure was Atkins herself. She rather liked her role as it was: pithy, exacting, with moments of humour; and there is something to be said for not wanting to relinquish a fine supporting role in favour of a part that was forever being rewritten, and therefore an unknown quantity. In the end it was decided that enough rewriting was enough: Atkins wasn't happy with all of the new material and a compromise was reached. But by the time the play went to London, Elizabeth and Mary's parts were of equal weight in the production.

These changes served the play well, as they opened up Elizabeth's story and gave a greater sense of her dilemma; however, they didn't help Sarah Miles, and Atkins walked away with the acting honours. When the play transferred to Broadway, Atkins went with it and Miles was replaced by Claire Bloom. The American notices for Atkins were excellent: "The life of the play comes with her," wrote *The New York Times* about her performance, and she was awarded a Tony Nomination for Best Actress, her performance, "brilliant and witty", being hailed as one of the finest portraits of the Queen yet.

The play has been less frequently revived than Schiller's *Mary Stuart* but is sometimes produced as a vehicle for two star actresses. Recent productions include one directed by Roy Marsden at the Mermaid Theatre in 1995. The venue, sadly now a conference centre, set the drama as visible to the audience on three sides, and starred Barbara Flynn[*] as Mary and Janet McTeer[†] as a 'regal' Elizabeth. Some felt McTeer not suited to the part and the production received poor reviews. Since then, the play has been rarely seen, most believing its original production to be its finest[‡].

| **"You just have to find her in you"** |

Eileen Atkins is one of the greatest actresses working today, but she is also, with regard to her own work, a pragmatist, and her no-nonsense approach to building a character is illuminating. She has a refreshing ability to research, then discard, and ultimately decides how to play a part strictly on its strength on the page and not what can be added to it from outer influences. *Vivat! Vivat Regina!* was no exception, where she delivered one of her finest performances and suggested that Elizabeth is a far more interesting part to play – and watch – than Mary Stuart.

---

[*] Flynn would play another version of Mary in *Elizabeth I*, opposite Helen Mirren.
[†] McTeer would find one of the great roles of her career as Mary in Phyllida Lloyd's *Mary Stuart* ten years later: a rare incident of an actress playing both Mary and Elizabeth.
[‡] In 2012, to celebrate fifty years of the Festival Theatre, at Chichester, *Vivat! Vivat Regina!* was briefly revived as a single reading. Atkins was special guest at the reading and interviewed after the performance by the director.

Portraying Elizabeth
Interview with Eileen Atkins

Eileen Atkins as Elizabeth*

"When we started working on *Vivat! Vivat Regina!* it soon became clear to Robert Bolt [the writer] that if he was going to get a good play of any kind, he would have to work the character of Elizabeth up a bit. As originally written it was a much smaller part. So the role was increased a little at Chichester Festival Theatre – the play debuted there in 1970 – and then in the break before we came into London he doubled the part. I had received some very good notices as Elizabeth, which Sarah Miles, who played Mary, accepted with good grace. I think had she not been the wife of Robert Bolt and the play not written for her, she might well have tried to get out of coming into London with the production; it was an uncomfortable affair.

I can't remember much about the production all these years later, except that I think it was very good in a schoolmasterly sort of way and that

---

* Like many before her, Atkins wore a putty nose for the part.

Elizabeth was a brilliant character to play. I read all the obvious books on her, though I didn't like Edith Sitwell's book *The Queens and the Hive*. I did feel that the material available at the time was lacking in the tiny, personal details that fascinated me about her. For example, proof positive, nobody seems to have been able to inform me about the real state of the Queen's hair loss. Now, of course, anybody who plays her shaves the top of their head back, but I was fortunate that I have a very high forehead so at least could look like her.

In terms of her character she must have had abnormal energy. I read somewhere that she spoke twelve languages, a huge amount. And when you look at her day, she was up and riding before breakfast, as I remember, and then back to her papers. One of the things I liked most about her was her eating habits: because I have great difficulty eating socially and don't eat as much as other people do, I was therefore very envious of the fact that she was able to say to hosts, "Utterly delicious. I would really like to enjoy it some more. Would you take it away so that I may enjoy it in my private rooms?" And I always want to say that when I am out having dinner!

I admired her immensely, even though I am certain that she could be vicious and vile, but then she had to be, she had to watch her back. But I didn't have an interest in her until I played her. Nearly everybody I have a passion for has been because of my work in some form or other. But I like tough leaders, like Churchill, which Elizabeth most certainly was. But to prepare to play her I read an enormous amount and that was hugely helpful and trickled through into my performance. But one of the great wrong things of acting real people is to go against the text to try and portray something about the character that isn't there on the page. You must take the script that you are given and say "yes" or "no" to it and play what you have got on the page. You should never read a lot and then say to the writer, "You know, she did this or that" – they won't be interested anyway. And then if you try and overlay what you have read into the part it doesn't work. You just can't push it. A lot of actors make this mistake: they do a vast amount of research which has nothing to do with what they have on the page. The only things that you can filter through into your performance are those not determined by the script itself: for instance, I read somewhere that she moved very swiftly, and I thought as her movement wasn't mentioned in the text that I would use this and that whenever I went on I would move at lightning speed, difficult in panniered costumes, but one learned to do it. So I tend to do any reading on the subject many months before and then shove it all away, certainly while I am rehearsing. And then with any luck you have a huge impression of the woman before you begin. And then you do your impression of her.

The actress Ellen Terry wrote in one of her lectures, when discussing Ophelia, that you must always have the idea in your imagination first, and then go and look at reality and do your research afterwards, but it is your ideas and imagination that will make it live. Bringing total reality onto the stage, without any choices, and saying, "Well, that is it," is not a good idea, she says, and I totally agree with her. It's not a good recipe for a successful evening in the theatre. For example, if someone like Mike Leigh really works on his choice of subject and uses his imagination and choices in the piece, taken from what his actors said in improvisation, well then that is acceptable. I'm not excited by it, but it is acceptable.

As to the way I looked as Elizabeth, I was in my mid-thirties, and it was in the days when I didn't quite have enough power, or didn't think I did, to have a greater say in the matter of Elizabeth's appearance, although the designer Carl Toms and director Peter Dews were both extremely helpful to me and they let me do a lot. I did like their suggestion, with the wig, to have the younger Elizabeth wearing almost a ponytail: scraped up and falling down the back through the headdress. I think I was one of the first people to be seen looking like that as the Queen, and since then we have had Cate Blanchett looking like that and several others, choosing to play her in a less frightening way than Bette Davis and Flora Robson. I got to play her from her first entrance into court almost to her death, which is a nice span to play when dealing with appearances. However, I didn't like the way I looked during Elizabeth's middle years. I had three wigs: for the first scene my own hair with the ponytail attached, then the middle-aged wig was clamped on and I really hated the style, a sort of horned look, a little like how women dressed their hair in the war in rolls. And I never felt right. I never saw the same look in any painting I studied, so that I would have liked to have done something about that. I think they wanted her softened, but I think if I had had my own way I would have had her hair flattened because that is the way you think of her, that is the way you think of her mind, as taut. I know she was very, very vain, so I suppose the designer could have excused it because of that, yet I don't think her vanity would have done that style and I don't know why. I was never happy about it.

In terms of the choices I made vocally, I felt about her as I did about

Virginia Woolf. I'm sure if I heard myself today speaking as Elizabeth I would cringe, but then, as opposed to now, one used a very different type of 'posh' voice! I've always believed that if you have a very brilliant mind, as she did, you tend to bring the voice up into the head, more than people who speak more from the heart, or loins, who tend to have more depth of voice. I think as a performer; therefore you tend to want to use a head voice.

I think the most convincing Elizabeth I've ever seen is Vanessa Redgrave's in *Anonymous*. God, she was good – although she wouldn't have been cast as Elizabeth forty years ago in *Mary, Queen of Scots* because back then she would have wanted to play the beauty and the passion, i.e. Mary. Now she is even more interesting as a performer and can do both. But I think Elizabeth was more than just the 'hard woman' that she has often been portrayed as. I think she had to be that on occasion, but she was much, much more than that. She was a clever woman, but she was someone who lived on the edge of her nerves as well. I don't think she was necessarily a calm person, and she had to control this. That is my feeling; it may have been something to do with her stomach. She certainly wasn't someone who could eat a huge hearty meal and then roll into bed! I think she was someone who lived on the edge all the time. Her prayers, that she wrote herself, are particularly illuminating and very beautiful and give one a real sense of how close she – like all the Elizabethans – was to death, which obviously sharpened her appetite for life.

One problem I had with the play was the enlarging of my role. I was actually very happy with what was originally written for me: it was short and sharp and to the point. And I had endless phone calls with Robert Bolt about it. What he did was the old trick with writers, that if they have a part that isn't quite coming up trumps and isn't playing correctly, then you get the other character to give the information necessary for that other part. So he wrote me a long speech at one point of how beautiful, how wonderful and how charming and how adorable Mary, Queen of Scots must be. And I said I *really* don't think Elizabeth is going to hold forth to her favourite [Robert Dudley] about how marvellous this other woman is. She might have thoughts in her *mind* about how gorgeous Mary might be, etc., but I don't think she is going to hold forth to either Cecil or Dudley about her. And so I wouldn't do it. So he shifted a little and I made some accommodations and between the two of us we managed to make it work. We remained very good friends. It isn't always a good thing to have more lines added to your role: a lot of the best parts are when the other poor sod has been speaking for a page and a half and you have the choice line at the end of it! And Elizabeth I felt was someone who got to the pith of the argument and came to it.

By the time the play transferred to Broadway I was much happier with the production, and Claire Bloom [who replaced Sarah Miles as Mary] was happy playing the other part and longing to do it. What is interesting is that it was written as a play about Mary and yet it actually became a play about Elizabeth. In England I always won the audience over but in America the matinees preferred Mary, probably because they were made up of middle-aged and romantic women. This is more the norm as people want their queens to be passionate and have love affairs, if they are sentimental. But in this play, and I believe in life, Elizabeth is just a darned sight more fun: funnier, wittier, sharper. And I would always rather see that than see someone having a mad, passionate love affair on stage. Also I would rather play that – not that I would have ever been cast as Mary or wanted to play her, not least of all because I'm too thin and too bony to play her. I've never had that kind of bosomy, seductive thing that people expect of Mary. And also I'm not very sympathetic to her. I think she is something of a silly cow, but then that may be because I have played Elizabeth! And I think we grow tired of the continual messes she makes of things. Also there is something about the British admiration of that quality that Churchill and Elizabeth both had: a toughness of mind that won't put up with a lot of shit, and a lot of wit in what they say. It is what we lack now in politicians. What goes on in Parliament today is the equivalent of slanging matches in a playground.

I'm very glad we didn't have a scene in which Elizabeth and Mary meet; I hate Schiller's play and think it *so* wrong! I've been offered the play several times and I will not do it. How dare Schiller?! We all know the absolute truth in this case; it is one of those rare times when it is definitely recorded: they did not meet. So why did he have to do it? I won't go to the play, unless I have a friend in it, so then I have to go. I like Harriet Walter's acting very much, and Janet McTeer's, but I didn't go and see their production* because I just can't bear the play. I think it is lacking in wit, lacking in humour, and I think each scene is a lot of 'drama' and I get bored with that. I don't say that Robert's is a great play. I still think there is another wonderful play to be written about the two of them.

I don't think I would like to have another crack at the part and I'm

---

* *Mary Stuart* at the Donmar Theatre, London, 2005.

certainly not film starry enough to do it on screen. But then that has been my own fault, and I'm so old it doesn't matter now, but I actually don't like filming; I totally chose not to do films when I was young: I don't like the atmosphere of a film. I don't mind television quite so much, at least in the old days, because it was filmed in studios and then you could do long takes, as on stage, and you could get more of the feeling of the piece. I hate this habit of: a few lines, then stop, then another few lines, stop. I literally only do movies for the money. It didn't matter to me one whit that others played my stage roles on screen, because I wasn't interested in the medium.

Fortunately, I've been lucky enough to play a satisfyingly wide range of roles on stage and I have never had a problem finding a link with the character I am playing, and I certainly didn't with Elizabeth, because everything is there – it is just a question of pulling it out. I can see how some people might find playing her a huge challenge, because she is autocratic and there is an inner violence to the woman, but, and I am like Judi Dench in this respect, we just get the part and try and morph into it. You just have to find it in you. You say the line and imagine yourself there and then you find it in you. In the end you can either do it or you can't. So you can either take a part and morph into it, and persuade huge numbers of people that you are that person, or you simply can't. You can learn technical things, good solid notes on voice and movement, but not "Oh, I feel true this morning". In our training my age group came in for a lot of that rubbish!

The performers of today, I think on the whole, are remarkably good and much better than we were. It may be a bit sweeping, but accents for example, they can all do a lot of dialect. When I was young most people would say they could do American and most of them were utterly appalling! I've always kept to the decision that one must not do an accent if you are doing it in the actual country you are in. And I believe that you rarely get a really naff young person come up who just can't act. I mostly have nothing but praise for them. But I don't follow Elizabeth as portrayed by other people. I think there are a few actresses who will no doubt play her one day: Anna Maxwell Martin, for example. I think she is a wonderful actress and she is wonderfully thin and spare and has a very good mind, just like Elizabeth. What would be a mistake is for a very beautiful actress to be cast or, worse, an actress who knows she is beautiful and is trying to prove a point by playing Elizabeth. That would be a huge mistake!"

❦ *Felicity Dean* ❧

"This final instalment of her story had the flavour of a great movie, perhaps involving Bette Davis in the starring role"
Elizabeth I 2017

THE *INDEPENDENT* DESCRIBED THE THREE-PART SERIES AS "WOBBLING a bit between drama and schoolbook history… [but] actually pretty good." Reviews were better than might have been expected of the Channel 5 series, though much was made of some of the weaknesses and the simplicity of the script. The 'pop-up' historians, Suzannah Lipscomb and Dan Jones, were praised for an engaging and modern style, that complemented the dark authenticity of the dramatic re-enacting of events from the Queen's life.

Much was made of the model turned actress Lily Cole taking on the role of Elizabeth, her name being the selling point of the project, and it was she who was the cover girl for all publicity. Because of her attachment, what might have been the latest in the ever-increasing market for historical docudramas, presented in an often chatty and modern way, attracted publicity and more viewers than a standard programme on Elizabeth might have done. Fortunately, what *Elizabeth I* doesn't do, despite its shortcomings, is tread the misguided path of historians dressing up in mob caps and cloaks against a backdrop that resembles a National Trust shop. Cole, when asked about wearing "all those silly ruffs – did you enjoy that?" replied that she did: "I'd normally feel quite guilty if I was bossing people around. But when you're playing Elizabeth I, you can really enjoy being superior." The lightness of the answer disguises a dedication to Elizabeth and, even if it might not have been fully realised in her finished performance, at least her intention towards the Queen was sincere.

The gloomy, menacing sets and edgy camera work does much to distract from the presenter's narrative that sometimes falls into over-simplistic bullet points, but what really sets the tone of the drama, if you're willing to hang around long enough for it, is the last twenty minutes when Cole exits, and part three is dominated by the presence of Felicity Dean in the guise of Elizabeth. It is a pity that Dean was not allowed to play those earlier scenes actually suited to an actress of her age. Cole is given these big moments from

Elizabeth's history and she misfires under the weight of such material. If Dean had been allowed the complete third episode, we might have had a last act to live up to the *Daily Express* comment that the final instalment could have been like a Hollywood movie starring Bette Davis.

> ## "I don't think she will ever be exhausted as a character"

Although Elizabeth is the driving force of the three-part docudrama *Elizabeth I*, I have chosen to place the interview with Felicity Dean in this segment of the book dedicated to cameo performances. Dean's time on screen makes up the final third of the final part, and therefore sits between cameo and leading role.

Fortunately what Dean brings to this time is an Elizabeth carved out of the stuff of history books, with a leaning towards a 21st-century insight into the ageing monarch, dealing with the last love of a romantically troubled life. Almost unrecognisable behind the flaky white make-up, Dean presents Elizabeth as crabby, haughty, humorous, vain, winsome, regretful and – at times – vindictive. It is also one of the most telling portraits of the Queen exploring her mortality.

Portraying Elizabeth
Interview with Felicity Dean

Felicity Dean as Elizabeth (© Brendan McGinty)

"DOCUMENTARY DRAMA USED TO BE CONSIDERED THE POOR RELATION of mainstream drama, but that's changing; and it definitely has its dramatic strengths. I discovered, when playing Elizabeth, whose life was long and spanned a great many events, to concentrate on only one period of her life allowed me to go deeper. Four actresses portrayed her life and I was playing her towards the end of her reign. Politically and personally her life was in turmoil. Economically the country was in a bad state, her youth and physical beauty were waning. As a monarch and as a woman she felt she was on a decline. She was fighting an ongoing war with Ireland[*], and then at this point she entered into an intense and devastating 'friendship' with a much younger man. As an actress, these contradictions, and how I imagined her conflicted emotional state, made her an immensely interesting woman to portray. She was ageing, powerful, one of the greatest rulers to have ever lived, yet now vulnerable and isolated and in love! On top of all that, she made the decision

---

[*] The last years of Elizabeth's reign saw the Nine Years' War in Ireland, a revolt headed by the Earl of Tyrone.

to have Essex, her younger man, executed when he betrayed her by trying to raise a rebel army against her.

So it was very interesting to have to focus on that period, and I felt her vulnerability greatly. Because of this, what really attracted me to doing the piece was that the scenes I had were quite dense, well written, with long speeches. These changed a little – not down to me, but because of what the production wanted to highlight about Elizabeth. And when I discussed this with Chris Holt, the writer and director, he was keen to illustrate Elizabeth in a dramatic form, rather than use the more common idea of a voiceover to present Elizabeth's narrative. And even if there were presenters, they became the links in the drama, which for me is the correct way to show this type of television.

Obviously, one looks at Elizabeth through a 21st-century lens which is post-Jung, post-Freud, so one has a psychological take on her character. But what makes her so fascinating is that she is an archetype – anything can be projected on to her. We never knew and never will really know about her. So you can bring your own ideas to what is going on within her. And it is important not to think about how anybody else has played her. Having said that, I did watch the entire series of *Elizabeth R* – full of information, and Glenda Jackson was quite marvellous.

Playing her, one of the key elements I wanted to find was how she sounded vocally. Visually, I don't look anything like her, as she was such a particular looking woman, and there is such a shorthand to her image – red wig, ruff, white face – but fortunately the audience will accept different actresses in the part because of this. The vocal portrayal I thought was more important, the reason being I felt her voice had to come from a very rounded, very centred place. Because that is who she was, who she had to be. So I believed she had to have a strong presence, as a route into her core. And because of the format, and time constraints, I had to walk onto the set absolutely word perfect, in order for me to be able to have the freedom to move about, to be physically in the space. We were filming in a Tudor manor, in the middle of winter, and it was freezing. We had roaring log fires, huge blazing candles, and it was just extraordinary, but in order to have the freedom and own the place, just like one does on stage, I had to be absolutely off the book, and aware of what I was intending to do. Obviously I worked closely with Chris, to discuss how to interpret the emotional dynamic as best as we could. After a while he trusted me and let me get on with it, and gave me minimal direction actually. He understood that I'm not the kind of actress that responds to micro-management very well. Where Chris helped me enormously was by guiding me through the challenge of bringing this powerful strong woman to a cinematic size, telling me when to do less and focus more, and when he was pulling the camera right back to give me free rein to let rip. Size of frame was immensely important. This is where director, director of photography and actor can collaborate. I thoroughly enjoyed working with Chris, and the director of photography Brendan McGinty.

I had conversations with Lily Cole – who played the Elizabeth who preceded me – about our interpretations, but because the format was disjointed, with such a vast jump historically, and with the age of Elizabeth jumping with it, we were in very different periods of her life. And you have to remember that you're given the script, you have a certain amount of time and those are the parameters that you have to work within. Unlike being on stage, where you can discuss, modify and make more choices, on television where the time constraints can be immense you have to be really disciplined. I was fortunate, though, that I had time to prepare to play her, a couple of months, and that really allowed me a decent amount of preparation time. And what I always do, if I'm playing somebody who has existed, or someone from Shakespeare or classical theatre, is to get a very clear and simple overview of the character. I want to know the story in its broadest context, which is what I did with Elizabeth's life. There is so much literature out there on her, you can almost go mad wondering where to start! So once the overview is there, I like to get a little more in-depth in the period I'm working on: I read as much as I can and then I looked at as many paintings of her as I could, one of my favourites being the Phoenix Portrait by Hilliard – even if they are propaganda.

She was a brilliant PR woman, one of the great PR people of any generation. I did notice that in later years she seemed to be painted at a side angle, sort of two-thirds, possibly because of the templates that artists had of her? If so, she obviously knew what suited her. You could say she knew how to take a 'selfie'!

I never felt when playing her, *Oh, this is just another job*! I felt it was a real privilege, as a performer, to have the opportunity to show a snippet, just a small chance, to play that incredible woman. And how was I going to garner all my personal strengths to pull down from the ether that energy. Because that to me was the essence of who she was, that extraordinary power, and I needed to bring that to my performance. This I believe was the absolute core of her. When tuning into the energy of Elizabeth I, it is a little like channelling a character. I had to use my antenna to try and pick up the essence of who this woman was. Like all characters of very high status there is often nobody above them, except God; there are many below and there are enemies and adversaries, but the supreme inner confidence that they must have is very, very enticing, and challenging to play. I had to remain very centred. The format, therefore, of drama-documentary, is very geared towards finding those moments of internalisation: the focus had to be right, to give the right snapshots of her life.

One of the things that really brought her to me was reading that when she was going to die, she refused to go to bed. I just thought that showed such fortitude and strength, even though she had an ulcerated throat at that time – she must have been in such pain and emotional turmoil – plus she had been betrayed by the man who gave her her last chance of happiness, the Earl of Essex. There had been so many dangerous events in her life, and yet she managed, somehow, to hold the country together throughout. This relationship with Essex, that my chunk of the drama focused upon, made me think that she went into the relationship with her eyes wide open. And I think the trap for dramatists is to make her into a Mrs Robinson kind of character, a glamorous older woman having a relationship with a younger man. But what I discovered was the painfulness of taking those steps to allow herself to be seduced by this glittering boy, that it was both agonising and brave; it was as if she was saying: I will open this doorway into my heart a little bit. And to some degree it was humiliating for her. But maybe the slightly masochistic hurt that it brought her, she found enlivening. Perhaps she was kept alive by it, even if it was perverse.

I liked very much that the script wasn't Shakespearian, but it wasn't modern. It tried to use phrases or vernacular that she might have or did use, and I think it managed to balance the accessibly of drama-documentary and something that had a period quality to it. You had to be quite dexterous linguistically to deal with it, but that was fine, I enjoyed that, and I thought it was important not to colloquialise anything.

I wanted her to look as authentic as I possibly could. I had ageing make-up, my face was blown with a hairdryer, latex was pressed upon it. Interestingly, the freedom of that make-up, the freedom of being made to look so far from how I'm often cast, was amazingly freeing. It's very liberating not to have to think about looking good, and part of being an actress is to constantly be aware of what you look like; it's a profession that is forever focused on that. And suddenly I was stepping into a different character and a different time zone, which was fantastic, especially being able to play somebody older than myself.

I don't think she will ever be exhausted as a character because we bring our own interpretation through our modern-day framework and understanding, and I think generations to come will do the same thing, and who knows what will be discovered and how actresses in a hundred years' time will play her. I think one could say the same thing about Shakespeare or Chekhov. Has it been done to death? Do we want to see it again? There will always be a different interpretation to be had."

9

Elizabeth: The Whole Story

❦ *Glenda Jackson* ❦

> *"Elizabeth must have been impossible!"*
> Elizabeth R 1970

FROM SARAH BERNHARDT'S FIRST TENTATIVE ATTEMPT AT bringing Elizabeth I to film audiences, it would take nearly sixty years to produce a performance and vehicle, on either stage or screen, that was truly worthy of the Queen, and would place her at the centre of its drama. It seems quite incredible that a story so rich, and a leading character so emotionally varied and remarkable, should take this time to come to fruition, but here at last, in *Elizabeth R*, the whole story of her adult life is played out for us, in six ninety-minute episodes. At its heart is a bravura performance, one that has stood the test of time and is seen by many as definitive. It would win Glenda Jackson two Emmy awards for Best Actress in a Drama Series, for the third episode 'Shadow in the Sun', and Best Actress in a Movie or Television Serial, and become the part for which she is best remembered.

The series came about because the BBC's *The Six Wives of Henry VIII*, starring Keith Michell, had been a major hit with audiences and critics, and it made sense to capitalise on this by continuing the story to the end of Elizabeth's reign. Six highly accomplished writers, John Hale, Rosemary Anne Sisson, Julian Mitchell, Hugh Whitemore, John Prebble and Ian Rodger, were employed to create an episode each that show actual events in her life where very little is imagined and relying heavily upon Elizabeth's own words. The sets are more accurate, showing the English court as more intimate, less showy and in keeping with Elizabeth's parsimonious personality. Very few exterior shots are used, due to costs of location shooting, and camera angles are often in close-up, giving an intensity to a drama that relies less on spectacle and more on an intimate knowledge of the workings of the court, its inhabitants and Elizabeth herself.

Having recently won her first Oscar, Jackson was a hot property and the only choice for the role, though she had done little television and wasn't keen on the medium. "Television seems to have all the faults of theatre and none of its advantages, and all the faults of film and none of its advantages," she said, but despite this she thought herself a good casting for the part: "I like Elizabeth. She's about eighteen people under one skin and she made sure no one ever really got to the central character. She was arrogant, selfish, flamboyant and thoroughly mean."

In episode one 'The Lion's Cub', Elizabeth exclaims that she may not be a lion, but is a lion's cub, which is a reference to her father. It begins with the arrest of Thomas Seymour and Elizabeth's servants for questioning by Edward Seymour, who was Lord Protector of the Realm for Elizabeth's brother Edward VI. It places the young Elizabeth in one of the most vulnerable periods of her life, the episode ending with the death of Mary Tudor, and Elizabeth being presented with the coronation ring. Jackson, with her head shaved to produce the famous high forehead, an effective false nose and her skin powdered to create Elizabeth's famed pale complexion, looks convincing as the Princess*. In reality, at this point in her life, Elizabeth was described as "proud and disdainful" which "much blemished the beauty of her person". And Christopher Hibbert writes "[She] was certainly most striking in her appearance with her reddish golden hair, her white skin, her long, slightly hooked nose, her extraordinarily long-fingered hands of which she was already so proud that she displayed them against her bodice or skirt in gestures that were to become instinctive…" Jackson presents great complexities and undercurrents to her character from the start, as Elizabeth deals with the constant questioning, threats and accusations that the Princess had to endure during much of her brother and sister's reigns. Thomas Seymour has attempted to kidnap Edward VI to gain control of the

---

* Jackson also learned archery and to ride side-saddle, play the virginal, dance and write, as Elizabeth would have done.

realm from his brother Edward. On his breaking into the boy's room, the King's dog barks and Seymour takes his sword to it. The attempted kidnap – quickly interpreted by many as an attempt on the King's life – and the pet dog's death mark the end for Seymour and the beginning of the most perilous time of Elizabeth's life, as she is accused of being in league with Seymour, who intends to marry her now that Katherine Parr is dead. "You have a guilty look and a guilty manner," states Robert Tyrwhit (Stanley Lebor), as he questions Elizabeth over her involvement with Seymour, going on to remind her that "The penalty for treason for a woman is decapitation or burning. Remember the death of your mother, Your Grace." A sharp intake of breath, and the lip that has been so steadfast in the face of adversity trembles. "You are not here to trap the Admiral [Seymour] but to destroy me," she replies. Flashbacks fill in the gaps between *The Six Wives of Henry VIII* and the present, as the camera takes on the eyes of Elizabeth (we hear Jackson's voice, laughter and breathing only) as she flirts with Seymour; firstly in the gardens of a suggested Sudeley Castle, as he takes a constitutional with Katherine; then as he wakes Elizabeth, throwing back her bed curtains and trying to tickle her out of bed; and thirdly being held by Katherine as Seymour cuts Elizabeth's skirts with his dagger. Each of these events happened (information gleaned during the questioning of Elizabeth's servants, Ashley and Parry). Kat Ashley (Rachel Kempson) appears in each of these flashbacks and brilliantly conveys her devotion to her charge but also her often misguided moral management of her. 'The Lion's Cub' places the Princess at a Damascene moment regarding her honour. Just as Cate Blanchett's Elizabeth will 'become' a virgin at the close of *Elizabeth*, so Jackson's Princess suffers a series of emotional breakdowns that make any question of "flattery", as she refers to Seymour's attention, out of the question.

Enter William Cecil (Ronald Hines) who, although known to Elizabeth, is not as yet in her confidence. Cecil would become the saviour of her reign, the guiding voice at her side. Hines' steadfast, measured performance beautifully captures this and plays well against Jackson's fiery, multilayered monarch. "Why do you risk yourself for me?" Elizabeth asks him. And Cecil replies that he respects the order of her father's succession. However, there was more to Cecil than this: he was too shrewd a negotiator not to see the problems arising at court – the fall of now *both* Seymour brothers, and the short-lived rise of Lady Jane Grey, a puppet monarch, manipulated by her father the Duke of Northumberland. Cecil played one faction off against the other, swore allegiance to Mary Tudor and even went to Mass, although he was not Catholic, to save his own neck and steer the country and Elizabeth in the right direction, both politically and on religious matters. He cleverly saw in the wise and popular Princess the future of England and hoped, and probably knew, that it would only be a short time before she would be Queen, for Mary was in her late thirties, still unmarried, and rumours of her sickly health were rife. Elizabeth confesses to Cecil that she has trusted no man since the death of Katherine Howard, but the seed is sown and their union as mistress and secretary now comes into play.

With Cecil's advice and interception, we observe a change in Elizabeth: her confidence returns, and she adeptly answers her questioners, leaving her enemies with the problem of how to control her and her popularity now that Edward VI is dead. Cecil informs Mary of her brother's death: "God be praised," Mary replies, as by this time relations between Protestant Edward and Catholic Mary, both religious fanatics, had completely broken down. Cecil, swearing his allegiance to the Catholic Queen, also tells her of Northumberland's plan to place his daughter upon the throne; cut to Mary's prisoners in the Tower, with the last shot the door of Jane Grey's cell as Jane "puts her hand to her throat".

Mary is now Queen; Thomas Seymour, "a man of much wit and very little judgement", as described by Elizabeth, has been executed, and Elizabeth is welcomed at the court. She wears white, her hair hanging loose, both signs of her purity; the difference between middle-aged Mary and young Elizabeth couldn't be more pronounced. Thomas Wyatt calls out, "God Save the Princess Elizabeth!" on Coronation Day as a trigger to the Wyatt rebellion*, and the religious tug of war between the two sisters ensues. Mary (Daphne Slater) is neurotic, paranoid and maniacal in her fervent determination to convert Elizabeth to her faith, while Elizabeth shows the negotiating skills for which she will become famous, parrying each attempt until she draws the Queen's fury with her resistance. Elizabeth is sent to the Tower. Jackson

---

*   Elizabeth's involvement in the plot by Wyatt to overthrow Mary (she denied any complicity) is left for the viewer to decide. Wyatt, the son of the poet Thomas Wyatt (a favourite of Anne Boleyn), organised a mismanaged rebellion in protest at Mary's forthcoming Spanish marriage, wishing to overthrow the Queen and place Elizabeth on the throne, with the wealthy Protestant Edward Courtenay, first Earl of Devon, as her consort. The uprising was quashed, and Elizabeth and Courtenay were placed in the Tower; Wyatt was executed.

is on fire with terrified fury, her bedraggled tresses about her face, as she steadfastly refuses to enter Traitors' Gate, sitting on the steps, leading from the water, in the pouring rain. Although there has always been argument that the Princess, due to her station, would not have entered through such a gate, and the Thames tide was too low at that point to have permitted such a journey, the image is memorably dramatic, effectively showing the jeopardy she is in. What follows allows Jackson to portray the mercurial mix of terror and majesty, as she battles to save her life, "a lamb to the slaughter", and those of her servants, Parry and Ashley.

In time Elizabeth is released but, now under house arrest back at Hatfield, the questioning and accusations continue. Cecil once again comes to her rescue: wearing the guise of Queen's interrogator, he actually has only Elizabeth's interests at heart. With the news of Mary's pregnancy, Elizabeth crumbles and is only steadied with Cecil's guidance (when they are alone together and he can reveal his true loyalty to her): "Stand firm... Be silent. Be still", filmed in a tight two shot that has the battle cry of Lady Macbeth's "But screw your courage to the sticking-place, And we'll not fail." Elizabeth regains composure, and Mary's delusion that she is pregnant is played out. Her husband, Philip of Spain (Peter Jeffrey), describes her as "old, ugly and barren", and sets his sights on Elizabeth, whom he pleasurably spies dressing, before stating his allegiance to her.

As Mary's condition worsens so the tide shifts and Elizabeth's safety and self-assurance grow. In time Mary dies, and it is fitting that the episode ends with Cecil handing over of the coronation ring to Elizabeth. Delighted, she tosses her cap into the air.

Episode two, 'The Marriage Game', by Rosemary Anne Sisson, cleverly shows the formation of Elizabeth the shrewd negotiator. Now she is the property of her kingdom, her body is no longer her own, but as she nimbly steps from marriage proposal to marriage proposal Jackson shows the formation of the mature woman in the place she was born to occupy: the top job. The episode is one of the few times the early stages of Elizabeth's reign are profiled: these apprentice years are usually sidestepped by the dramatist in favour of the demands of bigger moments of spectacle and crisis. With the death of Mary, Elizabeth takes up the reins of office with alacrity and assurance. A brief, and rare, exterior shot of Jackson riding through streets of cheering London crowds is followed by a scene showing the Spanish ambassadors complain of her conduct and comment on her youth and inexperience. By the time of the next scene such doubts can be dispelled. Hair up, business-like demeanour, Jackson enters a meeting, begun without her, and sits at the head of her council: this is obviously going to be a very different ruler from Mary Tudor. With office comes the pressure to marry, while Elizabeth is seen to conduct a liaison (at one point kissing passionately in front of her ladies-in-waiting) with her favourite, the handsome Robert Dudley (Robert Hardy), whom she promotes and names as her successor, to the consternation of her council, when she falls sick with smallpox and nearly dies*.

Dudley has his own story playing out, as his sickly wife, Amy, is found dead at the foot of a staircase at his country seat. The mystery was never solved and, though Dudley was found innocent, his name was forever tarnished by the scandal. Now, free to marry again, he cranks up his ambitions to marry the Queen and become King of England†. Elizabeth, though romantically attached to her favourite, with whom she has grown up and experienced so much, is aware of his objective and manages to keep one step ahead of him. She tells Burghley, her chief minister, as they discuss prospective husbands, "No one should be entirely discouraged." Though later she announces, "I am an absolute Princess, and I will marry at no man's bidding, so you may put that thought clean out of your heads! And I take it very unkind in you all, knowing as you do my heart, and my love for my people, to come and harry me this way!" From here on she begins to assemble the creation of Elizabeth, her legitimacy, virginity, and marrying herself to her people.

By the time of 'Shadow in the Sun', the third episode, Jackson's Elizabeth resembles the image of the Queen that we readily associate with her. The hairline is higher, the costumes more elaborate, the face whiter, harder: the myth of the Virgin Queen – even though she is continuing marriage negotiations with foreign princes – is almost completely formed. We even see Elizabeth sketched in the court garden, in natural light, a habit she adopted

---

* Elizabeth contracted smallpox in 1562, four years into her reign. At first, as there were no signs of the actual pox on her skin (her symptoms included a high temperature and a discomfort in her throat), she was distrustful of the doctor's diagnosis. In time, however, the pox came out and the country nervously predicted a future without Elizabeth, sparking images of rebellion, invasion and the strong possibility of a Catholic monarch on the throne. On Elizabeth's survival and return to health, her ministers put even heavier pressure on her to marry.

† The episode closes with a mistimed attempt at a secret marriage ceremony between Elizabeth and Dudley. One wonders, though, was it really Elizabeth's intention to share her crown, weaken her power, and succumb to the often fatal peril of the marriage bed or, as the episode title suggests, was it just a 'Marriage Game'; one suspects the latter.

so as not to cast a shadow upon her face, a clever weaving of the Queen's personal and public life.

The Queen's relationship with Lettice Knollys (Angela Thorne) is an unusual one: they were cousins (Lettice was a granddaughter of Anne Boleyn's sister Mary and mother of the future Earl of Essex) and spent a good deal of their childhood together. Lettice, attractive and vivacious, and younger than Elizabeth by ten years, would have many admirers at court and was married three times. When Elizabeth discovered Lettice's marriage to Dudley, she was banished from court and never forgiven*. Lettice, however, rallied, married again and saw the rise and fall of her son Robert Devereux, Earl of Essex, heightening further the animosity between monarch and subject. She would be returned to court in the more lenient reign of James I and would die in 1634 at the ripe age of ninety-one, a tremendous feat for the time, having outlived Elizabeth by thirty-one years.

The episode also deals with the proposed marriage of the Queen to the Duke of Alençon (Michael Williams), the son of Catherine de Medici, something that seems like a last stab at marrying her off, though none of the participants, Privy Council, Queen or Duke, ever seem completely behind it, for whoever Elizabeth unites with she chances falling foul of another nation, therefore better to carry on prevaricating over suitors, who are thinning as the episode plays out. She complains: "I am the Queen and alone, and that is what it is to be the Queen" and declares that marriage and war are "one and

---

* Elizabeth couldn't understand why her ladies-in-waiting, for whom she felt a particular responsibility, or courtiers for that matter, wanted to marry. She kept a tight rein on those closest to her, which caused a great deal of secret marrying, resulting in intense rages from the Queen when she found out, as she always did. She was under the impression that if she could devote her life to duty (in 'Shadow in the Sun' Elizabeth states that she is "married to her country", though she is not taken seriously at the time), then others should follow her example. She might complain about her spinsterhood, but took the radical, for the time, view that a woman didn't need to take a mate, and was more respectful of those who did not, promoting them throughout her reign. Jackson shows the simmering volcanic quality of the Queen's dealings with those who serve her intimately, at one moment relying upon them for comfort and advice, the next irritated and the butt of her anger and frustration. Of course, the real 'marriage' that the Queen undergoes, except for the one she chooses with her nation, is that which she conducts with her chief minister, Burghley. Here, their relationship is cleverly depicted as being one of deepest mutual trust: he was, perhaps, the only man Elizabeth ever did trust. Jackson and Hines beautifully suggest a partnership of principle, shrewd decorum and understanding. At one point Burghley, grown used to Elizabeth's sometimes maddening caution and indecisiveness, asks of the Queen: "Is it wise to wait and see?"; "Always," she replies with a twinkle.

the same thing!" One of the main voices of opposition to the match is that of Dudley, so it is neatly done when his marriage is revealed by the Duke's intimate adviser, Jean de Simier. Dudley is banished to the Tower, and the Queen, though tragically sobbing, declares Alençon England's next King. But the pronouncement is short-lived, as the terrified Queen confesses to the Earl of Sussex her fear of marriage and ultimately death, whether it be as her mother perished or through childbirth, for in Elizabeth's mind the two, like marriage and war, are forever a pair. She too has to come to terms with her own mortality as she confides to her ladies that she "want[s] not to feel time like a dead child in my womb". Dudley returns to court, but as the episode closes one senses he will never truly be pardoned.

The figures of Death and Mary Stuart were never far out of mind in Elizabeth's life, nor here in *Elizabeth R*: now they loom to the forefront of the drama in episode four, 'Horrible Conspiracies', by Hugh Whitemore. The casting of Vivian Pickles as Mary accurately imbues the Scottish Queen with the single-minded, misguided and sometimes irritating energy. Authenticity of script means that the Queens do not meet, and the drama ping-pongs back and forth between the English court and Mary's places of custody. The episode is imbued with menace, there is tension and fear – fear on the part of both Queens, but particularly Elizabeth as she gears herself up to make the most momentous decision of her life, while Mary, less the deluded martyr of some productions, hangs on to what majesty is still allowed her. Jackson's Queen is consumed by troubled emotions; deeply anxious, she becomes venomously cranky, aware of her own mortality, and conscious of what the future will bring if she does sign Mary's death warrant. The plotting of the Queen of Scots comes to light, her own person is repeatedly threatened, and when Walsingham (Stephen Murray) "counsels delay", she is quick to accuse him of placing her life at risk. So it seeps in that she must act decisively, but still she falters.

Jackson is marvellously effective at showing the frightened ageing woman behind the magnificent facade that is the Queen. Costumes are inspired by the Phoenix Portrait by Nicholas Hilliard, the Darnley Portrait (artist unknown), and the Sieve Portrait by Metsys the Younger. As fame and fantasy spread about Elizabeth, so her costumes become more theatrical and impressive, as she follows and sets fashions: no white is worn here (as it was in the previous episode) for there is no chance of catching a husband now. We also see Elizabeth in private: "God's death! First teeth, now stomach," complains the Queen to Walsingham as she takes her medicine in her bedchamber, wrapped in fur, her face a mask of discomfort, with John Dee, Elizabeth's astronomer, desperately searching for some spiritual sign. And we even see the Queen in bed, again advised by Walsingham, the matters of state forever near, as he forces her to choose a new location to house Mary. Elizabeth, frightened and frightening, yet also extremely amusing in her peeved repartee with her spy master, exclaims, after finding fault with all of his choices, "*Oh, leave me to rest! God's death!*" then punches her pillows harshly, embittered and resentful that the worries about Mary even contaminate her sleep.

The Queen of Scots is executed, and the, now familiar charade of whether Elizabeth gave permission or not is played out, as she tries to rid herself of what she ultimately sees as her guilt. What is left for Elizabeth is the contemplation of her cousin's death and eventually her own, as she chillingly tells Walsingham: "Peace? Ah no, you are mistaken. There is no peace for the dead… it is a busy time for my royal cousin. See, already the creatures are at work, crawling between her lips, entering her nose, burrowing beneath her eyes. Worms cluster in her belly, competing with foul maggots for the tastiest morsel. Even now, she is being invaded by a legion of grey flesh-eaters… picked clean by worms, flesh curdling with corruption, stinking like a blocked midden. So do not talk to me of 'peace' and 'God's good grace' – dying is a fearful process. I have known Death since I was a child; I have stared long into his white, unseeing eyes. I know him. When you are lying on your last bed, remember my words, cry out for mercy, bite deep into your lips, and recall how you plotted my cousin's most terrible end…" Sinister in its subtlety, 'Horrible Conspiracies' surfaces as the episode of *Elizabeth R* that deserves reappraisal, and also admiration for not having the Queens meet or inventing a romantic image of Mary.

'The Enterprise of England' skilfully plays out the months leading up to the attempted attack on England by Spain, weaving the twin dilemmas of both Elizabeth and Philip as they justify their actions before God. At one point they kneel, alone, and utter the same prayer, cutting from Elizabeth to Philip, in a moment of touching simplicity[*].

---

[*] God is paramount in both monarchs' actions, though the 'Allegory of the Tudor Succession' by Luca de Heere, a piece of Elizabethan propaganda, comes to mind: Henry VIII sits centre stage, Edward VI kneels to his left, while Mary Tudor and Philip enter, stage right, followed by Mars, the god of war, and Elizabeth enters stage left with the goddesses of peace and plenty, a sign of Protestant reform.

The comparison between the two ageing rulers continues, as neither is really in a position, financially or mentally, to go to war, and Elizabeth is in a foul mood for much of the episode as her ministers try to force her to do the one thing she doesn't want to: enter into conflict with her ex brother-in-law, who once, to her mind, saved her from the block. Her natural suspicion is heightened beyond measure, as she continually reminds both Burghley and Walsingham that they are to blame for the situation as they were the ones who tricked her into signing the death warrant for that "wretched woman" Mary Stuart.

Jackson shows the ageing Queen's wriggling discomfort as she wrestles with the prospect of war, alien to her being. She is waspish when declaring that she thought she had hanged Drake, but then somewhat admires the Dutch envoys for standing up to her. She illuminates our understanding of Elizabeth with her quicksilver, mercurial playing as she interacts with Dudley, one moment tender, the next jealous, haughty and then vengeful as she is reminded of his deceit over his secret marriage to Lettice Knollys. The Earl of Essex (Robin Ellis) makes his first appearance, and wariness simmers as Dudley observes the position of favourite shift from himself to his stepson. Elizabeth knows this, and plays upon it and pities him. She sees everything, and in a brilliant moment of volcanic eruption Jackson (in a piece of scripting by John Prebble that intercuts with the Queen's own words) declares, "I know you'd as life have a man on my throne. But God gave it to me. I am anointed by Him, and I am answerable to none but Him. My councillors depend upon me, not I upon them. I hold their lives and heads in my hands. You're dust that I've moulded. You are empty breath without my voice. I'm not deceived by Spain. There are men like you who would have Philip set power against me. But we are princes both, not common soil, and we know that we are bound by the will of God to preserve the peace of our kingdoms. Don't think you can trick me. I've such cunning that if I were turned out of my kingdom in my petticoat I would prosper anywhere in Christendom!"*

When the Armada comes, Elizabeth is what we want all leaders to be: brave and charismatic. She dons, not a breastplate, but a plate collar that

---

* "I am your anointed Queen. I will never be by violence constrained to do anything. I thank God I am indeed endowed with such qualities that if I were turned out of the realm in my petticoat I were able to live in any place in Christendom." A response to Parliament in 1566, on the subject of her marriage.

gives her discomfort: "God's death, this fancy corselet is crushing me!", and rides out to Tilbury on a white horse to speak to her army. She delivers one of the finest speeches of her reign, words that echo down the centuries and define her as a ruler and a woman, not a battle cry but a wiser declaration: one of defence and pride in the country and people she calls her own.

This dazzling episode is concluded with the revelation that Elizabeth was less motherly to her subjects after the defeat of Spain. Seamen injured and hungry are forgotten as the Queen tightens her purse strings as she contemplates the cost of war. And the news of the death of Dudley is brought to her. At first she cannot comprehend Burghley's news, then rages at Essex, signs and seals Dudley's last correspondence to her, 'His last letter', before falling to the floor, hoarsely sobbing.

The script of 'Sweet England's Pride', the final episode, spares no punches for the last act of Elizabeth's life. Not before or since have we seen so accurately the Queen's physical decline. What was hinted at in episode four, brought to attention in episode five, is grotesquely splendid in its full visual horror, as we view the white pancake and thick paint and rouge that defined Elizabeth's elderly appearance. Dealing with the rise and fall of the Earl of Essex, the continuing troubles in Ireland, the Queen's fragile life and the much discussed though never settled succession, Jackson's final Elizabeth is gloriously crabby, mean and flirtatious, yet can still deliver rousing rhetoric that demands the admiration of even those who plot her successor's easy journey to the English throne. She is sharp in her dealings with her ladies; one in particular who has gained the Queen's displeasure is referred to as "My lady tart!" And she bullies Francis Bacon into finding a way of repressing copies of *The History of Henry IV*, something Essex used to try to strengthen his claim to the throne. The Queen is tired, lonely, dismissive and watchful as those around her, who have advised her and she has trusted, begin to die off; chief among these is Burghley, whom Elizabeth has worked into the ground for forty years, from her accession until his death in 1598. He is replaced by his son Robert Cecil, Earl of Salisbury. Robert Cecil would later say of Elizabeth, that she was "more than a man, but less than a woman". A parallel to this new political relationship is the personal replacement of Dudley by his stepson Essex. Where once Elizabeth and Dudley had been the golden couple of the court, now Essex and the Queen make an odd match of wily would-be mother and grasping son. Jackson's Queen may wear Essex's miniature on her sleeve, but her heart does not rest next to it. This Queen would never have wrestled to the last with her emotions and contemplated giving up her crown to Essex, as Bette Davis's did in *The Private Lives of Elizabeth and Essex*: Jackson's Elizabeth is too mistrustful, clever and sly to ever permit matters to take such a course. Her allowing the Essex affair to get out of hand is due to her prevaricating, not her foolishness. He may be her "sun in splendour" but her knowledge that he is also "our pride" is not forgotten, her meaning double-edged: pride comes before a fall.

Death is at the Queen's elbow throughout the episode, like the painting 'Elizabeth with Time and Death' (see Chapter 4). But here she does not seem to fear the next step her life may take, and death is a friendly reminder of her own mortality, so when Essex finds the Queen soaking her feet, stripped of the vestiges of Gloriana, she does not scream in horror for him to leave, she merely welcomes him back to court and says they will talk more when she is dressed (by this time in her life, Elizabeth would have taken several hours to get ready to be seen by anyone other than her ladies). Jackson's Queen knows that she has created an immortal image of herself, but she understands that it is just that: an image.

With the defeat of Essex, that "hollow hero", and his uprising, Elizabeth's mood becomes increasingly melancholic. She delivers the famous 'Golden Speech', described by Bacon as "magnificent", to which Cecil replies, "Before it goes out, the candle always flares." After such glory – Jackson is decked out in a copy of the costume worn in the magnificent Ditchley Portrait – we see Elizabeth, sitting with her ladies, waiting to die. Cecil declares that to please her people she must go to bed. "Little man, the word *must* is not used to princes."* At which she decides to stand, and there she remained for the next four days, with her index finger in her mouth, contemplating her life, welcoming her death, looking, as Jackson herself described it, "Like a turtle". Her face made up, her robe gold, her hair about her shoulders, alluding to her virginity, she asks if the people love her, and upon hearing the affirmative states, "They have been good company". Walter Raleigh (Nicholas Selby) passes through the presence chamber and stops momentarily as he notes the empty throne. He joins the others waiting outside the Queen's bedchamber and, as Elizabeth remained standing, so those about her had to also. She is asked who is to be her successor: the King of Scotland? She shakes her head, nods, then shakes her head again and dies. The hair and gold of her robe

---

* "Little" makes reference to Robert Cecil's height, which was said to be 5' 4".

blaze, her finger, removed from her mouth, rests in her lap. In the script, Ian Rodger has courtiers already leaving their mistress, "moving fast down the corridor", presumably heading to Scotland and the preparations for the future of the realm. He writes that Elizabeth clasps a sword as she dies, removed by Cecil after her last breath; neither of these events take place in the final film – the passing is revered and poignant and real.

"Am I like anyone?" Elizabeth asks Dudley, in episode three, 'Shadow in the Sun'. But the question needs no response, for in *Elizabeth R*, in which the Queen's story expertly gives us the finest and truest telling of her history to date, both Elizabeth and Jackson are not like anyone, never could be, and remain the more remarkable for this fact.

"Everything you need is in the script"

For a performance of truly epic proportions, Glenda Jackson's approach to constructing the part of Elizabeth was as unfussy as the actress's reputation. Some critics of Jackson have accused her of merely forcing her own set of strident mannerisms into an Elizabeth that has more to do with 1970s' feminism than with the Virgin Queen. The fact that the script of *Elizabeth R* is so proficient adds weight to Jackson's reluctance to research, but her own instinctive understanding of the woman makes it clear that her casting was inspired. Like Eileen Atkins, Jackson's dismissal of anything that might be construed as pretentious in her craft only adds to the admiration we must feel for what she brings to the role.

Portraying Elizabeth

Interview with Glenda Jackson

Glenda Jackson as Elizabeth (Moviestore Collection Ltd)

"*ELIZABETH R* WAS SUCH AN AMAZING OPPORTUNITY: TO PLAY someone's life virtually all the way through without it becoming a trick of 'Oh, look, and now she is that age', and most importantly to work with the same group of people, which was quite unusual for television in those days – for something, in essence a nine-hour series, to work all the way through with that same team was very unusual. We had about three weeks' rehearsal before we started at the BBC studios, then a rehearsal period there, during which you had things like costume fittings, and then we'd actually shoot over the weekends. And I can't stress enough, the great thing about it was working with that same group of people, and those around us – that was just extraordinary. We had a fantastic cast, and up to a point we always had the same technical people with us as well, so that in itself was an enormous bonus. Some of the scripts were more literary than others, and they used so much of Elizabeth's own language, because so much was extant. And we shot it relatively chronologically.

Costume and wig fittings became progressively more time-consuming as she aged: at the beginning, for the earlier episodes – even though there were things like false noses to put on – it was mostly just a case of getting the wig on, at which the fitters were expert. Certainly though, at the end, I could be in the make-up chair for as much as seven hours. One of the ironic things was, towards the end of her life, the ladies of Elizabeth's court could also take that time to get ready to present themselves.

I obviously didn't resemble such portraits of her that exist and, along with the false nose, my hairline was shaved to replicate Elizabeth's very high forehead: this was much easier for me to have, and then the wig put on, rather than those terrible partial bald wigs where you could usually see the line! But the emphasis on getting Elizabeth's appearance correct was incredible. I remember one of the leaders from the Royal College of Embroidery, she and an art historian, towards the end of the series, because they were obsessed with getting the ruffs correct for those worn at the end of her reign, spent the whole weekend checking out portraits, and by seeing how the light had fallen they discovered how those ruffs had been made, which gives you some idea as to their attention to detail. There were difficulties, of course, with the costumes, especially the larger ones, as there was a huge difference between the materials of our age and her age – and at the end of her reign, with the huge skirts, on occasion they wore wooden wheels to keep the skirts out at the sides: we managed with canvas and things like that. And for the early part of her reign the corsets would have been made out of wood: we didn't have that, but it was interesting to know when playing her.

In terms of other forms of research I'm a great believer in the theory that everything you need as an actor is in the script, but when I got the part in *Elizabeth R* everyone I knew sent me books about her, but the two that I found most useful were *Elizabeth the Great* by Elizabeth Jenkins and *The Queens and the Hive* by Edith Sitwell. But there was also a book which was a compilation of extant memoirs about Elizabeth, and one of these was by one of her ladies-in-waiting, and described that when she was actually dying she was sucking her thumb, and that script ['Sweet England's Pride'] had originally had her clutching the mace, and I said, "This is bloody ridiculous, she wouldn't do that," but the idea of her sitting in that chair and sucking her thumb was something that I just thought was marvellous.

One of the amazing things about her time was how much of her actual words are still in the National Archive and, for me, one of the touching documents was one of Mary Stuart's letters in code, which Elizabeth's secret service cracked within about five minutes, and to actually hold that was quite extraordinary. Pretty much anything we wanted to see was made available to us. What I hadn't seen, and didn't see until the recent 'Elizabeth' exhibition at Greenwich, and found particularly touching, was a ring which opened, and one side was her mother and the other a portrait of her – that was very moving.

Essentially, although you can't make direct comparisons, and she was an *absolute* monarch, I think her greatest gift was indecision, though I don't necessarily think she was undecided, but her ministers and others could never pin her down and she always left doors open. I don't just mean on the subject of her marrying – though she was very astute in how she handled that – but I think on broader matters, certainly on what we would now call foreign policy*, she would keep people dangling. What she does seem to have been clear on was religion, and definitely on where her own power base was, and that was her popularity with the people.

In terms of her character, I think she must have been absolutely impossible to be around, certainly towards the end of her life, incredibly difficult, because her vanity was extremely high, but a challenge and enjoyable to play. Acting is a tremendously difficult thing to do well, and the longer you do it you realise how little you actually know, and how easy it is to act badly and how difficult it is to act well, so always the more complicated the person, the more interesting, though demanding, she is to play. I haven't seen all of the series – I need to buy the box set – but when I do watch *Elizabeth R* it's like everything, you think, "Oh God, why did I just do that? Why did I move then?" But it's too late and you have to take the rough with the smooth.

Because I knew so little about her, I went into playing her with very little preconceived opinion about her. What I knew when I started filming was what most people know. The areas, though, that I found most hard, were to do with her belief, her genuine belief that she had been chosen by God. And for someone like me – who, though I believe we are more than flesh, blood and bones, and I believe there is a spiritual aspect to us all – that religious belief is not something that I could tap into easily. In terms of how I moved

---

* Jackson felt that the episode 'The Enterprise of England' by John Prebble was "undoubtedly the best script of the series". It deals with the attempted invasion by Spain.

when playing her, this was entirely dictated by the fashions of the day, and no one knows how she sounded, so she sounded like me! The series in a sense was her home life, and her home was a court. And so we see her with people that she knew extremely well; there is very little that is filmed outside, or shows how she interacted with the people, with exceptions, the big one being the Armada/Tilbury Speech*, which must have been published, it must have been handed out – she couldn't have been heard by her whole army on that day. I'd seen Bette Davis's portrayals of her, and I thought Cate Blanchett, in the first of her outings, was *just marvellous*. I thought she really did capture what everyone had mentioned about the young Elizabeth, that she was like a flame, and she looked like a flame; I'm not so convinced by the rest of the film – but I thought *she* was just wonderful.

I've always said that *Elizabeth R* and series like that are forms of 'posh escapism': there is something inherent in all these historical dramas where you are over the first hump, because they are so far away in time, of asking people to suspend disbelief. They don't have to do that. It may be – and I don't think it's true of *Elizabeth R* or indeed the previous series that went before it, *The Six Wives of Henry VIII*† – that judgements are made and based on the mores and attitudes of our own time, which is something that

---

* The Tilbury Speech, which was published and handed out as the Queen delivered it, in full: "My loving people, We have been persuaded by some that are careful of our safety, to take heed how we commit our selves to armed multitudes, for fear of treachery; but I assure you I do not desire to live to distrust my faithful and loving people. Let tyrants fear. I have always so behaved myself that, under God, I have placed my chiefest strength and safeguard in the loyal hearts and good-will of my subjects; and therefore I am come amongst you, as you see, at this time, not for my recreation and disport, but being resolved, in the midst and heat of the battle, to live and die amongst you all; to lay down for my God, and for my kingdom, and my people, my honour and my blood, even in the dust. I know I have the body but of a weak and feeble woman; but I have the heart and stomach of a king, and of a king of England too, and think foul scorn that Parma or Spain, or any prince of Europe, should dare to invade the borders of my realm; to which rather than any dishonour shall grow by me, I myself will take up arms, I myself will be your general, judge, and rewarder of every one of your virtues in the field. I know already, for your forwardness you have deserved rewards and crowns; and we do assure you in the word of a prince, they shall be duly paid you. In the mean time, my lieutenant general shall be in my stead, than whom never prince commanded a more noble or worthy subject; not doubting but by your obedience to my general, by your concord in the camp, and your valour in the field, we shall shortly have a famous victory over those enemies of my God, of my kingdom, and of my people."

† Transmitted by the BBC in 1970. *Elizabeth R* was screened the following year, with the final episode, 'Sweet England's Pride', aired on the 368th anniversary of Elizabeth's death.

creeps in: we are inclined to be infinitely more judgemental, possibly, and also, to my mind, make false allusions to what is happening now, but I don't think that is the case in the period that we are talking about, when *Elizabeth R* was made.

I don't know, necessarily, if she is being reinterpreted over time, because the reinterpretation is essentially in the hands of whomsoever is presenting her; whether that increases our knowledge of her in any practical sense is probably not the case. It's also dependent upon how much money people think they can make out of her story. I don't think there is much more to know, as the practical details of her reign are there to be seen, they still exist: speeches, treaties, the enormous amount of actual history is there to be mined as you wish. Whether you know more or less about her as a human being is possibly dependent upon the way we like to rewrite history, which can be highly dangerous.

There have been other parts that I have preferred and have found more difficult, or challenging – when I played Stevie Smith[*], even before the curtain went up on the production, there was an outcry that I was totally wrong to play her – but in the case of *Elizabeth R*, to fit so much of the life into an hour and a half episode was unique, and she was *extraordinary*, there's no two ways about it!

The film *Mary, Queen of Scots* was something I did because I wanted to work with Vanessa [Redgrave], and it wasn't the greatest script in the world – we only had those two scenes together, which were completely untrue because they never actually met, and I think on that level, that was the reason I took the part. The film is MARY, *Queen of Scots* and very different, obviously, from *Elizabeth R*, and a film is very different to a television series. And there we are!"

---

[*] In *Stevie* by Hugh Whitemore, which Jackson played on stage and screen.

❦ *Anne-Marie Duff* ❦

"She is in the very soul of England. She is in the bones of this country"
The Virgin Queen 2006

THE VIRGIN QUEEN – PRODUCED BY THE BBC – SUFFERED FROM being eclipsed by the HBO miniseries *Elizabeth I* that was to be released at the same time, forcing the BBC to hold back transmission of *The Virgin Queen* until the beginning of the following year. As to its critical response, it was also outshone by the more opulent production and showier antics of Helen Mirren. But, in spite of such competition, this full retelling of Elizabeth's history, starting a little later than *Elizabeth R* but covering the same historical territory, has merit and is interesting for many ideas it attempts to suggest and question about Elizabeth. If Glenda Jackson's portrayal has been accused of a steely control that hints of coldness, in Anne-Marie Duff's performance (over four episodes, each constituting an hour drama) we are on the other end of the spectrum, and at times off the scale. With its incessant use of modern and traditional music (supplied by the Mediaeval Baebes), it occasionally resembles a pop video. Inspired by Shekhar Kapur's revolutionary retelling, it sits oddly between this and *Elizabeth R*, as if it doesn't have the conviction to settle in either camp. It is relevant to note that Sofia Coppola's *Marie Antoinette* was also released in 2006, another biopic with a firm feminist standpoint that tried to reinterpret another familiar historical figure. The turn of the century seems to have been a time to reappraise our feminist icons. *The Virgin Queen* also had to compete with *Gunpowder, Treason and Plot*[*], a fictional account of the lives of Mary of Guise, Mary, Queen of Scots and James I, released in 2004. Often a new wave of appreciation is whipped up for the House of Stuart, or even the series of Georges that came after them, but time and time again we return to the House of Tudor and those familiar

---

[*] Catherine McCormack played Elizabeth, a secondary role to the main activities happening in Scotland. The production is a mishmash of styles, and McCormack, usually excellent (her performance as Elizabeth David was extremely noteworthy), seems all at sea. The script which defines the Queen as a bitter villainess in the Florence Eldridge mode offers no room for even an attempt at portraying a real character.

larger than life personalities: *The Tudors* series was just around the corner when *The Virgin Queen* was aired. Written by Paula Milne*, *The Virgin Queen* conjures up a picture of what Tudor England might have been like for Elizabeth, with the emphasis on the female soul prevailing in spite of outward masculine adversity: Queen Mary might rule, but the pit bulls she seems to employ are the ones that wield the power and are out to bring down this heroine Princess. Because of this Elizabeth is haunted by traditional images of Henry VIII and Mary, Queen of Scots, as if they were being noted in a documentary. Anne Boleyn is repeatedly referred to as a whore in Elizabeth's presence (even the last line brings reference to her as Elizabeth's locket ring is opened revealing Anne's image), indicating that she's a bastard. The emphasis is always on the visual, and known historical information is fed us, as if we, as an audience, have to be shown our history by a series of familiar images. For example, Elizabeth the questionable daughter, possibly of ill repute like her mother, who bewitched a King, must not be allowed to bewitch in her turn. So, to survive she must reinvent herself.

Duff's Elizabeth does want to be Queen, and readily and joyously takes up the crown, yet there is a pervading sense that she has almost been forced to do so. Duff forever rushes from chamber to chamber, out of palaces, across fields, as if she wants to run away from her predicament. Liv Ullmann's Queen Christina, running from her duty in *The Abdication* (1974) comes to mind: hair running free, irresponsible and irrepressible.

---

* Milne told *The Daily Telegraph* that she was "increasingly struck how different generations of biographers or artists have portrayed Elizabeth according to their own needs. Indeed, creating portrayals of her in prose and drama is an industry in itself. She has been depicted as everything from courageous warrior queen to deadly nemesis of Mary, Queen of Scots, from unfulfilled lover to implacable stateswoman. She's been both the whimsical Faerie Queen and triumphant Gloriana..." Seeing Elizabeth as part Princess Diana, part Mrs Thatcher, thereby firmly stamping her own generational concept upon her subject and trying to defeat the 'Are you an Elizabeth or a Mary' question, Milne's Elizabeth's essence was that she had experienced "Losing love, for whatever reason, [this] reaches out through the centuries to all of us who have found love and lost it. As Elizabeth herself said in another context, 'All the rest is trifles'. This notion may be behind Sarah Bernhardt's view of the self-sacrificing Queen. Are not the interpretations by Helen Mirren (an equally emotionally surrendering portrayal), Duff, Bernhardt, and also Bette Davis (a performance more Mrs Thatcher than Princess Diana, but having to be included here because of the insistence on exaggerating the romantic elements of Elizabeth's life by Hollywood at the time) all similar in their sentimental standpoint, and because of this somewhat misguided? Elizabeth has to be a more dynamic character than one who has loved and lost.

Much of the imagery in the production is to be commended – it is beautifully photographed, and the first episode has dazzling scenes of Elizabeth travelling by barge, and Mary Tudor in church, but these are simply not enough to carry the production.

Anxiety prevails from the outset of the first episode, with the swift tread of Catholic feet, the confusion of identity between Elizabeth and her cousin Lettice Knollys (Sienna Guillory), the sounds of the prisoners in the Tower and the fear of the scaffold. All this sets the scene for a somewhat obvious retelling of Elizabeth's history. Everything is there as one would expect it to be, but haven't we seen it all before? It's as if 1950s' Hollywood has been morphed into a BBC budget. Joanne Whalley makes a neurotic Bloody Mary, less the desperate, sickly fanatic of Kathy Burke, more the famous portrait by Antonis Mor (1554): impressive, resolute and slightly mad. Her choice of a wandering Northern accent, however, is questionable. Tom Hardy plays Dudley as a loutish bad boy; his Dudley is a throwback to Errol Flynn's Earl of Essex: glamorous, non-conforming and sexy, but unrealistic.

And so we come to the Queen herself. Duff's characterisation is that of a spirit that will not be broken, but she is fighting a losing battle, creating a Queen that never appears to have a moment's stillness of mind or body, and even when established as monarch never looks as if she is in the right place or happy to be there. Whereas Glenda Jackson seemed consumed with both lightning speed and a deadly stillness, Duff's characterisation appears almost too human, too ordinary. Bette Davis's posturing and ever twitching palms might drive some mad, but there was a cohesive character created through such gesticulation; Duff shows the Queen, warts and all, but her showing doesn't enlighten.

The Virgin Queen loves a legend, and every episode is stuffed with them, including the inscription, made with a diamond, upon a window pane at the palace of Woodstock, where Elizabeth was held under house arrest in 1554:

> 'Much suspected by me,
> Nothing proved can be,
> Quoth Elizabeth prisoner.'

The series tries to burrow deeper into Elizabeth's psychology than any dramatic study has done before and by doing so recreates Elizabeth as a feminist martyr figure, whose lot it is to become a version of her paranoid sister Mary, prowling her palace in a breastplate, wielding a sword for protection*. This misses the point of Elizabeth's history completely, for she totally believed in her ultimate right to the Kingdom of England; and her accession isn't something that is foisted upon her: it is her *choice*, not her sacrifice, to accept the office and decide to occupy that throne alone.

By episodes two and three the image of Elizabeth has taken shape. To disguise the remains of smallpox, she adopts the use of a white pancake make-up, and decrees that her ladies-in-waiting must assume a more subdued wardrobe, establishing herself as the "One sun in the universe" around whom the ladies should orbit. But despite this outer likeness of Elizabeth, Duff's Queen still continues to burn within, as the incessant theme song – 'The Virgin Queen' from Martin Phipps and the Mediaeval Baebes – informs us†.

Elizabeth's response to a declaration from Parliament to marry as soon

---

* The last scene between the Elizabeth and Mary Tudor has Mary donning a similar breastplate for her own protection against Elizabeth's supporters.

† The song uses lines from a poem attributed to Elizabeth that she is said to have written after the breakdown of marriage negotiations with the Duke of Anjou, her 'Frog', in 1581, though there is another school of thought that suggests that it is more likely to be about her relationship with Robert Dudley, as would be supposed in the use of it here. In *Elizabeth R* ('Shadow in the Sun') a voiceover by Glenda Jackson narrates the poem as the Duke departs.

> I grieve and dare not show my discontent;
> I love, and yet am forced to seem to hate;
> I do, yet dare not say I ever meant;
> I seem stark mute, but inwardly do prate.
> I am, and not; I freeze and yet am burned,
> Since from myself another self I turned.
> My care is like my shadow in the sun –
> Follows me flying, flies when I pursue it,
> Stands, and lies by me, doth what I have done;
> His too familiar care doth make me rue it.
> No means I find to rid him from my breast,
> Till by the end of things it be suppressed.
> Some gentler passion slide into my mind,
> For I am soft and made of melting snow;
> Or be more cruel, Love, and so be kind.
> Let me or float or sink, be high or low;
> Or let me live with some more sweet content,
> Or die, and so forget what love e'er meant.

as possible* (this took place after her recovery from smallpox) is a passionate and heartfelt outpouring of sentiment, but lacking gravitas. So keen are director, writer and actress to present the Queen as an accessible heroine who becomes an icon that they ignore many real factors of her nature. And if these are hinted at, they are offered in a tongue-in-cheek manner that suggests that her actions are a game, and the viewer is in on the joke. Her famous "There shall be but one mistress and no master" epithet to Dudley, which is often dramatised as it presents Elizabeth's character in a nutshell, is an outburst of frenzied passion. After being kissed and embraced by Dudley, garbed in black leather, Elizabeth hysterically delivers her maxim, before falling to the floor, the onslaught of smallpox taking its toll. Dudley departs, threatening never to return, and the ailing Queen is surrounded by her ladies†. Duff says of Elizabeth and her bargain with her virginity: "[It] was a challenge to every man in the kingdom… to deliberately cease her power of giving life is an intensely powerful statement. For a queen, it was a deeply political statement, an incredibly effective tool wielded by Elizabeth over the men in her council and the men in her life."

Mary, Queen of Scots (Charlotte Winner), a shadowy figure in life, is given a further air of mystery in this series and is presented in portrait‡ form when Elizabeth is visited by Mary's emissary James Melville, employed to smooth over the issue of her second marriage to Henry, Lord Darnley. Once again this is a showing of history, not an informing, by another visual message: this is Mary Stuart. Just as Henry VIII, as a painting on a wall or in Elizabeth's dream, is never far away, so now Mary is an image that the viewer can identify with. Milne does not allow too much of Mary: the cousins do not meet, and she is a mystery, forever petting her dog, a turning figure as a door closes. More time is spent showing the web of intrigue and plots in

---

* The speech ended with these lines, some of which are used in the scene: "For although I be never so careful of your well doings and mind ever so to be, yet may my issue grow out of kind and become perhaps ungracious. And in the end this shall be for me sufficient, that a marble stone shall declare that a Queen, having reigned such a time, lived and died a virgin."

† There is also much that is inspired by Kapur's *Elizabeth*, including Duff's Queen sleeping in a bed adorned with hangings similar to those in *Elizabeth* and joined there by Robert Dudley; also reminiscent is the use of the camera travelling in and out of focus and the depiction of the novice Queen attempting to obtain order over her ministers and realm. Duff even wore some of the costumes donned by Blanchett in *Elizabeth*.

‡ The portrait, a gift from Mary for the Queen, shows Mary as a widow, a copy of one of the Sheffield portraits painted while she was in captivity, after Nicholas Hilliard, of which there are several in existence.

which she wrapped herself, and scant attention is paid to Mary's execution, although we might wonder how did the costume department imagine Mary could be executed while wearing a wired veil and headdress! Duff brilliantly displays the Queen's panic as she wakes from a nightmare wherein she herself is the victim of the executioner's block, begging God to forgive her: "What have I done?!" she exclaims.

Episode four, after a skip of ten years, brings us into the next romantic phase of the Queen's life, but misses out much that throws light upon Elizabeth as a stateswoman. Duff as the elderly Elizabeth is a painted gorgon, her costumes metallic, her heart by this time equally unresponsive. Much of the episode is taken up with the antics of the Earl of Essex (Hans Matheson), a leather-clad replica of Tom Hardy, and this is unfortunate as much of *Elizabeth I* is occupied with the same topic. Duff plays Elizabeth's death well, staring vacantly into the corner of her chamber, a finger to her lips, her gaze empty, before collapsing in slow motion. This would have been enough, had the director not thought it appropriate to crank up the Mediaeval Baebes to underscore the moment, and put a memory bubble of key moments of Elizabeth's life on screen, as if we were looking into her imagination. Duff stated at the time that "People don't appreciate what it was like to be English at that period, how different the national temperament was, how tactile, how fiery – more akin to the Latin temperament of today." There would be many who would dispute this idea of England at that time and suggest that actually Elizabeth and her reign caused emotional, romantic and sexual temperatures to drop, but in *The Virgin Queen* Duff has met her brief and created an Elizabeth who matches this belief.

10

The Queen in Comic Relief

❦ *Miranda Richardson* ❦

"I'll always be Queenie to some people"
Blackadder II 1986

MIRANDA RICHARDSON'S ELIZABETH HAS BECOME A COMIC masterpiece and, along with the part of Ruth Ellis in *Dance with a Stranger* (1985), is still the role with which she is most readily associated. For many, the performance sums up Elizabeth as films and dramas have failed to do, and gives surprising insights, creating a clear-sighted distillation of the passions that drove the woman. Taking inspiration from spoilt schoolgirls and Lewis Carroll's Queen of Hearts, Richardson's Elizabeth is a tyrannical, hysterical, immature, greedy, avaricious despot, who spits out vitriol in a mawkish Violet Elizabeth* voice and utters threats of execution with alacrity. Her behaviour – when sober – is that of a party girl, desperate for affection, constantly wanting to be entertained, with a quicksilver array of mood swings with which Richardson dazzles her audience, as if walking a psychotic tightrope of emotions. Ably abetted by the devoted Nursey (Patsy Byrne) and her adviser Lord Melchett (Stephen Fry, made to look like Francis Walsingham), Elizabeth's role in the six episodes mostly concerns setting tasks for Blackadder, many of which are erroneous or trivial.

---

* A character from the *Just William* series by Richmal Crompton, famed for her lisping voice and petulant attitude, source of the phrase "I'll scream and scream until I'm sick!"

Historian Elizabeth Jenkins writes in *Elizabeth the Great* that "Her blazing nervous energy was not a quality of sound health... Her frequent indispositions pulled her down alarmingly and 'very thin, the colour of a corpse' ... was a characteristic description of her appearance". She suffered from "gastric attacks, neuralgia and aching limbs". The precarious state of her health and the taxing demands of her role as sovereign caused unpredictable shifts of behaviour. Jenkins writes: "She once spat at a courtier who had disgusted her, she slapped the Maids of Honour when they annoyed her beyond bearing... She had a keen instinct for the dramatic and a capacity for passion... the Queen's vehement and ringing tones were to cut across many an argument at the council table." And in *Ladies-in-Waiting* the biographer Anne Somerset describes Elizabeth's "possessive nature [that] did not like to be parted from her favourite associates... [her] moods were subject to the vagaries of the affairs of State, and at times of political crisis her temper could be alarming and erratic... she even 'beat one or two of her ladies-in-waiting', and though at times she generally confined herself to purely verbal assaults on her ladies, her sarcastic tongue and withering wit still combined to render her an object of terror." Richardson's Elizabeth, therefore, cannot be dismissed as a comic skit, for she is more accurate than many would have imagined, bringing to her playing a shorthand to the real Elizabeth, laying bare her imperfect personality and bringing many of her inner demons to the surface. She would go on to reprise the role for a millennium special of *Blackadder*.

Portraying Elizabeth
Interview with Miranda Richardson

Miranda Richardson in *Blackadder II*, with Patsy Byrne (Everett Collection Inc.)

I WAS FORTUNATE TO TALK TO MIRANDA RICHARDSON, JUST OVER twenty-five years after she had played Elizabeth in the phenomenally successful comedy series *Blackadder II*. Of all the actresses I spoke to, this proved the hardest interview to prepare for: could I ask similar questions about preparation, motivation and interest in the character when dealing in comedic terms, as opposed to dramatic ones? I was soon put at my ease, for Richardson obviously approaches her comedy work with the same intensity as she does her dramatic performances. She pointed out that all good comedy has its basis in tragedy, for underlying all the humour in the series is the very real threat that any of the characters, including Queenie herself, could lose their power and end up on the executioner's block. Fear, therefore, is paramount to the drama, and adds the edge of hysteria to Richardson's playing, making Queenie hilariously funny and also terrifying with her quicksilver mood swings.

Richardson went on to explain that her initial idea for the part had come about because she had play-acted as a child with a friend, concocting a couple of spoilt, brattish schoolgirl characters whose vocal quality and petulant manner eventually became the basis of the iconic Queenie's personality. Richardson's grasp of Elizabeth seems to have taken the role to a higher level than was originally written by the creative *Blackadder* team. She certainly wasn't the first choice to play her: *Dance with a Stranger*, which brought her stardom, hadn't been released, and she was relatively unknown beyond her stage work. Auditions for the part consisted of varying versions of Bedale schoolgirls, but every actress tested appeared somewhat two-dimensional. Then in walked Miranda Richardson; Richard Curtis said, "Here was this astonishing actress, who did nothing like we expected it. Every line was odd, peculiar, weirdly pitched." Her vocal range in the part is particularly impressive: the delivery not only consisted of unusually placed words and phrasing, but also squeaks, yelps, cries and a whole arsenal of other noises. So she got the part and soon found herself weighted down with heavily researched costumes, as well as a mirror and a pomander*. Ben Elton would later say that without her the programme "probably wouldn't have worked".

Richardson felt that our continual interest in Elizabeth and our fascination with reinterpreting her for each new generation come increasingly from our celebrity obsessed culture. Elizabeth was one of the early superstars, the biggest of her day, bejewelled and magnificent, puffed up with her own importance and all powerful, and that for society is totally enthralling, rather like the interest people have in the Royal Family nowadays. Elizabeth's gift for theatre and for image make her all the more alluring, and when one thinks of the danger involved in her everyday actions, a theme all of the actresses I interviewed stressed, this only adds to her courage as well as her appeal.

When asked whether she would consider playing Elizabeth again, in a different context, presumably in a dramatic situation, she replied that of course the character was of immense interest but the material would have to be new, rather than a piece that had already been produced, as new writing was a main condition for her future work.

---

* Richardson, like Anna Massey, commented on the heaviness of her costumes.

11

The Return of the Queen: Actresses who have Played Elizabeth Twice

❦ *Flora Robson* ❦

'The actress who made worry into an art form'
The Sea Hawk 1940

FLORA ROBSON'S SECOND OUTING AS ELIZABETH IS DIFFERENT from her earlier incarnation, chiefly because the film was made by Warner Bros in America. Errol Flynn was thrilled with the casting, stating that it was a delight to play opposite an actress who wasn't only interested in herself, a definite dig at Bette Davis, his least favourite female co-star.

The movie, released in July 1940 and loosely based on the antics of Sir Francis Drake, was never meant to be historically accurate, but is chiefly impressive as a piece of pro-English propaganda. Presentations of the Queen often go into production during times of world conflict: *Fire Over England* as the world got ready for war; *The Private Lives of Elizabeth and Essex* in 1939 at the outbreak of World War II; *The Sea Hawk* just as America prepared to join the war; and *Elizabeth: The Golden Age*, brandishing the slogan 'Woman, Warrior, Queen' in 2007, as the Iraq War was underway. The release of *Fire Over England* in the United States had been held back, to generate sympathy for the British cause in World War II and to drum up support and allegiance from America. So Robson, at least on that side of the Atlantic, with the two films released in quick succession, became, along with Bette Davis, the recognised face of Elizabeth.

Flynn plays Captain Geoffrey Thorpe, the Sea Hawk of the title, another swashbuckling sea dog, just about on the right side of the law. At the court of Elizabeth ministers plead with the Queen to commission the building of a fleet to rival that of the Armada of Philip II of Spain, whose threat to invade increases daily. Philip wishes to conquer a country "as barren and treacherous as her Queen" and wreak revenge for England's habit of looting Spanish ships; Elizabeth is aware this is something of which Thorpe is guilty, but then we also know that Elizabeth is as greedy as she is mean, so although she does not condone Thorpe's actions she does not forbid them, as she likes to hedge her bets and is pleased to accept part of the swag.

All these characteristics are apparent in Robson's first four scenes. The character is aptly presented, but there is a definite change in Robson's delivery of the part. The influence of *The Private Lives of Elizabeth and Essex* is everywhere in this interpretation of the English court, as is the dialogue of Maxwell Anderson. It is therefore no surprise that the cinematographer and director are the same. Instead of the gracious, modulated introduction to England's Queen, the audience is privy to an entrance that almost outdoes Bette Davis's coming into court. We are given a huge fanfare by Erich Wolfgang Korngold, also responsible for the music for *Elizabeth and Essex*, and Robson veritably marches onto the screen, hips swinging, brandishing an ostrich fan. Warner Bros had sunk $1.7 million into the movie, and never is this more apparent than when the Queen swaggers onto the screen. We have seen Eldridge do it, then Davis, and now Robson gives us her version of the Elizabeth strut as the camera pans over the imposing set. Pitted against the excellent Claude Rains as a slimy Don Alvarez, seeking an audience with her to complain about England's misconduct on the sea, Robson conducts herself admirably: Rains is an adept scene-stealer but Robson holds her own against him, her recent screen work paying off with a new-found confidence before the camera.

Robson shows Elizabeth as woman in a man's world as she ticks off a sea captain: "Then hereafter you will allow me to determine in what manner England may best be served!" Just as Elizabeth seems set to take off emotionally, the drama is redirected and humour is introduced with the arrival of Captain Thorpe's monkey through a palace window, causing Elizabeth to be once more checked.

There is an impression of the familiar love triangle, though this time Elizabeth does not react in a neurotic, jealous manner. Don Alvarez brings his niece to England, Donna Maria, played by the sultry Brenda Marshall, and it will be she who catches Flynn's roving eye. Elizabeth is left without an emotional or sexual identity in the picture, as there is no inner quarrel or sacrifice with England winning over love, no demons questioning her decision to remain unmarried, no threat of another queen to take her throne. The threat from overseas (just as in 1940) is paramount to the Queen: it threatens all of England, and England and Elizabeth are the same, undivided, of one body.

Robson is allowed one moment of marvellous vitriol when rebuking Claude Rains – she demands Philip of Spain's portrait be removed from her wall: "It is enough that I have to listen to his tiresome complaints, without having to look at his arrogant face!" After which, toying anxiously with her pearls, as the business of England unfolds before her, there is little else for Elizabeth to do but to knight Thorpe. He has escaped capture and informed her that her minister, Lord Wolfingham (a rehashing of Francis Walsingham, Elizabeth's spy master, played by Henry Daniel), is in fact a traitor and an informer for Spain. And just as Elizabeth reluctantly did in real life, Robson instructs work to begin building a fleet to rival Philip's Armada. The picture closes to the cheering people proclaiming, "Hail to the Queen and to England!" Stirring stuff for a wartime American market.

Robson would play Elizabeth one more time on screen, and on this third occasion it would be in a sketch with the comedy duo Morecambe and Wise!

❧ *Bette Davis* ❦

> *"This Elizabeth was finer than my first"*
> **The Virgin Queen 1955**

BETTE DAVIS LIKED TO BE FIRST AT ALL SHE DID: FIRST LADY OF THE Screen, first female President of the Academy Awards, first performer to receive five Oscar nominations in a row and first actress to be honoured with the American Film Institute's Lifetime Achievement Award – the list goes on. If she had any desire to become the first actress to play Queen Elizabeth twice on film, she was beaten to it by Flora Robson.

The plot of *The Virgin Queen* has a timescale that is a decade earlier than *Elizabeth and Essex* and deals with Elizabeth's relationship with Sir Walter Raleigh, but whereas Davis had played a stylized Queen in her earlier film, suited to the movie's Technicolor fairy-tale appearance, and carried off the acting honours with aplomb, this time she is less at ease within the picture's boundaries and her second Elizabeth seems out of sync with the rest of the drama. Director Henry Koster tries to create a light, romantic spectacle: soft muted pastels fill the screen, and the women's costumes have a modern, 1950s appearance, that may be flattering but owe nothing to historical accuracy. Amongst all this froth, Bette Davis[*] sits or strides (her walk again much commented upon) in a blast of red and ginger and gold, vibrant, powerful and angry, and her performance is in perpetual simmer until the moment she suddenly ignites at the merest provocation.

The plot runs thus: by deploying the old trick of casting a cloak over a muddy puddle, Sir Walter Raleigh (Richard Todd) wins the attention of Queen Elizabeth in the hope that she will favour him and invest in his expedition to sail for America and return with treasure to present to her. The Queen takes a fancy to the handsome Raleigh, but Raleigh to one of her ladies-in-waiting (Joan Collins)[†]. The Elizabethan love triangle is deployed

---

[*] Davis hadn't appeared on screen for three years, taking time off to concentrate on her family and stage commitments, and *The Virgin Queen* was being touted as something of a come-back for the actress.

[†] The film does make some attempt at authenticity: the character Collins plays is called Bess Throgmorton – Raleigh's wife was called Elizabeth Throckmorton, and she was, indeed, a lady of the Queen's privy chamber.

again, though this time, as in *Fire Over England*, any romantic feelings that Elizabeth might have for the object of her attentions are not reciprocated.

All goes well for the ambitious Raleigh: he succeeds in winning Elizabeth's favour, confident that he will achieve his aim and set sail for the New World – that is until the Queen discovers that he has secretly married Bess, and she has Raleigh and Bess thrown into the Tower. Only when she visits the prisoner and tells him that she too was once held captive here does the Queen forgive them; and realising that she is no longer a lover in the eyes of the world, she bids him set sail, telling him: "You'll sail the ship yourself! This doesn't mean that I forgive you, nor that slut you married. I want the world you promised me... And those cargoes you bring back had best be rich!"

The film did relatively well at the box office, despite an advertising campaign that had images of Davis promoting the film as Margo Channing, her character from *All About Eve*, rather than as Elizabeth. The critics commented that Davis's performance was a "composition of shrewd intuitions about the complex sovereign" and that she "walked away with the picture".

Davis once more adopts the same jerky, twitching mannerisms as before; her scenes were shot in only eleven days and one can feel the speed with which the actress worked. She struts through her palace, waving her fans and ordering her ladies-in-waiting about, but, since her first embodiment as Elizabeth, Davis's acting style has become more mannered, and though the character can carry it, the gaudy set, blazing wigs and costumes combined create a performance in overdrive, as if, while away from the screen, Davis has been shackled like a pent-up racehorse, and now they are off and she is free, which judging by Davis's preference for work over her home life is probably not far from the truth.

In spite of its faults, it is a performance that cannot be ignored, and her fearlessness in again shaving off her hairline and eyebrows and succumbing to another unflattering make-up can only be admired. There are those who accuse Davis of showing off, and there is a degree of truth in this: a woman who, before she went to Hollywood, was happy with her appearance, only to find that the movie capital considered her ugly, made the decision that she would be different by refusing to adopt glamour, and would go out of her way to make herself unattractive when the part required it. Unfortunately for Davis, times had changed, and playing the same part, even at the correct age, led to comparison with her earlier portrayal.

This was meant to be Davis's big return to the screen ("The triumphant return to the screen of its fabulous first lady" was how the trailers described it), in colour, in Cinemascope, playing her favourite character in history. The result should have been another hit, desperately needed at that point in her career; it wasn't. What was needed was another script of the quality of *All About Eve*, rather than an attempt to recreate *Elizabeth and Essex*. Hollywood had changed its attitude towards her: she was pushing fifty and not where she had been at the box office five years before. Hollywood had also changed its attitude towards Elizabeth. Davis and Elizabeth went hand in hand, as did Charles Laughton and Henry VIII, and Hollywood no longer saw Elizabeth as a love interest. The love triangle of lady-in-waiting, courtier and Queen still existed, but now only in the Queen's mind. Delivering the line "Am I old, do I look old?" would have had no impact upon Davis in 1939; now it was as poignant to the actress as to the Queen.

Davis enjoyed being back before the cameras and tackling her favourite role. The only fly in the ointment was her relationship with Joan Collins, an actress Davis did not admire, thinking she was coasting on her looks and lacked ability before the camera. Collins thought that Davis was "terrifying", and recounts that Davis made it increasingly difficult for her to put one of her shoes on in a particular scene, by never keeping her foot still. When Collins grasped the foot between her knees so Davis couldn't fidget, and was successful in finally getting the shoe on, Davis winked at Collins and told her she was learning. Despite their animosity, Collins thought highly of Davis and was greatly impressed with her discipline, and her belief that vanity didn't have a place when creating a role. Only Glenda Jackson matches Davis's desire to be as truthful as she could be when creating the look of the Queen. In *The Virgin Queen* Davis excels, and in one scene, in her bedchamber, we not only see Davis's forehead shaved, but when she whips off the curious, pixie-style skullcap we observe that the cranium has a realistically bald wig, with only a few strands of grey hair*.

As in *Elizabeth and Essex* the Queen is alone at the end of the movie. She watches, with the aid of a telescope, as Raleigh's ship prepares to sail, then she returns indoors, with the faithful Dudley at her side†, to affairs of

---

* Davis had similar caps made for real-life use, famously shocking the audience at the 1955 Oscar ceremony when she came on wearing an Elizabethan-style dress and pixie cap to present the Best Actor award. The effect slightly backfired: given the actress's recent absence from Hollywood, many thought she had been ill and had lost her hair!

† Dudley is played here as an elderly statesman by Herbert Marshall, a familiar Davis co-star from the 1940s.

state: she can spare no more time for affairs of the heart. In the previous film, Davis begs Essex to take her throne; this Elizabeth is a more cunning animal, and though the last frame has the Queen dropping her head, as though in defeat, it will no doubt be only a matter of time before she resumes her duties and carries on as before. For this Elizabeth, no man is a match for England.

❦ Glenda Jackson ❧

"I'd much rather have Vanessa's part"
Mary, Queen of Scots 1971

BETTE DAVIS SAID OF GLENDA JACKSON, IN THE EARLY 1970S, THAT "[she] is going to have an incredible career. She makes me think of myself. She hasn't got the motion picture beautiful face, and neither have I. But she cares and is dedicated. That counts." There is much truth in the words of the indomitable Miss Davis, for if ever there were two actresses linked in style and temperament then Davis and Jackson are just that. Jackson rightly had grave misgivings when she signed on to repeat the role of Elizabeth in a picture whose quality falls far short of *Elizabeth R*, which had only been completed six weeks previously.

Jackson didn't want to feel bored in the role, and she was often heard to complain, "I'd much rather have Vanessa's part."* Later she would admit to doing it for the money, and insisted that her scenes be shot in three and a half weeks. Trevor Howard, who played William Cecil, and had most of his scenes with Jackson, commented that he had just spent over a year filming *Ryan's Daughter*, and now he had to complete *Mary, Queen of Scots* at breakneck speed! The cast and crew had to put up with it, as the producers wanted Jackson, who was at the pinnacle of her career, having just won an Oscar for *Women in Love*, and who would go on to win two Emmys for *Elizabeth R*. The two performances of Elizabeth would lock in to the public's imagination: Jackson was Elizabeth, much as it had been with Bette Davis in the '40s and '50s.

Jackson was dissatisfied with the filming process and the finished picture, which didn't get off to a good start even before filming began. Jackson wanted a rewrite that didn't allow the two Queens to meet; this was refused and, although inaccurate, they are two of the most affecting scenes in the picture. To win back some control over her performance, Jackson had her head shaved once again (in fact it had hardly grown back from filming *Elizabeth R*), even though she was warned that she might experience

---

* Vanessa Redgrave played the title role.

problems with hair growth afterwards. One thing she didn't do, though, was to wear a putty nose, as in *Elizabeth R,* which is a pity as it would have given her look more authenticity.

Unfortunately, the material itself, and the actress's boredom with the part, combined to produce a dissatisfying whole. Jackson overacts, but then the script gives her little room to manoeuvre into another gear, as the film is so loaded in Mary's favour. Certainly this Elizabeth is the Queen as villain, and there is little chance to see into her soul, except to show she is jealous of the younger and more beautiful monarch. Unlike the script of *Vivat! Vivat Regina!* there is no equal playing time between Jackson and Redgrave; Mary is the film's lead, although so saintly is she that Elizabeth becomes a welcome injection of much-needed vitriol into the action.

The plot of the film follows that of *Mary of Scotland* and begins with the death of Mary's first husband (Francis, the Dauphin of France, son of Catherine de' Medici) and her return to Scotland as a young widow to rule, now that her mother, Mary of Guise, regent in Mary's absence, is dead. To reach Scotland, Mary wishes to travel through England, but the "bastard and heretic" Elizabeth refuses Mary safe passage, and she must take the more perilous route of going by sea to the coast of Scotland. And then we are introduced to Elizabeth: director Charles Jarrott, who gave us *Anne of the Thousand Days,* and saw the life of Mary Stuart as a companion piece to that of Anne Boleyn's, adds fuel to the rumour that Elizabeth "consorts with her Horse Master" by setting our introduction on a curtained barge, where she is serenaded by her then Master of Horse, Dudley, and is later seen in his arms. This is a very different Elizabeth from the woman Jackson created in *Elizabeth R.* Without the putty noise, she appears softer, her face less angular; her costumes are sumptuous, showy, then when the time comes to present the older Mary and Elizabeth, Redgrave's dress changes to that of the Catholic martyr, while Jackson's Elizabeth is forced to be seen in either her bedchamber, ill, old and weary and in her nightgown, her famous red tresses gone, or, for her penultimate appearance, in the most gaudy get-up ever seen in Tudor England. The final meeting between the two sovereigns has Jackson in a patchwork of fabrics and fur, with a jaunty green felt cap on a brilliant red wig, that wouldn't have looked out of place on Bette Davis's virgin Queen. The odds are against Jackson from the outset, but with her winning humour, wit and her dazzling sense of timing – fine chemistry is created with Trevor Howard and with Daniel Massey as Dudley – she is fiery, flamboyant and funny: Jackson may have the smaller role, but she does have the more entertaining part.

Once back in Scotland there is little to do but show Mary as a victim, and then, when her world spirals out of control, as a martyr. The reinvention of herself, as a sacrificial heroine of the Catholic cause, is a reinvention worthy of Gloriana herself. Redgrave plays Mary for sympathy for all it is worth, and it is a tribute to her genius as a performer that she pulls it off and makes Mary so convincing and attractive a heroine. Throughout the picture the familiar concept that Mary ruled with her heart, Elizabeth her head, is played out. At one point in their last meeting, Mary expresses her wish to die and become a martyr, forcing Elizabeth to do the thing she fears most – order the execution of an ordained sovereign. As she exits the chamber at Fotheringhay, Elizabeth states tenderly: "If your head had matched your heart, it would be I who would be awaiting death." Robert Dudley enters to escort his mistress from the room, and kneels before Mary and kisses her hand, while Elizabeth watches. Mary is not only a martyr but more of a woman than Elizabeth, and the image of Dudley before Mary shows a jealousy burning in the embittered eyes of the virgin Queen. All that is left for Elizabeth is pomp and majesty, as Mary predicted in their final meeting, and the closing shot as the credits roll is of Elizabeth sitting in state, resplendent in mourning, holding her cousin's prayer book, alone, weeping*. The title card, stating that the throne passed to Mary's son at Elizabeth's death, implies a final personal triumph for Mary.

---

* In fact Elizabeth seems to have undergone complete physical and mental collapse at Mary's death, locking herself away for days, consumed with guilt and denial (certainly not sitting under canopies of state), no doubt a combination of shock and repulsion that she had been forced into this situation by her ministers, which implies that the Divine Right of the Sovereign was beginning to slip even then. Had Elizabeth had her way, she probably would have kept Mary prisoner for the rest of her life, in the hope that she would die quietly from ill-health, or that some well-meaning Protestant would murder her. This contradicts reports that the French ambassador, who "arrived to plead for clemency for Mary [was told by] Elizabeth… that matters had gone too far for that. 'This justice was done on a bad woman protected by a bad man'… If she herself was to live, Mary must die."

❧ *Cate Blanchett* ❦

"An echo in the room"
Elizabeth: The Golden Age 2007

OF THE FOUR ACTRESSES TO PLAY ELIZABETH FOR A SECOND TIME, Glenda Jackson was reluctant, Bette Davis and Flora Robson were enthusiastic, both admitting to feeling an ownership of the part, but Cate Blanchett found the prospect: "[a] daunting path to tread", considering those that had gone before, and took "a long time to come round" to accepting the role. She was wise to be cautious: each of the other actresses' second attempt at the character was less well received than their first. She was drawn, once again, to the "Rock and Roll... Bollywood aesthetics" of the picture's director and felt that "enough time had passed to do something different and unique..." She might have been prudent to have been more concerned with the script (which was pared down drastically) than with the visual opulence that director Shekhar Kapur offered.

Playing the Queen fascinates Blanchett: "Her reign was so long, and English culture really emerged... she was a remarkable diplomat." And she was impressed by "how stable she was able to keep the empire..." Interestingly she admits that she "enthused herself with all the interpretations" and as much research as she possibly could before she "funnelled it all into the script"*, proud that she was now a "better actor, ready to do something different this time", although she felt there was still "an echo in the room" of the previous film and character.

For Blanchett, one of the chief attractions, along with working with the same creative team as on *Elizabeth*, was the "ageing process" of the character; this is interesting, as Blanchett was still in her thirties, when historically Elizabeth is in her fifties. Unlike Davis and Jackson, who revelled in the opportunity to look as authentic as they thought possible, Blanchett

---

* The starting point for the film's writer, William Nicholson, was "a woman who has achieved power, and knows that any relationship – marriage, a sexual encounter – would dilute it." Kapur wanted to show the difference between the personalities of Elizabeth and Philip of Spain: she the "embodiment of tolerance, pitted against [his] fundamentalism", subjects as relevant now as they were then. "If Elizabeth had not become divine, the Armada would have invaded England, and [we] would have been talking Spanish. It was very important that the tolerant divine should win."

remains looking much as she did in her earlier incarnation of the role. She would later comment: "If Botox had been available in her day, Elizabeth would have been first in line." This Elizabeth has decided against the chalk-like mask of the earlier film's closing moments when Elizabeth 'becomes' a virgin, and instead looks the age of Blanchett herself, giving Elizabeth a timeless, eerie quality; she is old, but not old, as if everyone has aged at the court except the Queen[*]. Presumably the intention was to show Elizabeth to the world through the eyes with which she saw herself, in this case as an eternal Gloriana, a goddess, whose youth is not a painted decaying mask but a reality. Blanchett's Queen is a portrait in 3D, created by a template from the school of artists who painted Elizabeth in her later years, each dictated by the Queen herself as to how she should be depicted, in this case as divine.

The film deals with the execution of Mary Stuart, Elizabeth's relationship with Sir Walter Raleigh and the defeat of the Spanish Armada, a trio of key incidents in the second half of her reign. Liberties have been taken with the history, chief among them the aforesaid difference in Elizabeth's age, and also the depiction of Raleigh (portrayed by Clive Owen) as playing a critical part in the downfall of the Armada, a victory due more to the skill of Sir Francis Drake. But these discrepancies, and there are many, matter little to the finished product. *Elizabeth: The Golden Age* is a series of paintings, producing a stunning backdrop to the world in which Kapur casts his characters. This world reflects not only how life was presented by artists of the time, but the opinions of the English people as well: Elizabeth is England and she is tolerant, even of her Catholic subjects; Philip II is Spanish, therefore foreign, the enemy. Elizabeth is bathed in white, telling us she is not only pure but also good. Philip, by comparison, as Mary Tudor was in the first film, is devilishly dark. It is an epic movie: history is told by images on stained glass or on flags, or on sets that look like the vast canvas of George Gower's Armada Portrait, depicting Elizabeth on board ship, her hand resting on a globe, and behind her the Spanish fleet, tossed about on a stormy sea, with the English ships in a haze of calm and victory.

This is history told as a fantasy: the palaces are tall and cathedral-like, the villains are dark, devious and one-dimensional and the biggest fantasy is

---

[*] In this picture Cecil is not shown or mentioned – Walsingham is the Queen's chief minister, as well as her spy master (excellently portrayed by Geoffrey Rush) – neither is Robert Dudley seen, he who was to play such a crucial part in the war with Spain and would die soon after the English victory.

that Elizabeth could still be fertile. But we do have, and perhaps more than in any other depiction of Elizabeth, a sense of the Queen's body being that of the nation. We start with Elizabeth being inspected by her physicians to see if she can still conceive, and we end with a recreation of the Ditchley Portrait by Marcus Gheeraerts the Younger – Elizabeth, bathed in a heavenly glow, spins around on top of the world, in the form of a globe, at her feet.

Blanchett's second Elizabeth has an air of world weariness that at times borders on camp. But beneath this exterior lurks vulnerability and, as the Queen removes her wig, complaining of the lines on her face, she is answered by her lady-in-waiting that they are smile lines. "When do I ever smile?" she replies, and scratches her scalp, so peels away the Queen, revealing all of the woman's fear of assassination, ageing, of never being kissed again, of murdering Mary Stuart, of simply being alone. She is not bitter, as Bette Davis's Elizabeth could be, but she is resolved, despite the hope that there is more to her lot than just being Queen of England. With Blanchett and Kapur's modern interpretation of her, Elizabeth is a woman with the hope of obtaining it all, career and man, even if she knows it can never be possible. She has had her man (who could forget Elizabeth in the arms of Joseph Fiennes' Dudley in *Elizabeth*, before she "becomes a virgin") and we understand this just by the raising of an eyebrow in Raleigh's direction: she has been a woman who has known a man in the biblical sense, and now she must, alas, be a queen with "no master". The only thing she cannot be is a man, but as she states, "I'm my father's daughter"; perhaps that is enough?

"Some people will love it, some will hate it," Blanchett mused after the film was in the can, and it did indeed cause something of a stir, not just because of the liberties it took with history. The Vatican had something to say about what they saw as an "antipapal travesty" in the representation of the Catholic faith. The picture does indeed cast aspersions, as did the English at that time about the 'True Faith'. However, it is refreshing to see Elizabeth no longer a cinematic villain and the enemy of Mary Stuart. In fact Blanchett's Elizabeth could be said to not need God since she is herself a god, and maybe the Vatican took umbrage at this too? As she tells the Spanish ambassador, in one of the most famous scenes from the film: "I, too, can command the wind, sir; I have a hurricane in me that will strip Spain bare if you try me!" Blanchett's hand twitches with rage, before she composes herself; her voice deep, she bellows at the retreating figure of the slimy, swarthy ambassador, then wobbling, visibly shaken, at the threat to her nation. This is Elizabeth epitomised: mother to her people, war leader, and once most eligible princess in Europe. Philip wanted her hand (now he wants to put his daughter, the Infanta, who carries a doll of the Queen of England, on the throne in her place), and their history and her rejection of him at the start of her reign has much to do with his 'Enterprise of England' and desire to bring Elizabeth's kingdom to its knees. This scene alone is worthy of Blanchett's Academy Award nomination*.

But Philip and the Spanish stand little chance against England, not just because the weather is in England's favour but because of their Queen. Donning a breastplate isn't enough for this Elizabeth: she garbed in full armour like a cross between Joan of Arc and Henry V; with a wig of long tresses, she mounts a white charger and addresses her troops at Tilbury, rousing them to battle; her courage knows no bounds; the effect is electrifying. But we see the chink in her armour, as does Raleigh when she tells him of her fear of invasion, in a touching speech that makes the audience aware of the risk to Elizabeth and the consequences for herself, and England, had they lost and been invaded by the Spanish†. And then, that night, she wakes and steps out onto the clifftops, barefoot, in her nightgown, looking like a female Prospero, communing with her country as she stares out to sea. The war leader Elizabeth states that "We cannot be defeated", and we believe her.

The relationship between Elizabeth and Bess Throckmorton (a lacklustre Abbie Cornish) is given more credence than in *The Virgin Queen*. Here Bess is the highest ranking lady-in-waiting, who will be allowed to meet the Queen's gaze as others cannot, typified by Raleigh's attempt to do just that. She sees the Queen at her most intimate, so much so that a lesbian flirtation is hinted at, something that has never been suggested about the real Elizabeth. The other players of influence are Walsingham, as in *Elizabeth*, and a new voice of power, Dr Dee, whom the Queen respects, fears and looks to for guidance‡.

---

* Blanchett lost to Marion Cotillard, for her performance as Edith Piaf.
† At a moment of intimacy between the two, Raleigh questions whether the Queen is liked for herself. "Now you grow dull," she snaps. One wishes for more moments such as these from William Nicholson's script.
‡ The real Dr Dee was highly thought of at the court: not only was he patronised by the Queen but by Cecil, Walsingham, Dudley, Hatton and Sir Philip Sidney. His influence was large, he was key in the Queen's acceptance of the Gregorian calendar, and his Christian beliefs strengthened Elizabeth's respect for him – he was undoubtedly more than just a quack.

The other key relationship for Elizabeth in the film is the one she shares with a Scottish sounding Mary Stuart, also shown in a dark light by Samantha Morton*. Rightly the Queens do not meet, and rightly Mary is the harbinger of a string of plots to rid the world of the English Queen and place herself on the throne. "They call her the Virgin Queen," Mary muses. "Can it be that no man will have her?" One of Mary's conspiracies, 'The Babington Plot', almost comes off as Anthony Babington (Eddie Redmayne in one of his first screen roles) comes face to face with the Queen at prayer. Wielding a pistol, he proclaims, "Elizabeth – whore!" before being struck by her god-like quality, her purity, and once again light†. This is Elizabeth 'Woman, Warrior, Queen' as the billboards proclaimed, who can stop the pulling of a

The Rainbow Portrait, attributed to both Isaac Oliver and Marcus Gheeraerts the Younger, c1600-02 (World History Archive)

---

* Like Anne Boleyn, Mary Stuart possessed a French accent and the ways of a Frenchwoman, having spent so much time at the French court.

† As Elizabeth herself did, this image of the Queen in church rivals that of the Virgin Mary herself. With the dissolution of the monasteries by Henry VIII, Elizabeth, some fifty years later, saw that there was an opening for a new virgin to take the Virgin Mary's place.

trigger with her divine glance. Redmayne crumbles before the camera, and so does Mary's plot: the executioner's block is but moments away. The scene shows Elizabeth ready to die for her country, for in this staging of her story she is the heroine to Mary's villain. Yet, valiant though she is, we see behind the facade of Gloriana a real sense of her fear at the prospect of invasion; "I am always afraid," she tells Raleigh, her own mortality at threat.

The closing scenes of the film show Elizabeth as carer, and finally mother. She visits the sick and aged Walsingham lying in bed beneath the Rainbow Portrait*. She then cradles Raleigh and Bess's baby, bringing an odd dimension to the familiar love triangle; she says, in voiceover: "I am a mother to my people." The image of Elizabeth holding a child she will never have is somewhat foreign to us, but it is a fitting climax to a remarkable and fine portrait of the Queen by the creative team and star that also gave us the more critically acclaimed *Elizabeth*.

Reviews on the whole were favourable, with the odd sour note. ("A kitsch extravaganza aquiver with trembling bosoms, booming guns and wild energy" was how *The New York Times* described it.) And there were some who asked, "What new emotional journey is possible for such a frozen personality?" Blanchett felt justified in her decision to return to "the old trout in the red wig". She also said: "I had a sense that through returning to the role, you can delve deeper into it… What is revealed about her depends on where you shine the light."

A third film, covering the latter years of the Queen, is planned; Kapur says: "The first film was the journey from innocence to ruthlessness –what is lost

---

* The Rainbow Portrait, painted at the turn of the 17th century and attributed to both Isaac Oliver and Marcus Gheeraerts the Younger, is the most fantastical and symbolic of all the portraits of Elizabeth. So called because the Queen carries a rainbow in her right hand, bearing the motto 'No rainbow without the sun', she is dressed like a goddess, her hair piled with the most opulent of headdresses and drop pearls, her body swathed romantically in a cloak covered with eyes and ears, symbolising that she sees and hears everything, and on her left sleeve a large serpent representing wisdom is entwined. Although showing a youthful Elizabeth, the portrait was painted when she was in her late sixties, and was commissioned, supposedly, by Robert Cecil, her chief minister (the son of William Cecil, who had inherited his father's position), for a visit from the Queen, where a shrine to Astraea, the goddess of justice, was part of the festivities. The painting now hangs at Hatfield House, Cecil's seat, in the new house built after the Queen's death in the time of James I. The Old Palace, where Elizabeth lived before she was proclaimed Queen, and site of the oak that she was supposedly under when she learnt of Mary Tudor's death, is still part standing; what remains is the Great Hall, considerably smaller than the new building. It is fitting that the painting features in *Elizabeth: The Golden Age*, its dreamlike aesthetics perfect for the director's intention for the movie.

is the quest for power. The second is about divinity and immortality – where people in absolute power start to aspire to the divine and the immortal… The third one is about mortality – what happens when those who aspire to become immortal have to face their own death. It's about Elizabeth saying, I have been divine, yet I am not so loved by God that I will be immortal."

CONCLUSION

'The Daughter of Debate'

Cate Blanchett in *Elizabeth: The Golden Age*
{Laurie Sparham, Universal Pictures}

'THE DAUGHTER OF DEBATE' WAS A TERM ELIZABETH USED TO describe Mary, Queen of Scots in a poem, 'The Doubt of Future Foes', that she wrote in approximately 1568. But the sobriquet describes Elizabeth herself just as well. Not only in her own time, but ever since, she has been the source of constant scrutiny, argument, re-examination and interpretation. Never has a monarch, with the possible exception of Henry VIII (much of his fascination being the misfortunes of his wives), captivated audiences for so many years. Very little new information has recently come to light, and probably won't now, but we are continually riveted by each new characterisation. The word 'reinterpretation' has to be stressed when

Elizabeth is created for screen or stage, as writers stamp ideas of their own time and understanding of her, along with a heavy dose of artistic licence, upon their characterisation. This would delight Elizabeth. The knowledge that she is still being discussed and revered after all this time could only bring satisfaction to a woman who exercised a control upon her own image that was so extreme. The fanatical policing of her own marketing made sure that she was ever youthful and above mere mortality. So, with each new portrayal of her, the debate will continue.

There is no definitive Elizabeth, one that is closer to the Queen than all the others, for with all the positives of a performance there may be as many negatives. "We all have the germ of every other person inside of us," said Dame Sybil Thorndike, who played Elizabeth in 1928 at the Arts Theatre, London, in *The Story of an Immortal* by George Moore. This dispels any preconceived notion that an actress must resemble the part she creates. Follow Thorndike's theory, and Jackson, Davis, Blanchett and others can all enjoy inimitable triumphs as the Queen.

Personally I would rank Glenda Jackson above all other Elizabeths, in *Elizabeth R*, not just because of her magnificent, intuitive understanding of the Queen, but also because of the piece itself. Each episode constituted a complete film, and many of her own words were used within the text, heightening the dramatist's conception of her, and the viewers' understanding. The old adage that truth is stranger than fiction also applies and, by sticking to the facts, we have a greater sense of how extraordinary Elizabeth was, and a more compelling narrative. At about the same time as Jackson was starring in *Elizabeth R*, Eileen Atkins was winning rave reviews from scholars and critics alike for her interpretation of Elizabeth. Although I did not see the production, from what I have read, and what I know of the actress's work and ability, I can safely guess that here too was a performance of clear-sighted greatness. Anna Massey's Elizabeth I did see, and she fully convinced in the role, bringing a humour and deftness behind the weary facade of the ageing monarch, aided by her personal appreciation of the woman. Bette Davis is another favourite; I value her interpretation because she, against all the odds of her looks, the inaccuracies and weakness of the script, the triteness of many Hollywood depictions of English history, and her own distinctive acting style, finds a fire within that is, in its own way, Elizabeth. Cate Blanchett, along with Shekhar Kapur, created a completely original Elizabeth which balanced modern insight against Elizabethan propaganda.

Three women, to me, have handed the baton of portraying the Queen on to the next: Bette Davis, Glenda Jackson and Cate Blanchett. Each has created her Elizabeth in ways that have renewed interest in the monarch and defined her own career, making Elizabeth the character for which she is best remembered.

Anna Massey made a profound comment about Elizabeth when she said that she was a "woman of *all* time", but not only that, her character is as we see her, also an amalgamation of those who have played her successfully. By being interpreted by so many great actresses, she has become defined by them: she is the neurosis of Bette Davis, the fire of Cate Blanchett, the majesty of Flora Robson, the wit of Eileen Atkins, the curdled, vain charm of Anna Massey, the vulnerability of Vanessa Redgrave, the resourcefulness of Lalla Ward, the fear of Harriet Walter, the anger of Greta Scacchi, the chameleon quality of Miranda Richardson and the sheer extraordinary brilliance of Glenda Jackson. She is Everywoman and she is unique. She is all of the above, and much, much more.

Appendix I

Queen Elizabeth's Locket Ring

While discussing Elizabeth with Anna Massey, the subject of the Queen's jewellery came up and in particular the famous locket ring with the double portrait enclosed within its setting. On opening the clasp, the diamond 'E' reveals miniatures of Elizabeth and her mother Anne Boleyn. The ring formed the closing shot of *The Virgin Queen* starring Anne-Marie Duff. Ms Massey was fascinated by the ring, describing it as a real "knuckle duster". Although knowing some of its history, I decided to find out more, and in doing so began to query the veracity of one of the images, however much I wanted to believe its identity to be that of Anne Boleyn.

The Queen wore the ring for the latter part of her life, and it was only removed from her finger on her death, such was her attachment to it, when it was taken to James VI of Scotland, soon to be James I of England, as proof of her death. It became a star player in the 'Elizabeth' exhibition in Greenwich in 2003 and has always been of interest to historians and the public alike. Today the ring is kept at the Prime Minister's private residence at Chequers.

The recognised assumption is that the ring was a gift from Edward Seymour, 1st Earl of Hertford, the son of Edward Seymour, 1st Duke of Somerset (Somerset was the brother of Elizabeth's first stepmother Jane Seymour and later brother-in-law of Katherine Parr). If it was a gift to seek the Queen's favour or advancement, the Phoenix emblem immediately places the Earl as a possible giver, as both he and Elizabeth used it as their badge, the Queen most famously in the Phoenix Portrait by Nicholas Hilliard. If all these assumptions are to be agreed upon, then I believe the picture facing that of Elizabeth's is *not* in fact that of her mother Anne Boleyn, as has been assumed.

For someone of the Seymour clan, and not a Boleyn or Howard (the Howards were the Queen's cousins), to give the Queen an image of her

The ring: supposedly brought to James I as proof of Elizabeth's death
(Heritage Image Partnership Ltd)

mother seems a peculiar choice, particularly when we know that Elizabeth only spoke of her mother on two recorded occasions during her reign, such was the stigma attached to Anne. Not that she derided her mother, far from it: she chose to advance relations from her mother's lineage and was aware and proud that she had many characteristics associated with Anne. Yet, for Elizabeth, it was safer to glory in the memory of her father, who had none of the negative traits (witchcraft and adulterer being the foremost) attached to his character that had been to Anne's. Interestingly, over the centuries the reputations of Anne and Henry have somewhat, and quite rightly, been reversed. With these questions taken into account I wondered why should Hertford present Elizabeth with it. Was there a special understanding between them, or was the likeness in fact somebody else?

My theory now takes into account the recently re-identified image that for years historians thought of as Lady Jane Grey. Approximately twenty years ago, the painting, in the National Portrait Gallery, was acknowledged to be Katherine Parr, Henry's sixth wife and Elizabeth's fourth stepmother.

This conclusion came about because a recently discovered jewel inventory, from Queen Katherine's time, noted that the jewels were the very same as those that hang from the waist of the Queen in the portrait. We should have suspected something all along, as Jane Grey only sat for one image in her lifetime; this has recently been discovered and is also hanging in the National Portrait Gallery. She was known to favour much plainer clothes, appropriate to her staunch Protestant practices, and a likeness would not have been painted in the nine days of her reign, and certainly not commissioned in her successor Mary's reign, or even Elizabeth's, when the Grey family was still tarnished by disgrace.

If we now look at this new image of Katherine Parr, and think of the woman in terms other than the slightly matronly character with which she is associated in the other three portraits that we have of her, and if we remember that the French hood, the headdress most commonly associated with Anne Boleyn – although forbidden at court after her fall – made a reappearance in the time of Katherine Howard, and was worn at court well into Elizabeth's reign, then couldn't the likeness be that of Katherine Parr, a woman of learning whom she greatly admired and tried to emulate, rather than the bewitching Anne Boleyn? Katherine was widely regarded as the main maternal influence in Elizabeth's upbringing, and Elizabeth always held great affection for the Queen, so why wouldn't Hertford, no doubt wanting to keep favour and strengthen his own connection to the crown, emphasise this through Katherine Parr?

Appendix II

The Interviewees

Anna Massey

ANNA MASSEY, DAUGHTER OF ADRIANNE ALLEN AND RAYMOND Massey, and sister of Daniel Massey, enjoyed a career spanning five decades and proved herself one of the country's most accomplished actresses, with success in film, theatre, television and radio.

She shot to fame overnight in 1955 in *The Reluctant Debutante*, starring alongside Celia Johnson, playing the part in London and New York. She made her film debut three years later in John Ford's *Gideon's Day*. Other stage work includes *Double Yolk*, her hugely acclaimed performance as Annie Sullivan in *The Miracle Worker*, *The Glass Menagerie*, *The Prime of Miss Jean Brodie* and her award-winning Ariadne Utterwood in the Old Vic's production of George Bernard Shaw's *Heartbreak House*. In the '80s and '90s she appeared with the National Theatre Company in *King Lear* and in *Moonlight* at the Almeida.

From the 1970s Massey became familiar on television as Mrs Danvers in the original television adaptation of *Rebecca*, *Mansfield Park*, and as Gwen John in *Journey into the Shadows*. More recently she appeared in *The Sleeper* and *He Knew He Was Right*. But perhaps her finest moment came in 1986 when she played Edith Hope in the BBC's version of Anita Brookner's *Hotel du Lac*, her painfully acute performance winning her a BAFTA.

Film work ranged from Hitchcock's *Frenzy*, the cult *Peeping Tom*, and *Bunny Lake is Missing* with Laurence Olivier, to costume work such as *The Corn is Green* and as Miss Prism in *The Importance of Being Earnest*, earning her an Olivier Award.

Her vast audio work includes *The Sceptred Isle*, and the crime drama *Daunt & Dervish*, which she also created, both for Radio 4.

She has played Elizabeth I more than once, on radio, and on stage in the National Theatre's 1996 production of Jeremy Sams' version of Schiller's *Mary Stuart*, her last stage appearance. In 2004 she was created a CBE and in 2006 published, to great acclaim, her autobiography *Telling Some Tales*, which she subsequently read on Radio 4. She died in 2011.

Harriet Walter

TRAINED AT LAMDA, HARRIET WALTER THEN CUT HER TEETH WITH touring theatre companies Joint Stock, Paines Plough and John McGrath's 7:84 company, before joining the Duke's Playhouse Lancaster. As well as working with successful fringe companies, her name went on to be connected with The Royal Court, Royal National Theatre and the RSC. Her breakthrough came as Ophelia opposite Jonathan Pryce's Hamlet at the Royal Court, where she also played in *Cloud Nine*, *The Seagull* and *The Lucky Chance*.

Further success came in the late '80s playing Imogen in *Cymbeline* and an 'iconic' Masha in John Barton's production of *Three Sisters*. The 1990s saw further praise for performances with the RSC, including *The Duchess of Malfi*, and the National Theatre in Tom Stoppard's *Arcadia*.

She has also become well known as a film, television and radio actress, with work as diverse as Dorothy L. Sayers' sleuth Harriet Vane, *The Men's Room*, *Downton Abbey* and more recently *Spooks*. Film performances include a delightfully calculating Fanny Dashwood in Emma Thompson's *Sense and Sensibility*, *Young Victoria*, the Oscar-nominated *Atonement*, *Babel*, and more recently *The Sense of an Ending*.

Other stage work has included *Life x 3* for the National Theatre, which gained her an Olivier Award nomination, *The Three Sisters* and *Twelfth Night* winning her an Olivier Award, the West End hit *Dinner*, *Antony and Cleopatra* with Patrick Stewart, *Macbeth* alongside Antony Sher for the RSC, and her Evening Standard and Olivier Award winning performances of Schiller's troubled Elizabeth I, first at the Donmar Warehouse, before transferring to the West End and Broadway, where she garnered a Tony nomination in 2009. Recently she appeared again at the Donmar Warehouse, in all-female productions of Shakespeare's *Henry IV* and *Julius Caesar*.

In 2003 she published *Other People's Shoes*, part autobiography and part 'Thoughts on Acting'.

She was made a CBE in 2000 and a Dame in 2011.

Greta Scacchi

BORN IN MILAN, GRETA SCACCHI IS THE DAUGHTER OF AN ARTIST/ art dealer and a dancer/antiques dealer. When her parents separated she returned with her mother to England. On her mother's remarriage the family moved to Australia, but by the 1970s she was back in England and pursuing an acting career; she studied at the Bristol Old Vic, one of her contemporaries being another Elizabeth: Miranda Richardson. Scacchi shot to worldwide fame as a distinguished film actress in the early 1980s, giving illuminating performances in *Heat and Dust*, *Jefferson in Paris* and *The Coca-Cola Kid*. Her stature as one of the industry's leading actresses was confirmed with her portrayal of Lady Diana Broughton in the smash hit *White Mischief*.

By the 1990s she was a lead player in Hollywood in Robert Altman's *The Player* and the thriller *Presumed Innocent*. The decision not to take the part of Catherine Tramell in *Basic Instinct* marked a sea change in her career.

She began to take parts which had less to do with her beauty and more to do with her versatility as a performer. Since that time, she has developed into an engaging character actress with roles as far reaching as Margaret Thatcher, the Empress Alexandra (she received an Emmy Award and a Golden Globe nomination for the latter) and the emotionally torn Laura Crocker-Harris in the remake of *The Browning Version*. She garnered a further Emmy nomination in 1997 for *Broken Trail*, and through the 1990s worked in Europe as well as Britain. She also took stage roles – *Old Times*, *Easy Virtue* and *Miss Julie* – as well as television offers, and as of today she has one of the most wide-ranging careers of any actress. She is fluent in English, French, German and Italian.

Her more recent West End performances include in Terrence Rattigan's *The Deep Blue Sea*, John Osborne's *The Entertainer* and playing Bette Davis in *Bette and Joan*. She has also starred in several major motion pictures, including *Beyond the Sea*, *Brideshead Revisited* and *The Falling*, and on television *War and Peace*, and portraying Cassandra Austen, Jane's sister, in *Miss Austen Regrets*.

In 2008 she played Schiller's Queen Elizabeth at Sydney's Ensemble Theatre and was nominated for a Sydney Theatre Award as Best Actress.

Eileen Atkins

BORN IN CLAPTON, EAST LONDON, EILEEN ATKINS BEGAN HER career as a child performer in working men's clubs during the war. Billed as 'Baby Eileen', she was proficient in toe tap, an advanced form of tap dancing. Her mother, having been told by a gypsy that she would have a daughter who would be a famous dancer, pushed Atkins to pursue a career in musical revue. Atkins, however, had other ideas and wanted to forge a career as a serious actress, and has since spoken of her dislike of her early dancing years. She gained a place at the Guildhall School of Music & Drama on the teacher training course, but instead took part on the acting course, unbeknown to the school principal.

On graduating she made her stage debut at Regent's Park Open Air Theatre in 1953, and from then on has worked continually in all major media, though her first love has always been the stage, and upon this she has focused on both sides of the Atlantic. Stage work includes: *The Killing of Sister George, Cymbeline, A Delicate Balance, John Gabriel Borkman, Doubt* and *Honour*. More recently she has been seen in *The Sea*, Pinter's *The Birthday Party*, *The Witch of Edmonton* at the RSC and a piece of her own devising about the actress Dame Ellen Terry. She has been nominated for, and won, countless prizes, including Tony, Olivier and Drama Desk awards. For her work as Elizabeth I in Robert Bolt's *Vivat! Vivat Regina!* she was awarded the Plays & Players Award and Variety Award for Best Actress of 1971.

She has also carved out a highly successful career as a writer, firstly with her friend Jean Marsh, creating the massive hits *Upstairs, Downstairs* and *The House of Eliott*; and on her own she has become synonymous with the work of Virginia Woolf, as a performer in *A Room of One's Own* and *Vita & Virginia*, the latter co-starring her friend Vanessa Redgrave and later Penelope Wilton, and as a writer supplying the screenplay for *Mrs Dalloway*, which also starred Redgrave.

She has paid less attention to screen and television and therefore has remained less well known, stating that her contemporaries Maggie Smith and Judi Dench have made movies and appeared on television, while she has "ploughed away at the classics". In the last few decades, however, this has been addressed and she has been seen in *Gosford Park*, *Last Chance Harvey*, *Jack & Sarah* and *Vanity Fair*. On television she recently won a

BAFTA and an Emmy for her performance in *Cranford*. Other television work includes *Bertie & Elizabeth*, *The Lost Language of Cranes*, Alan Bennett's *Talking Heads*, *Doc Martin* and most recently playing Queen Mary in *The Crown*.

She was made a CBE in 1990 and a Dame in 2001.

Felicity Dean

BORN IN LONDON AND EDUCATED IN SUNNINGDALE, DEAN BEGAN her film career playing another Tudor queen, Lady Jane Grey, in *The Prince and the Pauper* in 1977, after which she was dubbed, "One of the 10 Women to Watch" in that year by *Cosmopolitan* magazine. Other film work includes *Steaming* opposite Vanessa Redgrave and *The Whistle Blower* with Michael Caine.

But it is for her television and theatre appearances that Dean is best known, carving out an impressive career that has ranged from Shakespeare to comedy.

On stage she has worked with the RSC and the Royal Court. She originated the role of Annie in *Good* by C. P. Taylor, the production transferring from the West End to Broadway. Other stage work includes *An Honourable Trade*, *Twelfth Night*, *The Taming of the Shrew* directed by Jonathan Miller, and *The Churchill Play*. Her work for the National Theatre includes Richard Eyre's production of *John Gabriel Borkman* opposite Paul Scofield, Eileen Atkins and Vanessa Redgrave, and *The Coast of Utopia* directed by Trevor Nunn. Recently she has won plaudits portraying Pamela Harriman in *Swimming at The Ritz*, and Princess Margaret in *A Princess Undone*.

Her television credits have been extensive and have included *The Professionals*, Guinevere in *The Legend of King Arthur*, *The Far Pavilions* opposite Ben Cross and Rupert Everett, and the Lynda La Plante series *Trial & Retribution*. She starred alongside Judi Dench in *The Last of the Blonde Bombshells* and has been a familiar face in crime dramas such as *Rosemary and Thyme*, *Midsomer Murders*, *The Inspector Alleyn Mysteries*, *Hetty Wainthropp Investigates* and *Lovejoy*.

Her most recent film performance was in *The Wedding Video* with Harriet Walter, Rufus Hound and Robert Webb.

Glenda Jackson

DURING HER RENOWNED ACTING CAREER, GLENDA JACKSON HAS played a wide array of real-life characters on stage and screen, including the poet Stevie Smith, actresses Patricia Neal and Sarah Bernhardt, assassin Charlotte Corday, Tchaikovsky's wife Nina Milukova, Nelson's lover Emma Hamilton and human rights activist Elena Bonner. Her work has won her Academy Awards, New York Film Critics Awards, Emmy Awards, a Golden Globe, a Tony and many others. Her first performance of Elizabeth won her three Emmys, and for her second – in *Mary, Queen of Scots* – she received the Evening Standard Award.

Her portrayals of Elizabeth have been lauded as some of the finest acting recorded, and her reputation as an actress is unsurpassed. Today she is, along with Vanessa Redgrave, Judi Dench, Maggie Smith and Eileen Atkins, regarded as one of the finest actresses of the post-war years.

She was born in Birkenhead in 1936, and after training at RADA joined the RSC in 1964, working alongside such luminaries as the director Peter Brook. While at the RSC her colossal stage presence was quickly noted, prompting some reviews to suggest that the production of *Hamlet*, in which she starred, should have been re-billed *Ophelia*. Her admiration for "the Bette Davis school of acting: big, bold and brash" soon had film directors calling, and she became something of a muse for Ken Russell, working with the radical director six times. After appearing as Cleopatra on the *Morecambe and Wise Christmas Special* – something she refers to as "the apotheosis of my career" – she was offered the part of Vickie Allessio in the comedy *A Touch of Class*, co-starring George Segal. She received her second Oscar for the film and some of the finest reviews of her career. She proceeded to intersperse her dramatic film career with comedies, something which surprised audiences who had only seen her up until 1973 as something of a heavyweight, dramatic actress. As her film career flourished, she continued tackling stage work as diverse as Ibsen and Pinter, Shakespeare and Genet.

In 1992 she retired from acting and stood for Parliament as a Labour candidate, winning the seat of Hampstead and Highgate. She held the position of Member of Parliament until standing down in 2015. She then resumed her acting career, making an award-winning, triumphant return to the stage playing the title role in *King Lear* at The Old Vic and more recently on Broadway, where she also won a Tony for Edward Albee's *Three Tall Women*.

She was awarded the CBE in 1978.

Miranda Richardson

MIRANDA RICHARDSON IS ONE OF BRITAIN'S BEST LOVED AND MOST highly respected actresses. Hailed as "the greatest actress of our time" by a critic at the Edinburgh Fringe, where she was performing in *Orlando*, she has worked successfully in film, theatre, television and radio.

Born in Southport and trained at the Bristol Old Vic school, upon leaving Richardson moved into rep work, before making her West End debut in *Moving* at the Queen's Theatre in 1981 and later winning an Olivier award for *A Lie of the Mind*.

Famous for playing complicated, layered women, she was soon in demand for television roles: Queenie in *Blackadder II*, *Secret Friends*, *Dance to the Music of Time*, *After Pilkington* and as an emotionally troubled Queen Mary in *The Lost Prince*.

Always interested in challenging new writing, Richardson has also carved out one of the most impressive film careers of recent years, hitting our screens in 1985 as Ruth Ellis, the last woman to be hanged in Britain, in Mike Newell's *Dance with a Stranger*, a film that instantly shot her to stardom and critical recognition and won her the Evening Standard Award for Best Actress. She has gone on to present audiences with a bewildering gallery of characters.

She received Academy Award nominations for *Tom & Viv* and her tour de force in *Damage*, and further film awards for *Enchanted April* and *The Crying Game*.

Refusing offers from Hollywood, most notably the part of Alex Forrest in *Fatal Attraction*, she chose to concentrate on film, television and stage work in England, becoming associated with London's Royal Court and National Theatre, stating, "I would rather do small roles on TV, stage or film than one blockbuster that made me rich but had no acting. And if that's the choice I have to make, I think I've already made it."

Recent work has included: *Mapp and Lucia* and *And Then There Were None* for television, and *Belle*, *Testament of Youth* and *Churchill* for cinema.

SOURCES

Books

A History of Britain by Simon Schama
Elizabeth by David Starkey
Elizabeth the Great by Elizabeth Jenkins
Elizabeth the Queen by Alison Weir
Elizabeth's Women by Tracy Borman
Elizabeth R by Roy Strong and Julia Trevelyan Oman
Flora Robson by Janet Dunbar
Glenda Jackson: A Study in Fire and Ice by Ian Woodward
In the Frame: My Life in Words and Pictures by Helen Mirren
Ladies in Waiting by Anne Somerset
Leading Ladies by Boze Hadleigh
Mary Queen of Scots by Antonia Fraser
My Wicked, Wicked Ways by Errol Flynn
Other People's Shoes: Thoughts on Acting by Harriet Walter
Queen Elizabeth's Wardrobe Unlock'd by Janet Arnold
Sarah: The Life of Sarah Bernhardt by Robert Gottlieb
Telling Some Tales by Anna Massey
The Lonely Life by Bette Davis
The Virgin Queen by Christopher Hibbert

Periodicals and Websites

Australian Stage
CinemaSource
Daily Mail
Grazia magazine
musicOMH
Radio Times
Stage Noise (www.stagenoise.com)
The Daily Telegraph
The Guardian
The Independent
The New York Times

The Spectator Australia
The Sunday Times
The Sunday Times Magazine
The Telegraph Magazine
The Times
Time Out
Vanity Fair Magazine
You magazine

Also by the author

Bette & Joan
Storm in a Flower Vase
Mrs Pat